lessons of one of history's finest physicians of souls. In this work Spurgeon lives again not merely as a preacher but as a teacher of preachers for his generation and ours. Eswine honestly explores the strengths and weakness, theology and practice, personality and passions of Spurgeon to guide us on a path toward sound, gracious, and Spirit-empowered preaching for our time.'

Bryan Chapell,
President and Professor of Practical Theology,
Covenant Theological Seminary, St. Louis, Missouri

'As hard as it may be for 21st century preachers to believe, Charles Spurgeon dealt with many of the same challenges today's preachers face. In *Kindled Fire*, Zack Eswine allows us to sit at the feet of this powerful pulpiteer and gain insights from the life and ministry of one of the greatest preachers in the history of the church. Throughout the pages of this fascinating book, the reader feels drawn into Spurgeon's presence and receives valuable counsel as if from the great preacher's own lips. This is a volume that is both enjoyable and rewarding.'

Michael Duduit, Editor,
Preaching Magazine

KINDLED FIRE

How the Methods of

C H Spurgeon

Can Help Your Preaching

Zack Eswine

MENTOR

To my dear friend and father in the Lord, Bob Smart,

who in a used bookstore in Muncie, Indiana,
first introduced a searching college student to
the benefit of preachers who have gone before us, and to
the necessary ministry of the Holy Spirit
for the preaching of the Word.

Copyright © Zack Eswine 2006

ISBN 1-84550-117-9

10 9 8 7 6 5 4 3 2 1

First Published in 2006
in the
Mentor Imprint
by
Christian Focus Publications Ltd.,
Geanies House, Fearn,
Ross-shire, IV20 1TW, Scotland

www.christianfocus.com

Cover design by Alister MacInnes

Printed and bound by
Bell & Bain, Glasgow

CONTENTS

Part Four: The Preacher's Limitations

ACKNOWLEDGMENTS

This book began as a Ph.D. dissertation which Michael Graves gave many hours to read, edit and ask thoughtful questions about. Michael's care and gift of teaching were an immense help to me and a good model for me. I am deeply thankful to David Calhoun and Bryan Chapell, my colleagues and friends at Covenant Theological Seminary, for their time, care, conversation and reading. Andrew Young also gave helpful insight by his willingness to read portions of an early draft.

I am also thankful to the board of trustees at Covenant Theological Seminary for allowing me a writing sabbatical to complete this book. Rick Matt, Rebecca Rine and my colleague Robert Peterson gave their editing direction to this work during two different phases of its writing over the years. Their suggestions were tremendously helpful to a pastor more at ease with speaking than with writing. Thanks also to Malcolm Maclean for his time and comments, to Dane Ortlund for conservation and prayer and who developed the topical index for the book, and to Tates Creek Presbyterian Church for their encouragement during the time of my writing sabbatical

Most of all, I thank my family and friends whose love, support and sacrifice of time have blessed my heart with hope. Nathan and Abbie have loved and prayed for me and Caleb has encouraged me with his laughter. With more than words can express, I am especially grateful to my wife Shellie. Her steady faithfulness and encouragement kept my feet on the ground and moving forward, reminding me of God's heart for His church and His gracious intention to strengthen His pastors.

INTRODUCTION

Charles Spurgeon is well known to the evangelical world as the 'Prince of Preachers.' But lesser known are the similar challenges that his times and ours share. The decline of effective preaching, moral decay within the churches, and the cultural assault on the validity of biblical Christianity converged and formed the context in which Spurgeon preached the gospel. As the threat of these darkened clouds and swirling winds inched closer, casting their sun-blocked shadow over the flowers and trees, roads and villages, Spurgeon cried out to God to anchor the pulpit for his generation and give it a voice again, the voice of the one who can speak to storms and silence them. Facing our similar challenges, preachers today can learn from Spurgeon to cry out for 'kindled fire' and to preach as if such a fire could, indeed, rise again from God for our generation.

Kindled Fire

'Kindled fire.' The metaphor calls to mind a once-blazing flame now cooling into slowly fading embers, perhaps at a campsite in the late hours of a long night. To kindle a fire is to step out into the chill of morning darkness and to stoke blackened wood into heated contact with patches of brown bark and skinny twigs. The result is an intensified illumination in the night which produces a renewed heat amid the sunless cold.

For Charles Spurgeon, 'fire' referred to that authority, that ardour of soul, that unnatural earnestness which could, in the context of God's Word, fill the preacher and his congregation when these were graciously visited by God's Spirit. That such a fire could be kindled refers to the local and intensified or awakened presence and working of the

Holy Spirit in and through His preachers and His people. 'Fire' is the Spirit's provision. Kindling a spiritual fire depicts the fresh stoking and blowing of God's empowering and manifest presence.

But why should God's preachers and people require kindled fire? Doesn't the fire from God's Spirit always burn full among them? Sadly and importantly, the Bible reminds us, and the history of preaching confirms, that as preachers and as congregations, we are readily able to forget our need of fire in the night. Often our blaze grows cool and what a generation finds in its pulpits is a dissipating smoke.

The Fashions of the Times
Every generation must have its joust with those who are ambitious to intimidate and threaten the advance of the gospel. Every preacher must face his fears and flatteries within the vice of these temptations. Consequently, the church must continually decide upon which source it will lean for relevance and gospel power in its pulpits. Essential for preachers is the ancient truth that 'there is nothing new under the sun.' Thus, we should not be surprised that Spurgeon's times offer significant parallels in substance with our contemporary times.

Beginning in 1865, Spurgeon gave an annual conference address to the alumni of his Pastors' College. Over the next twenty-seven years, the decline of ministerial power amid the issues of the age formed his recurring theme.[1] 'It is hard to win attention to the Word of God,' he lamented. 'We all feel that a hardening process is going on among the masses.'[2] Elsewhere he concluded, 'Revelation which is unchanging' is not considered 'fast enough for an age of which it may be said, "Change is its fashion".'[3]

Spurgeon was not alone in his assessments. A host of Victorian voices agreed that 'the pulpit is no longer a power in the country.'[4] Such sentiments sound foreign to those of us who often regard the nineteenth century as a golden age of preachers. But though many of our preaching heroes lived during that century, their numbers may indicate not a golden age of culture, but rather God's grace given to preachers to counter an age in decay. We must remember that the roots of this 'hardening process' which Spurgeon observed lay externally in the soils of Darwinism, rationalism, and the higher critical movement. Add to these the French Revolution and the Enlightenment and one remembers the dominant secularism which was growing throughout Europe.[5] These external pressures began to cave in on the church, forming what Spurgeon called a 'squint' in the pulpit. The Bible was no longer clear in the vision of preachers. They began to set their eyes on both Moses and Darwin, looking 'to revelation and speculation' for their sermons.[6]

But challenges to the necessity and centrality of preaching arose from other cultural quarters as well, focusing discussions of relevance and power in the pulpit on cultural concerns. Preachers at the turn of the twenty-first century may be surprised when they look at this list of nineteenth-century challenges closely. Hindrances to preaching arose from:

- The expansion of media access through the penny press, which minimized laymen's dependence upon a local preacher and enabled them to pay less attention to the preacher's authority in the community.
- Skepticism, suspicion and doubt resulting from Darwinism; higher critical skepticism challenging the claims of the Bible; human reason becoming a more trusted authority.
- Shorter attention spans due to the frenetic pace of the culture, material gain, illiteracy and the perceived dullness of logic.
- A renewed attention to rhetoric, eloquence and scholarship for respectability in society.
- An increased preference for artistry over sermons as architecture, music and other forms of art were increasingly sought to counteract the decline in church attendance.
- Material opportunity hindering clergy willingness to serve 'lesser' calls.
- Seminaries seemingly unable to train pastors for the realities of ministry, which were too demanding.
- Time demands hindering sermon preparation and communion with God. Pastors felt that they were

spending their time doing everything other than prayer, preaching and care for people.

- The plagiarizing of sermons arising as a needed relief from the demanding pace of ministry.[7]

Spurgeon summarized these concerns in a letter to the readers of his sermons in 1892. He wrote: 'Our nation is fast learning to forget God.... In too many instances ministers of religion have propagated doubt and the result is a general hardening of the popular feeling, and a greatly-increased neglect of public worship.'[8]

Challenging the Sermon

It is helpful for twenty-first-century preachers to recognize that these sweeping cultural challenges in the nineteenth century fueled movements which began to publicly challenge the role and practice of preaching itself. Some of this dialogue was captured in the journals of the time. As one observed, if the 'sermon cannot be altogether got rid of, it can of course be shortened...the standard length being reduced from half an hour to a quarter.'[9] The idea of a sermon lasting less than half an hour was echoed by others. Albert Evans sounded what to him was a hopeful note, stating that sermons had 'improved certainly as regards length,' and vary rarely approach an hour long.[10] 'In an average church,' Evans observed, 'the sermon still touches, or almost touches, the twentieth minute.' Another compared this growing sentiment with an earlier generation. 'That impatience with anything over half-an-hour which, more or less, characterises the modern congregation, was a feeling with which our ancestors had no sympathy.'[11] Such statements offer a corrective to assumptions which describe the nineteenth century in sweeping terms, as those who uniformly loved dry, storyless, passionless sermons which lasted over an hour in length and were comprised of extended logical argument.

The twenty-first-century preacher will marvel to learn that long before television and postmodernism, keeping attention and shortening sermons was a pulpit concern. We are surprised because we often forget Solomon's advice that it is folly to say that earlier times were better times. Just as in our day, some of Spurgeon's contemporaries began to express their desire that preaching should hold a lesser place in the practice of the church. They believed sincerely that such a measure would prove more attractive for the culture. 'There are those who hold the opinion,' said William Davies, 'that the function of the pulpit is now utterly decayed, that there is no more use for it, that it must inevitably grow more and more effete, until it shall no longer retain an existence among us.'[12] Louisa Merivale, though differing with Davies in his application of this sentiment, concurred with this belief: 'For ourselves, we should prefer being able to go to church occasionally without having to listen to a sermon at all.'[13]

Others urged the use of story in connection with shorter sermons, noting (in their enlightenment and print-oriented context) that 'an average person can only handle fifteen minutes of bare argument.'[14] The author of this article in *Tait's Edinburgh Magazine* then begs preachers:

> Will not great men – eloquent orators – remember sometimes that they were little children and had little thoughts and loved little things and were easily impressed with any pleasing incident? A tale of tenderness tenderly told occupying four or five minutes in the telling, would have kept them up then, through a quarter of an hour's 'dry as dust logic'.[15]

Keeping in mind what an average person can bear was becoming increasingly important. Challenge to dry and abstract discourses filled with bare logic grew long before television arrived. 'I want something for *today* – for overburdened men and women in this year of our Lord 1869,'[16] was the increasing summons. Give us 'something *live* and something that has bearing on our daily work, something that recognizes the seething elements about us and their bearing on the questions of conscience and duty we are hourly called on to settle. Oh, if the clergymen would only study their fellow men more.'[17]

These searchings for renewed power in the pulpit led many to combine shorter sermons with story, art and architecture. Dr. Allon in 1888 worried about this trend, wondering how concessions 'to ritual and music' might impact how

churches view preaching.[18] In 1921, Alfred Garvie, Principal
of New College, London, similarly noted the damage subtly
done when worship is more readily connected with art than
with the preaching of the Bible. 'Where devotion is divorced
from truth [in one's view of preaching],' Garvie said, 'it is to
be observed that the external aids – "the dim religious light"
of the pictured window, the symbols of the sculptured stone
or the carved wood, the suggestion of the human costume,
picture, and gesture, the stimulus of music and song – become and must become more prominent.'[19]

Spurgeon resonated with his generation's search for
power in the pulpit. He recognized the loss of attention and
the creative need for regaining it.[20] He certainly agreed with
the need for story and decried the 'articulate snoring' of de-
corum-bound preachers whose souls no longer 'sweat.'[21] But
he warned against those 'doctors' and 'deep thinking' men
who put aside the Bible for new schemes of pulpit attraction
and power and he lamented preachers who felt they 'must
link to the preaching of Christ all the aids of music and
architecture.'[22] Whether we agree with Spurgeon on these
points or not cannot detract us from the central conclusion
that an earlier age and earlier preachers had to wrestle
with the questions that we in the twenty-first century are
wrestling with. Significantly, a student of preaching may
learn from Spurgeon that these discussions of skepticism,
attention spans, story, art, media and sermon length, while
important in their own place, may veil the primary need
of the hour. According to Spurgeon, the hope for regaining a relevant and powerful pulpit amid a declining age is
not found 'in the preacher' nor 'in the crowd,' nor is it 'in
the attention' the preacher 'can attract.' The only hope for
regaining kindled fire in the pulpit is 'in God, and in God
alone.'[23]

The Pentecostal Flame
Specifically, Spurgeon's concern was that discussion for
regaining power in the pulpit was prone to leave out the
necessity of the Holy Spirit in connection with preaching. 'I
am persuaded,' Spurgeon revealed, 'that so far from speaking too frequent upon this matter, we do not often enough
extol the Blessed Spirit, and certain ministries almost ig-

nore his existence. You might attend some chapels and not even know that there was a Holy Ghost at all except for the benediction; and were it not for the liturgy, and the "'Glory be to the Father, and to the Son, and to the Holy Ghost," there are many of our national edifices where you might never know that a Comforter had been sent to us.'[24]

In contrast, Spurgeon prayed that every preacher who would profess to preach the gospel would 'learn to speak in entire dependence upon the direction of the Holy Spirit,' for the Spirit is the 'secret influence' from God – a person whose influence is able to make a sermon 'powerful upon the conscience and converting to the heart.' According to Spurgeon, a preacher must become convinced of this and learn to declare that 'It were better to speak six words in the power of the Holy Ghost than to preach seventy years of sermons without the Spirit.'[25]

The absence of this conviction among preachers troubled Spurgeon. He feared that the decline in Christian influence witnessed in his Victorian age was nothing less than *'an evident withdrawal of the Holy Ghost,'* a grieving *of the Spirit in the churches.*[26] If he was right, the greatest need of the hour for preachers and churches was neither to find new methods nor to remain stagnant in age-limited decorum. Rather, they must 'come back' to God in Christ, and seek a return of His gracious effusions of power for their generation.

For this reason, Spurgeon could not approach preaching without viewing all of its aspects from the vantage point of the Holy Spirit's person and work. Spurgeon's explicit references to the Spirit in preaching seem often and notably absent among his reformed and evangelical grandchildren. For example, it is difficult to imagine such successors crying out from our pulpits today: 'May the Lord answer us by fire, and may that fire fall on the ministers and then upon the people! We ask for the true Pentecostal flame...this we must have, or our ministry will be in vain.'[27]

Because of abuses among our number and our right concern to uphold sound teaching, we are often concerned and rightly so, to uphold what is biblical regarding the person and work of the Spirit. But when in a generation our references to the Spirit and preaching become veiled, implied or only assumed, sometimes another kind of 'abuse' emerges which is equally ruinous for preachers and people. A generation begins to look at preaching as a merely natural or a merely rhetorical event. When this happens, a generation of preaching has no distinguishing characteristics in its approach from that which is customary for non-Christian speechmaking. Furthermore, a generation that only knows what it does *not* believe concerning the Spirit is put into a dangerous situation, having no practical teaching for how to live on the basis of what it *does* believe about the Spirit.

Perhaps some of us as preachers rarely talk about the need for the Holy Spirit for relevant and powerful preaching because we are simply distracted by the fashions of our times. After all, we at the turn of the twenty-first century are called in the West to preach amid watershed changes and tectonic shifts in the cultural landscape. In the midst of shifts from print to visuals and from modern to postmodern perspectives, we are busy discussing how preaching can remain relevant and effective, often focusing our homiletic discussions with little attention to the Holy Spirit of God.

Training Ministers Suitable for the Masses

One of the ways in which Spurgeon attempted to recover an explicit connection between powerful preaching and the Holy Spirit was to train students for the ministry. 'Wherever a great principle is to be advanced,' he said, 'prudence suggests the necessity of training the men who are to become advancers of it.'[28] For thirty-five years ministers of the gospel were trained in a two to three year program of ministerial curricula at a college over which Charles Spurgeon resided as President.[29] The uniqueness of Spurgeon's College did not lie in the fact that it was the only Baptist option for ministerial training. There was the college at Bristol and Rawdon College, Leeds. Regent's Park College at Stepney and 'a college founded at Bury in Lancashire which was later moved to Brighten Grove,'[30] were also available. But what Spurgeon longed for were 'ministers suitable for the masses.' By 'the masses,' Spurgeon meant everyone, including the common people and the poor. As Spurgeon later acknowledged, 'No College at that time appeared to me to be suitable for the class of men that the providence and grace of God drew around me.'[31] By 'class of men' Spurgeon referred to men with a deficient education and few financial resources. He believed that such deficiencies ought not to hinder a called man from ministerial training and he intended to do what he could to remove the hindrances. He hoped that such a college would be useful in the hands of God to kindle a fire despite the spiritual decline in London and beyond. Starting a college to train preachers was for him, 'the simplest mode of influencing for good the Church and the world.' He found precedent in the Lord's training of the twelve, in John Calvin's college in Geneva, and in the establishing of such colleges that he had heard about among missionaries in China and Jamaica.

These biblical and historical precedents were given room to take root in Spurgeon's ministry by an unexpected and ordinary moment. Some of the members of New Park Street complained to Spurgeon that one of his converts,T. W. Medhurst, was preaching in the London streets. Medhurst's uneducated speech was an embarrassment to himself and to the church. Accordingly, Spurgeon had a talk with the earnest but uneducated man. The young street preacher agreed that he spoke with mistaken English and that he had other noticeable flaws, but he nonetheless declared to Spurgeon, 'I must preach, sir; and I shall preach unless you cut off my head!' Spurgeon recounted to the complainants what Medhurst had said. To this they replied, 'Oh!, you can't cut off Mr. Medhurst's head, so you must let him go on preaching.' Spurgeon agreed and added, 'As our young brother is evidently bent on serving the Lord with all his might, I must do what I can to get him an education that will fit him for the ministry.'[32] The rest, as the expression goes, is history.

The Purpose of this Book

What would it have been like to sit in Spurgeon's classes? I hope this book gives a sense of what students would hear Spurgeon say about preaching if he were to speak with them in the hall, from the pulpit, or on a walk down the streets of London.

Thus, the purpose of this book is to enable preachers to 'apprentice' with Spurgeon for a season in order to learn from him about preaching. It is hoped that such an internship will prove valuable for contributing to preachers as they mine resources for gospel relevance and power in the twenty-first century. But how could Spurgeon help?

The twenty-first-century preacher in the West will recognize some profound similarities with Spurgeon and his times. It is true that postmodernism and Enlightenment rationalism are very different philosophies. But their results are similar in that they promote widespread skepticism and doubt regarding the authority of the Bible. Furthermore, it is true that the printing press, and not the Internet, spread information rapidly throughout England during Spurgeon's times. But the results are common, introducing a media-access to information which reduces the perceived necessity of the local preacher and supports a local suspicion of clerical authority. The debates about the use of art and sermon length at the turn of the twenty-first century are no different in substance than those found in England at the turn of the twentieth. The effect of attention span and the need for story to accompany logic are not new topics of discussion for preachers. In addition, pressures which reduce time for sermon preparation and engender the temptation for shallow or borrowed sermons are nothing essentially new.

Moreover, we have something else in common with Spurgeon's day. Many of us are trying to offer solutions for renewed relevance and power in the pulpit, with little mention of the Holy Spirit of God.

Conclusion
Spurgeon taught his students to seek a 'kindled fire' as the source for renewed power and relevance in preaching. Below is a sample of the kind of prayer that Spurgeon's students and congregational members would have heard from him amid the spiritual decline of their generation.

> Come, Holy Spirit, we can do nothing without thee. We solemnly invoke thee, great Spirit of God! Thou who didst rest on Abraham, on Isaac and on Jacob.... Spirit of the Prophets, Spirit of the Apostles, Spirit of the Church, be thou our Spirit this night, that the earth may tremble, that souls may be made to hear thy word, and then all flesh may rejoice together to praise thy name. Unto

Father, Son and Holy Ghost, the dread Supreme, be everlasting praise. Amen.'[33]

Opening his eyes after praying such a prayer from his heart, I imagine he would have turned and looked out over us preachers of the twenty-first century with this exhortation. 'Let the fire be kindled, brethren! Let the fire be kindled by the Holy Ghost!'[34]

PART ONE:
The Preacher's Story

Key Points to Look for in Chapters One through Three:

- Training for ministry is not dislocated from real life and real people. God's providence is integral to preparing the preacher. A man's calling is rooted in a man's story. Preachers are mentored by God by means of living in a place and knowing a people.

- The Spirit of God is the authority over Christian ministry and ministers. A man must have a double call from the Spirit – a call to Christ and a call to the vocation of elder. Such a call must find confirmation as the would-be preacher relates to people, evidences gifts and lives in community.

- Possessing a personal lifestyle already committed to building-up and reaching both Christians and non-Christians is a prerequisite for vocational ministry.

- A preacher must settle and surrender his commitment to the authority and sufficiency of the Bible as he faces the needs and challenges of his generation.

- A preacher is neither the first to preach the gospel nor will he be the last. He preaches in light of those who have gone before him and for those who will follow. A preacher therefore needs theological mentors. These mentors shape the substance of his preaching.

- A preacher believes that truth exists in the world and that God is the one who has revealed it by means of the Bible.

Overview for Part One:

A preacher is, first of all, a human being. A preacher cannot separate his call, his gifts, nor his ministry from his own life nor from the lives of those around him. These relate to one another. Preaching is a task which flows from an integrated man. Therefore, a preacher has two schools from which to learn – the classroom and the community. Who he is in the pulpit is the result of who God has been to him during the real pains and joys of his actual life. A preacher must come to terms with who he is and where he is from, including the limitations and strengths of both. He can look to God for consistency of life and ministry, not just in terms of his morals, but also in terms of his integrity to the people and places from which the Lord has taught him and prepared him for ministry. The Bible, which has been God's means of grace in the preacher's life, also possesses the sufficiency in God's hands to meet the demands of that preacher's generation. The preacher must trust God and His truth as the means for renewed relevance and power in the community. 'Kindled fire' awakens a man to his story as God is writing it and to the Word as God has written it.

1

MYSTERIOUS AGENCIES:

Preparing our Hearts

Courage, ye warriors of the cross! Christ is with you for your captain. Sound your trumpets and advance to battle! If Christ and his angels, and the providence of God all work with you, who can be against you?[1]

By looking at the boy, the human eye cannot often discern what God may intend for the man. If one had asked the young Charles Spurgeon what he might like to be when he grew up, the boy might have dreamingly answered, 'I'm going to be a huntsman.'[2] After all, that secret spot behind the old congregational meetinghouse often and amply supplied his boyish imagination. From there, Charles could eagerly gaze upon those red-coated riders who charged on their noble steeds chasing foxes into the mysterious adventures of Stambourne woods.

Preaching the gospel and becoming a leader among Christians would not have occurred to the boy Spurgeon. In fact, even as a young man, he could deeply doubt his abilities in preaching, particularly when falling short of expectations for preachers which he had read in a homiletics textbook. He was not alone in this sometimes hesitance about his preaching. One woman, 'as fine a Christian matron as ever breathed,' earnestly dissuaded Charles from preaching.[3] Even the future Mrs. Spurgeon, though she later lamented it, early commented that the young preacher's 'countrified manner and speech excited more regret than reverence.'[4]

It may not sound so suprising then that for the young Spurgeon, 'A request to go and preach would have met with a decided negative.'[5] Like many a faithful pastor before and after him, and like many of his students, 'very frequently' Spurgeon could 'inquire within' himself whether he should 'resort to some form of secular labour, and leave the ministry.'[6] Perhaps at times his boyhood imaginations of living a huntsman's life seemed appealing. Many preachers have known these haunting hesitations which can creep into the attics of a called man's thoughts and whisper doubts to him.

The one thing that Charles was convinced of, however, was that every person's life is a story which God is personally writing. 'Leave out God,' he once said, 'and you cannot write the story of anyone's career.'[7] A force beyond the boy's imagination and equal to the young man's hesitation was therefore active. The learned awareness of this activity has been known to steady a leader's trembling courage and settle a follower's unassured steps. It is what enables one to look back and 'connect the dots' of one's life in order to make sense of a present crossroads. It is what enables one to look forward beyond what threatens.

In 1855, the then twenty-one-year-old preacher at Park Street identified this larger working when he published, for the strengthening of families, what he called *A Puritan Catechism*.[8] In it, he asked: 'What are God's works of providence?' Copying the Westminster Shorter Catechism, Spurgeon answered, 'God's works of providence are his most holy (Psalm 145:17), wise (Isaiah 28:29), and powerful (Hebrews 1:3), preserving and governing all his creatures, and all their actions (Psalm 103:19, Matthew 10:29).'[9] In every circumstance, Spurgeon believed that God's preserving and governing presence was powerfully and wisely active along with whatever he thought within himself or faced outside of himself. The Christian learns to say, 'No matter what, God is at work, too!' A preacher's anchor for ministry is held firm within the rock of God having called him to the work. This calling, which we will explore in chapter two, is demonstrated through the activity of providence.

In this chapter we will explore the story of God's calling Charles Spurgeon to preach. From it, we preachers learn

to look for God's workings in our own stories in order more clearly to identify the providential workings of God's Spirit, shaping us for the pulpit.

Deacon Vinter's Scheme

Every preacher has a 'first sermon'. Charles' hesitation to preach found a suprising remedy at St. Andrew's Street Chapel. It was there that Charles first preached. How it came about was that Deacon Vinter often arranged for young men to go and preach to local gatherings of village folk. Recognizing potential in the boy, Vinter chanced to invite young Charles to a preaching opportunity under the guise that Charles could offer support to the young man who was scheduled to preach. Unbeknown to Charles, Mr. Vinter had made the same arrangement with the other lad. Each of the young men thought that they were traveling together in order to support the other – each supposing that it was the other who was supposed to preach! When the two teenagers discovered the ruse, it was too late, and one of them had to bring a word to the people who had gathered. Realizing that he must 'tell a few poor cottagers of the sweetness and love of Jesus,' Charles felt the necessity to pray 'for Divine help' and to depend 'upon the power of the Holy Ghost' in order to 'at least tell out the story of the cross, and not allow people to go home without a word.'[10] The result of Deacon Vinter's scheme was the first sermon that a hesitant Charles Spurgeon ever preached. This was quite an unusual start for one of Christian history's finest preachers! Prior to facing the thousands who would one day gather to hear him, Spurgeon was pushed through his hesitance into preaching to a handful. The teenager's preaching left the meager cottage-gathering alive with interest, however. They wondered how old this preacher was who gave the word with such power. The result was their earnest invitation that Charles would come soon and preach Christ for them again.

A preacher must not take his meager start or its circumstances lightly. 'No matter what, God is at work, too!' Spurgeon appealed to divine providence in order to describe his beginnings in the ministry. 'I have felt placed by Providence in such a position that I had no wish to avoid the duty.'

Charles asserted that he was 'compelled' by providence and an inner impulse into the ministry.

> Before I thought of going to a Sabbath-school to teach, someone called – asked me – begged me – prayed me to take his class. I could not refuse to go; and there I was, held hand and foot by the superintendent, and was compelled to go on. Then I was asked to address the children; I thought I could not, but I stood up, and stammered out a few words. It was the same on the first occasion when I attempted to preach to the people – I am sure I had no wish to do it – but there was no one else in the place who could, and the little congregation must have gone away without a single word of warning or invitation. How could I suffer it? I felt forced to address them, and so it has been with whatever I have laid my hand to.[11]

God used other circumstances to prepare Spurgeon. For example, as a Non-conformist he was for three years 'a Cambridge man.' But he could not obtain a degree. At Cambridge, he became a part of the Cambridge Lay Preachers Association. There, he traveled by foot, walking three to eight miles through local villages, preaching to ordinary folks in 'a farmer's kitchen, a cottage or a barn.' He felt that this 'talking upon plain gospel themes in a farmer's kitchen' was a good preparation. 'To make the very poorest listen with pleasure and profit is in itself an achievement,' he said. 'Beyond this, it is the best possible promise and preparation for an influential ministry.'[12] Here, Charles learned to preach the gospel to plain people with plain speech in ordinary places. Likewise, taking tracts to the poorest districts and teaching Sunday school required Charles to learn to communicate gospel mysteries plainly. Of teaching children, Charles said: 'If I was ever a little dull, my scholars began to make wheels of themselves, twisting round on the forms on which they sat,' and the naughty ones would say, 'This is very dull teacher, can't you pitch us a yarn? I learned to tell stories partly by being obliged to tell them [in order to get their] attention again.'

In these and like situations, Charles Spurgeon was learning to preach the gospel by providential means. The foundations of his plain-speaking, care for the poor and his evangelist's heart were dug in these cottages and barns in hamlets and villages.

The Great Means of God's Hand

Long before Deacon Vinter's plan, or the student's asking 'for a yarn,' however, divine providence was writing with the pen of faithful women in Spurgeon's life. To begin with, Charles was raised in a steady atmosphere of preaching and Christian endeavor. It is not so for every valued preacher called by God. Some find Him calling them from a family broken and void of gospel grace. But Spurgeon, like Timothy in the New Testament, had a mother and grandmother who certainly and actively taught him the Scriptures in childhood. When asked on one occasion why God had given him the position he held in Christ's church, Spurgeon thoughtfully and profoundly gave two reasons: 'My mother, and the truth of my message.'[13] It was his mother Eliza's counsel, for example, which drew him to saving faith in Christ's cross-providing promises. 'I had been some years seeking Christ, and I could not believe that He would save me,' Spurgeon recalls. He shared this with his mother, who replied that 'she had heard many people swear and blaspheme God, but one thing she had never known: She had never heard a man say he had sought Christ, and Christ had rejected him.' In a letter wishing his mother a happy birthday, the fifteen-year-old said to her, 'You, my Mother, have been the great means in God's hand of rendering me what I hope I am.' Referring to Eliza's 'Sabbath-evening addresses' at home, Charles spoke of his possible calling one day to the ministry. With the courage needed for such a call in mind, he wrote warmly, 'I love you as the preacher to my heart of such courage, as my praying, watching Mother.'[14]

Charles' grandmother was no less active. She gave a small allowance to the boy for every one of Dr. Watts' hymns that he learned by memory. Though killing rats for his grandfather paid him a larger sum, a fact Spurgeon humorously recalls, he meaningfully asserted that, 'No matter on what topic I am preaching, I can even now, in the middle of any sermon, quote some verse of a hymn in harmony with the subject, the hymns remained with me, while those old rats for years have passed away and the shillings I earned... have been spent long ago.'[15] Further, his grandmother's prayers formed the context of his own life of prayer. Charles imagined his grandmother's lament and longing for her grandson's faith. He imagined what it would be like for his grandmother to see him from heaven. 'I see her as she said, "Behold, he prayeth; behold, he prayeth." Oh! I can picture her countenance. She seemed to have two Heavens for a moment – a double bliss, a Heaven in me as well as in herself – when she could say, "Behold, he prayeth."'[16]

Another, lesser known woman used in Spurgeon's life was 'an old cook in the school at Newmarket' by the name of Mary King. From her, Charles learned his first lessons in theology. He felt that he learned more from her than he did from the minister of the chapel. She possessed 'good strong Calvinistic doctrine,' he said. The two would converse about the vitals of the faith and the doctrines of grace. 'There are some Christian people who taste and see, and enjoy religion in their own souls and who get at a deeper knowledge of it than books can ever give them.' This cook was such a woman. 'I do believe that I learnt more from her than I should have learned from any six doctors of divinity,' Spurgeon declared. Charles would later publicly refer to Mary in his first book, entitled *The Saint and his Saviour*. In her later years, Spurgeon had the 'pleasure of supplying the financial needs' which Mary had.[17] He reminds by his gestures that even the greatest preacher is not too proud to learn from and thank the choicest of God's people, even if in the world they come to us in meager clothes.

Did Spurgeon's grandmother, mother and this ordinary cook at a school know how God was using their daily faith in Him to shape one of His future heralds of the gospel? Sometimes providence strongly prepares us by the most ordinary relationships. Sometimes amid our ordinary life, God is using us to strongly prepare another for extraordinary ministry.

Looking at the Moon
Providence also afforded faithful men to Charles. John Spurgeon was Charles' father. He was a pastor at some distance from home but faithful to the young boy and his family. Charles would stay up late into the night telling

his father of his new-found faith in Jesus Christ.[18] Like any son, Charles wanted to be like his father, but this became especially true as Charles grew in Christ. Leaving his boyhood imaginations of huntsman and riders aside, Spurgeon's new-found zeal for seeing Christ win sinners to Himself aroused an exclamation of respect for his father and longing for his father's labors to be his. 'How I long for the time when it may please God to make me, like you, my Father, a successful preacher of the gospel! I almost envy you your exalted privilege. May the...increase of the Spirit rest upon your labours!'[19]

But of the men in Spurgeon's life, it is James Spurgeon (1776–1864), Charles' grandfather, who was especially important concerning the preparation of Charles Spurgeon the preacher. Charles lived for a time with his grandparents. James preached for over fifty years, often preaching to upwards of 600 people in the old meetinghouse where his grandson once dreamed of red-coat riders. As young Charles listened to James Spurgeon preach on a towering pulpit which was nestled below a 'huge-sounding board,' Charles wondered what might happen to his grandfather if that huge board ever gave way during the sermon! 'I thought of my Jack-in-the-box,' Spurgeon recalled, 'and hoped that my dear grandpapa would never be shut down and shut up in such a fashion!'[20] But when the grandson was older and no longer imagining jack-in-the-boxes during sermons, he recognized the importance of the chapel ministry to those who had known his grandpapa as their pastor. 'No earthly house will accommodate a sounder or more useful ministry than that of my grandfather,' Charles Spurgeon testified.[21] 'Wherever my grandfather went, souls were saved under his sermons.'[22] One person who heard Charles preach in the very beginning of his young ministry declared, 'I heard your grandfather, and I would run my shoes off my feet any day to hear a Spurgeon.'[23]

But James not only preached and pastored – he seems, providentially, to have intentionally discipled his young grandson. Spurgeon's autobiography reveals many anecdotes to this end. On Sunday mornings, for example, Charles was to sit in the parlour with his grandfather while his grandfather made preparations there to preach. Likewise, though 'forbidden to stay there when grandfather was meditating,' Charles knew the garden, and the grass walk 'which looked upon the fields' that his grandfather often used 'as his study' – walking 'up and down...when preparing his sermons.'[24] Similarly, on Monday afternoons James would take Charles with him for tea with his neighbor and friend in ministry, the Rector James Hopkins.

Added to these together-times with grandfather was family worship. Each morning throughout the week Charles was allowed to read the Scriptures at family prayer. The young lad's persistent questions moved James to ask his young grandson, 'Well, dear, what is it that puzzles you?' The answers to such persistent questions, particularly how grandpapa described the 'beast with seven heads' in Revelation or the 'bottomless pit,' created an environment of regular Scripture reading with the freedom to learn. This atmosphere made lasting impressions on the young boy.[25]

It was his grandfather that strengthened the easily frightened young boy with a sense of courage. The Charles Spurgeon who surprisingly says that he 'always loved safe things,'[26] would also say, 'I have always been grateful to [my grandfather] for teaching me to act according to my belief whatever the consequences might be.'[27] It is his grandfather's Christward encouragement that must lie providentially behind such journal entries as April 27, 1850. Charles, then fifteen years old and in the first year of his second birth, writes:

> Fear, begone! Doubts, fall back! In the name of the Lord of hosts I would set up my banner. Come on, ye demons of the pit, my Captain is more than a match for you; in His name, armed with His weapons, and in His strength, I dare defy you all. How glorious 'twould be to die by the side of such a leader! I am a worm and no man, a vanity, a nothing; yet hath He set His love upon me, and why should I tremble or fear?[28]

When hounded by the expectations of the homiletics textbook, and wondering about his abilities in ministry, Spurgeon turned to his grandfather for much-needed support and encouragement.[29] When the time came for young

Charles to live again with his father and mother, his sorrow-
ing grandfather said these words to his young heart: 'Now
child, to-night, when the moon shines at Colchester, and
you look at it, don't forget that it is the same moon your
grandfather will be looking at from Stambourne.' And for
years, as a child, Spurgeon says, 'I used to love the moon
because I thought that my grandfather's eyes and my own
somehow met there on the moon.'[30]

A preacher who does not have the Christian family that
young Spurgeon had can still learn this principle of providence. God shapes preachers by bringing people to mentor
them. Though Timothy did not have a father to teach him
the things of God, an Apostle Paul would one day call him
'son'. Calling to ministry will ordinarily find its forging in
a relational context. The Bible says 'as iron sharpens iron,
so one man sharpens another.' Therefore, look to Him who
gives the blessing of people to mentor us.

Old Roads and Mr. Knill
Perhaps because of the mighty labor which Spurgeon would
be called to or perhaps because of his own weakness, some
extraordinary events of providence were given in his life.
Long before Vinter's plan, various events indicate the working of divine providence in preparing Spurgeon for a call to
preach. Surely Thomas Roads saw such an event when he
was encountered by the young child. Charles had heard
his grandfather James agonizing about Thomas and his
wandering from the faith. Soon after, the boy snuck outside
and burst into the bar where 'Old Roads,' as he was known,
was sitting with his 'pipe and mug of beer.' As Roads tells
it: The little child 'points at me with his finger, just so,
and says, "What doest thou here, Elijah? Sitting with the
ungodly; and you a member of the church, and breaking
your pastor's heart!"' Old Roads was smitten in conscience
and went to his pastor (Charles' grandfather) and sought
forgiveness, a forgiveness he demonstrated in faithfulness
to Christ through the end of his life. 'To think,' reflected Old
Roads, that 'an old man like me should be took to task, and
reproved by a bit of a child like that!'[31]

Another remarkable moment, baffling to many, but sweet
to Charles,[32] caught the attention of the whole Spurgeon

family. It was on occasion of a visit from Mr. Richard Knill. This pastor and missionary, after spending some time with the family, noticed the ten-year-old boy and invited him to meet for a walk at 6:00 a.m. 'With many a story he preached Christ to me, and told me how good God had been to him,' Spurgeon recalls. Then, 'he knelt down in that arbour, and prayed for me with his arms about my neck.... He heard my childish talk with patient love, and repaid it with gracious instruction...for three successive days.' When it was time for Mr. Knill to leave, the whole family was gathered for morning prayer. Then, Spurgeon says: 'In the presence of them all, Mr. Knill took me on his knee, and said, "This child will one day preach the gospel, and he will preach it to great multitudes. I am persuaded that he will preach in the chapel of Rowland Hill."'[33] Years later, when the then-famous Charles Spurgeon preached in Rowland Hill's chapel, Charles was filled with emotion as he told the story of Rev. Knill's statements from when he was a young man.

Beneath an Old Oaktree by the River Medway
In addition to using situations and relationships to write the preacher's story, God also endows the preacher with certain talents and later with certain gifts. The nature of Charles' talents were evidenced in his love for reading, studying and learning. His brother said that 'he never did anything else but study. I kept rabbits, chickens, and pigs, and a horse; he kept to the books.'[34] Keeping to his books began early for Charles. His grandfather's and his father's libraries led him to read Puritan authors, the poems of Milton and Cowper, and the dramas of Defoe and Shakespeare. An amusing anecdote regarding Charles' natural penchant for study arose when Charles publicly corrected his uncle's math problems while his uncle was teaching math to Charles' class. His uncle determined that Charles would better employ his time by taking his books and studying by himself 'beneath an old oaktree by the river Medway.' Charles happily obliged![35] These habits of voracious reading and personal curiosity formed the adult Spurgeon who at sixteen years old was preaching the gospel with doctrinal depth. This is the Spurgeon who was said sometimes to read up to eight books each week in the course of his ministry.

Spurgeon also showed an early talent for creativity and writing. In 1846, the twelve-year-old created *The Home Juvenile Society.* This was a magazine with volume numbers that contained bits of wisdom related to prayer and following Christ. *The Sword and Trowel* found its seeds here. In addition, Charles had a natural talent for speaking. Whenever he spoke as a boy, people were interested. Whether it was his speaking to the Sunday school classes or with those to whom he gave gospel tracts, Spurgeon's speaking was attended with a certain power. Large crowds began to gather to hear Spurgeon speak, in the Sabbath school for example, even before Waterbeach and long before the Park Street Chapel.

'All that men have,' Spurgeon declared, 'they must trace to the great Fountain, the giver of all good.' For this reason, a minister must learn to content himself with the measures given him by God. From this contentment he must strive, not to equal other men, but to use what God has given him to its fullest.

> One man finds himself successful, and he supposes that if everyone else could have been as industrious and as persevering as himself, everyone must necessarily have been as successful. You will often hear remarks against ministers who are godly and earnest men, but who do not happen to have much attracting power, and they are called drones and lazy persons, because they cannot make much of a stir in the world, whereas the reason may be, that they have but little talent, and are making the best use of what they have, and therefore ought not to be rebuked for the littleness of what they are able to accomplish. It is a fact, which every man must see, that even in our birth there is a difference. All children are not alike precocious, and all men certainly are not alike capable of learning or of teaching. God hath made eminent and marvelous differences.[36]

The Unseen Agency
That God makes eminent and marvelous differences among people in order to write their stories informed not only how Charles looked at his own preparation for his calling but also how he viewed what God might do in the context of

his sermons. The adult Spurgeon recognized that the same
providence that was at work in his situational, relational
and natural arrangements was connecting his sermon to
the stories of those who came to hear him preach. The fact
of providence reminds the preacher that the Holy Spirit 'is
everywhere in the midst of his Church' and 'comes forth'
to put himself into direct contact with a human spirit.[37]
Therefore, unseen to the preacher and audience, prior to the
pulpit event, God may act as an 'unseen agency' in the life of
an individual through the circumstances of ordinary living.
Faith is strengthened then when the preacher recognizes that
more than his sermon is taking place for the strengthening
of his hearers and the writing of their stories. 'The forces engaged upon our side are not confined to the pulpit,' Charles
urges. Throughout the week, the cares and joys that people
experience are God's means of preparing them to receive the
preaching. The preacher may doubt and feel powerless until
his 'eyes are opened' and he sees 'horses of fire and chariots
of fire round about the prophet of the Lord.' Yes, 'mysterious agencies are cooperating with the ministry of grace.'[38]
When the preacher sees the fruit of his sermon received in
the heart and connected to the actual lives of people with
its effectiveness, he will know that 'it was nothing but God
in providence ploughing the field for the seed.'[39]

'Mysterious agencies' and 'ploughed fields' describe the
combination of relationships, situations, talents and con-
versations which form the story of a person or a community.
These combine 'like servants' of God who everywhere carry out
'his secret directions.' 'Though they are little aware of it,' these
scenes of the story 'are led to work together for the same pre-
destined end.'[40] Such an unseen agency 'ploughing the fields'
through the week, enables an audience to feel at times as if
the preacher knows them personally as he preaches according
to the appointed ways of the Spirit: 'As our Lord seeks souls
by his providence he also seeks them by the *Word*. It is very
wonderful how the Word of God will come home to people. It
is a part of every preacher's business who is sent of God, so
to preach that persons in the congregation may perceive that
he speaks of them.'[41] The preacher and his sermon therefore
becomes the instrument of an unseen agency, a pen in the
hands of God by which He writes the pages of a person's

story in the world. In this same manner, God 'spoke' into Spurgeon's life by the arrangement of words, relationships, situations and talents. As a preacher, Charles recognized that he participated in the stories that God was writing in the lives of those who came to hear his messages.

Conclusion

Kindled fire begins with the provisions of God's providence. These form a life made ready to ignite with the touch of God's Spirit. Students of Spurgeon can learn to preach by first examining the ways of divine providence that continue to shape their stories. Preachers will benefit from wisdom when they consider the people and circumstances that God has brought into their lives and reflect with gratitude and humility what God has used them to teach. By these beginning reflections, the hand of providence begins to surface more clearly. Wisdom is gained and gratitude is born as a preacher learns that his calling began long before he was ready. The first thing a preacher can learn from Charles Spurgeon is this: A preacher's calling begins with God and is formed in the story of God's providence.

Questions for Learning and Discussion

1. What strikes you most when you read this chapter?

2. What do you believe the Bible teaches about divine providence? From what Scriptures do you draw your convictions concerning this subject?

3. Who are the people that God has used to prepare you for ministry?

4. What circumstances and situations have brought you challenge and taught you about walking with God and ministering to His people?

5. What natural talents and capacities has God given you? In what measure have these been given? What talents has God not given you so that you must humble yourself in dependence upon what God is doing in others?

2

THE CALL OF HEAVEN:

Clarifying our Work

Men of zeal and ability, if you love Jesus, make the ministry your aim; train
your minds to it; exercise your souls towards it; and may God the Holy Spirit
call you to it, that you also may preach the Word of reconciliation to the dy-
ing thousands. The laborers still are few, may the Lord of the harvest thrust
you into his work.[1]

On Sunday morning, March 11, 1866, Spurgeon made this
appeal to the Holy Spirit before his congregation: 'by the love
of souls, aid me in my great anxiety to supply the needs of
the age with a ministry called of God to preach his truth.'[2]
In this statement, Spurgeon saw the remedy for the 'needs
of the age' as a particular kind of preaching formed by a
particular kind of minister. The preaching must magnify
God's truth. The preacher must be a specifically 'called-
by-God' man.

This 'anxiety' for 'called of God' men to preach God's truth
was aptly expressed nine years earlier. During a Sunday
morning in 1857, Spurgeon preached a sermon entitled, 'The
Sound in the Mulberry Trees.' In this sermon, he instructed
his listeners regarding the peculiar calling of a preacher.
'No man has any right to address a congregation on things
spiritual,' he said, 'unless he believes that God has given
him a special calling to the work, and unless he has also
in due time received certain seals which attest his ministry as being the ministry of God.'[3] Similarly, his students
would have heard from him that a minister of the Word
must possess two things. First, he must possess '*Special*

---

gifts, such as perception of truth, simplicity, aptness to impart instruction, some degree of eloquence, and intense earnestness.' Second, he must possess a *'Special call.* Every man who is rightly in the ministry must have been moved thereto of the Holy Ghost.'[4]

From these instructions, the student of preaching learns that preaching begins with the Holy Spirit. Preaching cannot legitimately take place without the Spirit's sanction and authoritative call. A preacher therefore fulfills his task within the context of the authoritative permission of the Holy Spirit. To preach without this calling is to act without the authority of God's Spirit. 'No man may intrude into the sheepfold as an under-shepherd,' Spurgeon warned. 'He must wait for the call from above; and if he does not so, but rushes into the sacred office, the Lord will say of him and others like him, "I sent them not."'[5]

This sobering truth beckons the man of conscience to ask how one can know that he has been given this call by the Spirit. The instructions from Spurgeon noted above form four basic guides to recognizing a legitimate call. First, the Spirit will give to the man who would preach an increasing understanding of 'the work' of the sacred office. In addition, the Spirit will give an effectual and vocational call to that work. Furthermore, the Spirit will give inward confirmation that the preacher's call is from God. Finally, the Spirit will give a preacher outward 'seals which attest his ministry as being the ministry of God.'

The Sacred Office
The Spirit first gives a preacher an increasing understanding of the nature of the work. By this 'work' Spurgeon meant 'the sacred office' of 'overseer' or 'pastor' or 'elder.' He did not refer to 'occasional preaching, or any other form of ministry common to all the saints, but to the work and office of the bishopric, in which is included both teaching and bearing rule in the Church.' This work, Spurgeon said, 'requires the dedication of a man's entire life to spiritual work, and separation from every secular calling.'[6] As we will explore in chapter thirteen, Spurgeon believed that men and women in every station in life were valued ministers of the gospel and were called to serve and share the gospel with all their

capacities. He put this every-member conviction into practice and the interdependent ministries of pastor and people
at the Metropolitan Tabernacle remain a relevant model for
gospel ministry. But when he referred to regular preaching Spurgeon meant it as the 'special duty' of the 'sacred
office.' 'I do not believe, as some do, that it is the business
of everyone of us to preach,' he said.[7] This sacred office is
a calling reserved, not for every man, but only for those
men whom God has specifically gifted and called for this
purpose in the church. As a ministerial student, he would
have explained it to you in the following way:

> We believe that the Holy Ghost appoints in the church of
> God some to act as overseers, while others are made will-
> ing to be watched over for their good. All are not called to
> labor in word and doctrine, or to be elders, or to exercise
> the office of a bishop; nor should all aspire to such works,
> since the gifts necessary are nowhere promised to all;
> but those should addict themselves to such important
> engagements who feel, like the apostle, that they have
> 'received this ministry.' 2 Corinthians 4:1.[8]

The purpose of the sacred office must also comply with the
purposes of the Spirit. The office is not a means for exaltation or earning one's merit with God. Exaltation and merit
depend upon the prerogative and provision of Christ alone.
Therefore, if a man looks to his position as a minister as
the measure of his standing before God, that measure 'will
certainly fail thee,' Spurgeon warned. This is because of the
quality of the office. 'There is nothing in the most sacred
office in the church to preserve us or our characters.'[9] The
quality of the sacred office is not a preserving power but
an identified function within the body of Christ. The sacred
office reveals the earthly means by which God teaches and
oversees His people. A primary biblical metaphor Spurgeon
appealed to was that of a 'watchman.' A watchman is called
to oversee a particular place, which Spurgeon identified as
one's appointed 'sphere of labor.'[10] As a 'sentry' appointed by
God to labor in this place, the minister is to preach the truth
with all his heart, and to seek to give meat in due season to
all over whom the Holy Ghost hath made him an overseer.[11]

Though the preacher 'cannot, like Elisha, raise the dead; nor, like Isaiah, pour forth eloquent predictions; nor, as Ezekiel, foretell certain coming and immediate judgments; yet,' Spurgeon believed, 'like them, we are commanded to teach, to warn, and to encourage.'[12]

The preacher learns from Charles Spurgeon, then, that to aspire to the work of regular preaching is to aspire to the office of overseer or 'preaching elder' for the church in an appointed place. In that place, the sacred officer lives for the welfare of those entrusted to his care. Their good in Christ is his ambition. So, he teaches the Bible to them and relationally instructs, corrects and encourages them as he cares for their lives. To this end, Spurgeon felt that one must 'read carefully' the qualifications written in 1 Timothy 3:2-7 and Titus 1:6-9 if he were to aspire to the office of preaching. These qualifications are meant to enable a man to examine himself.[13] He must ask himself, 'Have I been called by God to this sacred office among His people?' 'Has God gifted me for this work?' 'Do I have a love for the welfare of souls?' Answering such questions in the affirmative is an important indication of a call, an indication that to teach and care with all one's heart as a watchman for the welfare of souls in a particular place is a desire of one's heart. Answering in the negative is an indication that a man has been fit by God for some work other than the sacred office among His people.

The Forked-Flash from Heaven
Second, the 'work of preaching' must originate not with preachers, but with God. In Acts 20:28, the Apostle Paul urges the Ephesian Elders to 'pay careful attention' to themselves 'and to all the flock, in which the Holy Spirit has made [them] overseers.' Regularly, Spurgeon uses this same language to identify his own ministry or to spur others on in theirs. He founds this conviction on the resonance which the preacher has with the Old Testament priest and the Old Testament prophet. 'I believe the office of the ministry, though not like that of the priesthood, as to any particular sanctity, or any particular power that we possess,' Spurgeon said, 'is yet like the priesthood in this – that no man ought to take it to himself, save he that is called hereunto, as was Aaron.'[14] Or, like the prophets, how can preachers

'justify their office,' Spurgeon asked, 'except by a similar call?'[15] Preaching has always originated with God and it still does. 'You may all preach if you can,' Spurgeon urged, 'but take care that you do not set yourselves up in the ministry, without having a solemn conviction that the Spirit from on high has set you apart.'[16]

Consequently, before a preacher can be called to speak for Christ, he must be called to salvation in Christ. Such a conversion to Christ arises from an effectual calling from God. In his *Puritan Catechism*, Spurgeon asks: 'What is effectual calling?' He answers: 'Effectual calling is the work of God's Spirit (2 Timothy 1:9) whereby, convincing of us our sin and misery (Acts 2:37), enlightening our minds in the knowledge of Christ (Acts 26:18), and renewing our wills (Ezekiel 36:26), he does persuade and enable us to embrace Jesus Christ freely offered to us in the gospel (John 6:44-45).'[17] The Spirit does not give such ministerial work to those who are strangers to Him. The Spirit who calls a man to ministry will be the same Spirit who first called the man to Christ. The Spirit and the man know one another from a prior fellowship.

Regarding this first coming to Christ, Spurgeon distinguished two kinds of calls – that which is general and that which is effectual. For example, in a sermon delivered on February 11, 1855, Spurgeon responded to a note written to him asking a question about this initial call to Christ. 'There are two calls,' Charles answered. The 'general call' is 'made to every man.' All who were listening to Spurgeon's preaching that morning were called, he said, in that general 'sense.'

> The other is a special call.... While I stand here and call men, nobody comes; while I preach to sinners universally, no good is done; it is like the sheet lightning you sometimes see on the summer's evening, beautiful, grand, but who has ever heard of anything being struck by it? But the special call is the forked flash from heaven; it strikes somewhere, it is the arrow sent in between the joints of the harness.[18]

'The general call,' said Spurgeon, 'is given by the minister, it is all that he can give...then there comes with the gen-

eral call to the chosen of God a particular and special call
which none but the Holy Ghost can give.'[19] The implication
for preachers is that those who are meant to call men and
women to Christ generally are those who have themselves
been called to Christ personally and effectually. Preaching
is described as a 'kindled fire' because even the man who
preaches must have been effectually awakened into new
life in Christ. Only the Spirit of God can kindle such dead
wood in the soul.

When describing his own conversion to Christ, Spurgeon
points to the Holy Spirit and casts his experience into this
framework of general and effectual calling. He says:

> When, for the first time, I received the gospel to my soul's
> salvation, I thought that I had never really heard it before,
> and I began to think that the preachers to whom I had
> listened had not truly preached it. But, on looking back,
> I am inclined to believe that I had heard the gospel fully
> preached many hundreds of times before, and that this
> was the difference, – that I then heard it as though I heard
> it not; and when I did hear it, the message may not have
> been any more clear in itself than it had been at former
> times, but the power of the Holy Spirit was present to
> open my ear, and to guide the message to my heart.[20]

Spurgeon had heard the general call time and again by
means of his grandparents and parents, through men such
as Mr. Knill and through the many Puritan books he had
read and local sermons he had heard. But it was not until a
cold Sunday morning amid a storm of snow that the forked-
flash from heaven came. Hindered from walking further in
the challenge of weather, the young man turned aside into a
Primitive Methodist chapel. 'The minister did not come that
morning' because he was 'snowed up,' Spurgeon recalled.
'At last a very thin looking man, a shoemaker, or tailor, or
something of that sort went up into the pulpit to preach....
He was obliged to stick to his text, for the simple reason
that he had little else to say.' The text was 'Look unto me
and be ye saved all the ends of the earth.' After ten minutes
of calling the people to look unto Christ for salvation, the
man looked at Charles sitting under the gallery and fixed

his eyes there. Then, the unexpected preacher with little to say and mispronouncing his words, looked earnestly into Charles' eyes that wintry morning and said, 'Young man, you look very miserable and you always will be miserable – miserable in life, and miserable in death – if you don't obey my text.' Then, 'lifting up his hands, he shouted, as only a Primitive Methodist could do, "Young man, look to Jesus Christ. Look! Look! Look! You have nothin' to do but to look and live."' That morning, the Spirit of God effectually called Charles Spurgeon to Christ. Charles did 'look' and from that time on Christ was his own dear Lord.

When considering the work of gospel preaching, a man learns to examine himself. 'Have I this effectual calling from the Spirit of God? Have I been born anew in Christ Jesus by His Spirit?' It was to the Savior's words in John 3:3 that Spurgeon turned to admonish his hearers:

> You are a member of the church; you have been baptized; you take the Lord's supper; perhaps you are a deacon, or an elder; you pass the sacramental cup round, you are just [about] all that a Christian can be, except that you are without a Christian heart.... Well, take heed, take heed! It is an astonishing thing, how near the painter can go to the expression of life, and yet the canvas is dead and motionless; and it is equally astonishing how near a man may go to a Christian, and yet, though not being born again.[21]

In sum, if one would preach Christ as redeemer for others, he must have a specific call from the Spirit to do so. This means that he must be able to declare Christ as his own redeemer – and this can only come by the effectual calling of the Holy Spirit of God. So Spurgeon urged the souls who were listening to his sermon, 'O my soul, by the power of the Holy Spirit! Call [Christ] this morning, thy Redeemer.'[22]

Needing More than a One-Sided Revelation
'His own personal salvation being secure,' the would-be preacher must now 'investigate as to the further matter of this call to office; the first is vital to himself as a Christian, the second equally vital to him as a pastor.'[23] For Spurgeon,

the nature of this 'special calling' refers to an inward and personal belief that one has been called to public ministry, confirmed by outward 'seals' of the Spirit. The inward and personal belief begins with an intense desire that may ebb and flow but never leaves. 'You were not forced to be ministers,' Spurgeon reminded preachers. 'You were not compelled to enter upon this sacred office. By your own choice you are here.'[24] Spurgeon's recognition of 'inward desire' imitates the Apostle Paul who said, 'If anyone aspires to the office of overseer, he desires a noble task' (1 Timothy 3:1). Spurgeon's early letters reflect his own growing desire to preach the gospel. To his mother, Charles wrote: 'I hope you may one day have cause to rejoice, should you see me, the unworthy instrument of God, preaching to others.'[25]

Personal desire and choice must have a particular object and possess a particular quality, however. A man must first inquire as to the object of his desire. What is it that he thinks he is choosing when he desires the work of preaching? Many 'young men,' he said, 'mistake whim for inspiration and a childish preference for a call of the Holy Spirit.'[26] The object of the desire must be the spending of one's life in the care of souls. 'If any student in this room could be content to be a newspaper editor, or a grocer, or a farmer, or a doctor, or a lawyer, or a senator, or a king,' Spurgeon says elsewhere, then 'in the name of heaven and earth let him go his way.'[27] In other words, the minister of the gospel must possess 'an intense, all-absorbing *desire for the work.*'

'If a man can detect, after the most earnest self-examination, any other motive than the glory of God and the good of souls in his seeking the bishopric, he had better turn aside from it at once.'[28] Fame, self-respect, seeking a position for influence or personal power, seeking a respectable profession, or hastily choosing on the basis of a season of feeling – none of these fits the object or quality of desire required for the special call of the preacher. For this reason, when a man possesses the right object and the right quality to his desire, he must demonstrate in his personal practice the kinds of gifts requisite for the sacred office and seek the outward confirmation of the community of believers who can attest to the validity of the inward desire. 'I have often marvelled that some people should think themselves called to preach when they have no ability,' Charles said. 'As I tell them, "If God calls anybody to fly, he will give them wings, and if he calls them to preach, he will give them ability to preach." But if a man has not the ability to preach, I am sure he has not the call.'[29]

Inward desire requires demonstrated practice and outward confirmation. The one who would preach must ask, 'Do I already practice in some measure the character and calling of the preacher?' 'Do God's people affirm that I have such character and gifts for preaching?' Spurgeon remembers:

> Two years ago, some man wrote to me a note, telling me that it had been said to his heart and God the Holy Spirit had revealed it to him, that I was to let him preach in this chapel. Well, I just wrote to him, and told him that was a one-sided revelation and that as soon as ever God revealed it to me that I was to let him preach here, then he should; but until then I did not see that the revelation was quite a square one. Why should it be revealed to him and not revealed to me? I have heard no more of him, and I have not had it revealed to me either; so that I do not suppose he will make his appearance here.[30]

For Spurgeon, a man must possess an inward desire for preaching. This inward desire is one-sided, however, until it lives in the context of a community confirmation.

Looking for the Seals
By community confirmation, Spurgeon did not mean formal ecclesiastical sanction. 'The rightly ordained minister,' says Spurgeon, 'is ordained not by the laying on of bishop's or presbyter's hands, but by the Spirit of God himself, whereby the power of God is communicated in the preaching of the word.'[31] Spurgeon never took the title 'Reverend' and was not formally ordained by an ecclesiastical body. Rather, for him, the question of calling was confirmed if the Spirit of God demonstrated His power as the man gave himself to the preaching of the Word in the community. By this, Spurgeon did not mean merely an aptness to teach. The preacher is one in whom 'sound judgment,' 'gentle manners and loving affections,' firmness, courage, tenderness and

sympathy must join administrative gifts to rule well. These qualities form the context of character out of which the man will preach the word of God. 'If such gifts and graces be not in you and abound,' Spurgeon says, 'it may be possible for you to succeed as an evangelist, but as a pastor you will be of no account.'[32]

In this construct, therefore, Spurgeon's appeal to the Spirit's calling leads the would-be preacher away from academic achievement as a 'seal.' However, Spurgeon's appeal to the Spirit's confirmation through instrumentality does not lead him into contemplations of mysticism for affirming a call from God. Rather than a 'one-sided revelation,' Spurgeon asserts that the Spirit of God uses ordinary and communal means to communicate His special call.[33] In sum, these ordinary and communal means include: personal and inward desire for the work, demonstrated abilities for the work, community confirmation of character and gifts for the work. Added to these seals is the desire to tell unbelievers about Jesus and the fruit of such desires shown in the conversion of others to Christ. A call to the ministry must flow from 'an irresistible, overwhelming craving and raging thirst for telling to others what God has done to our own souls.'[34]

For these reasons, at the beginning of a man's ministry, Spurgeon was not concerned how 'learned' the would-be preacher was. Preachers could gain the necessary learning and Spurgeon's College was aimed at that purpose. What mattered in the first place was desire, demonstrated ability, conversions to Christ, and confirmed gifts. Hear how he questions his students in order to help them discern the nature of their calling. He begins first by asking about their practice in the church and the demonstrated impact of that practice. 'Have you tried to address a Sabbath-school?' he asked. 'Have you gained the attention of the children? Having tried to address a few people, when they have been gathered together, have you found they would listen to you after you had preached?' Notice that Spurgeon assumes that an aspiring preacher is already testing his gifts among the body of believers in practical ways. Then Spurgeon asks about how the body of believers responds to the man's attempts to minister in the church. 'Had you any evidence and any sign that would lead you to believe that souls were blessed under you? Did any of the saints of God who were spiritually-minded, tell you that their souls were fed by your sermon?' While the man learns to resist seeking flattery or self-centered attention in response to his ministry, he does require the honest feedback of God's people as to the encouragement he is intending for them by the work. Spurgeon follows with a question about how sinners responded to the man's ministry and of conversions to Christ. 'Did you hear of any sinner convinced of sin?' he asked. 'Have you any reason to believe that you have had a soul converted under you?'

If a man answered negatively to these questions, particularly if a man answered that no one had been converted to Christ through his ministry, Spurgeon gave a challenge:

> If you will take one's advice for what it is good for – and I believe it is advice which God's Holy Spirit would have me give you – you had better give it up. You will make a very respectable Sunday-school teacher, you will do very well in a great many other ways; but unless these things have been known by you, unless you have these evidences, you may say you have been called and all that; I don't believe it. If you had been called to preach, there would have been some evidence and some sign of it.[35]

The purpose of this sifting process is to determine an eloquence that is from the Spirit and not from man. The Spirit of God must not only attend the preacher's way with power in preaching, but the Spirit also must originate the preacher's capacity for it. Spurgeon's convictions regarding these seals for one's calling arose not only out of his theological heritage, but also from what he practiced. Once effectually called by Christ, Charles immediately started to share the gospel. He began by praying for and sending tracts to some of those he knew and had 'tempted to sin' in his youth. The districts in the town of Newmarket formed the sphere for his young concern for souls. He would walk to visit the poor within his reach, and 'from house to house' he would tell as best he could 'the things of the kingdom of God.'[36]

He also started to find ways to serve in the community of believers. Spurgeon began to teach young boys during Sunday school. In this context, Charles was asked once to address all of the Sunday school classes. He was asked again. The third time, Charles was asked to speak regularly to all of the classes; a request which he declined out of respect for the other teachers. But whenever it was Charles' turn to address the whole group, older people started attending. 'Ere long,' Spurgeon remembers, 'in such numbers,' the 'auditory looked more like that of a chapel than a school.'[37] In this context Spurgeon's inward desire was expressed in demonstrated abilities, growing character, conversions to Christ, and outward confirmation from the church.

Conclusion

How then does one know if he is called to the sacred office? He learns of the sacred office and aspires to it. In the context of community, a man's inward aspirations are confirmed by outward seals of ministry effectiveness. A man who grows in assurance that his calling is from God is like a deeply anchored ship in the midst of the winds and waves. He may be tested but he will not be moved off course. Such a man 'cannot help it.... Friends may check him, foes criticize him, despisers sneer at him, the man is indomitable; he must preach if he has the call of heaven.'[38]

Questions for Learning and Discussion:

1. What strikes you most when you read this chapter?

2. Tell the story regarding the way God has effectually called you to Christ.

3. Describe the object and quality of your desire for the work of preaching.

4. In what practical ways are you sharing your faith and serving in the community of believers? What fruit are you seeing? How are sinners responding? What confirmation are you receiving from the community about your gifts?

5. Examine 1 Timothy 3:1-7 and Titus 1:5-9. In what areas of these qualifications do others affirm you? In what areas do you see your need of grace to grow?

6. In light of these reflections, what will your next step be?

3

THE OLD TRUTH:

Settling our Convictions

Our only safety lies in adhering tenaciously to the old truth, and seeking a fresh baptism of the Holy Spirit, that the life of God may be continued in our midst. Hold fast the form of sound words.[1]

As a student of President Spurgeon's College, a person would learn that preaching requires that one endeavor to learn the Scriptures. But by this, the President meant something specific. Like all preachers, Spurgeon had theological mentors, books and a heritage from which he learned the old truth. How Spurgeon taught the Bible, and what he meant by 'the old truth,' reflected these mentors.

The Pastors' College was unashamedly Puritanic. Spurgeon believed 'the Puritanic school' to embody 'more of gospel truth...than any other since the days of the Apostles.' Moreover, a student of Spurgeon's school would learn 'the old fashioned' evangelical doctrine – the 'old theology of the Westminster Assembly's Confession.' Of this Confession of Christian faith, written in the mid-seventeenth century, Spurgeon declared: 'Let wiseacres say what they will, there is more truth in that venerable Confession than could be found in ten thousand volumes of the school of affected culture and pretentious thoughtfulness.'[2] Spurgeon's exaggerated statements underscore the enthusiasm of his convictions.

For these reasons, Charles regularly prayed that the 'hand of the Spirit' would bring about 'a great and thorough revival of religion in the land.' He longed for a 'kindled fire'. The instrument the Spirit would use, he believed, was to

give again 'the old truth' of the Bible that Luther, Calvin,
Bunyan, Whitefield, and the 'Puritan age' had proclaimed.
The result of this 'kindled fire' would be a 'golden age of
preachers,' he thought. A golden age filled with 'great divines
and mighty ministers.'[3]

Just as a preacher learns to know himself as God sees
him by examining the providence and calling of God in
his life, so a preacher learns to know God and himself by
means of the company he keeps. Preaching and preachers
form a craft and a guild that pre-date and outlive our time.
Spurgeon was a good student in this regard. A preacher can
learn from him to ask the question: 'On whose shoulders
am I standing when I enter the pulpits of my generation?'
'Am I committed to preaching the "old truth"? If so, what
does this actually mean?'

That Old-Fashioned Book

To begin, the 'old truth' from the Spirit cannot arise from
preaching something other than what the Bible teaches.
Kindled fire requires the Bible. 'Brethren,' Spurgeon declared, 'we shall not adjust our Bible to the age; but before
we have done with it, by God's grace, we shall adjust the
age to the Bible.'[4] Spurgeon's commitment to the Bible led
to his eventual withdrawal and public censure from the
Baptist Union during the 'Downgrade Controversy' of the
1880s. For Spurgeon, the inspiration of Scripture, the virgin
birth of Jesus, the substitutionary atonement of Christ, and
the reality of heaven and hell were non-negotiable amid the
undercurrents of higher criticism, the rationalistic theology
from Germany and the rise of biological evolution.[5]

This same commitment to preaching the Bible aroused
criticism at the turn of the twentieth century from men like
Lewis Brastow in his *Representative Modern Preachers.* Cit-
ing an 'intolerance of the modern spirit and method,' Brastrow asserted that, 'The up-to-date man is not interested
in Guthrie or Spurgeon.' Describing Spurgeon's 'dogmatic
provincialism' and 'exegetical crudeness,' Brastrow asserted
that Spurgeon 'contributed little or nothing to the thought of
the church.'[6] Time has shown how wrongly Brastrow underestimated Spurgeon's contribution. For our present point,
however, it is important to note how Spurgeon's scriptural

commitment led him to seem old fashioned and crude to men like Brastrow. The same year he was censured by the Baptist Union, Spurgeon reissued for his students Dr. Louis Gaussen's book entitled, *Theopneustia: the Plenary Inspiration of the Holy Scriptures*. In the preface, Spurgeon writes: 'The turning point in the battle between those who hold the "faith once delivered to the saints" and their opponents lies in the true and real inspiration of the Holy Scriptures.... It is a delight to turn from the fantasies of the new school to the certainties of the Word of God.'[7]

Therefore, texts from both the Old and New Testaments formed the docks to which Spurgeon tied his sermons. His preaching about the person and work of the Holy Spirit and/or the role of preaching in the church was no exception. Some may rightly challenge Spurgeon's explanations from the biblical text here and there, and may at times wish for closer exposition. But all must admit from Spurgeon's sermons that it was the biblical text, and not some other text, that Spurgeon diligently sought to explain and apply for his hearers. For him, the 'old truth' centrally meant the truth as taught in the Bible.

Spurgeon's students could not have missed this central aspect of his convictions. Spurgeon was very willing to challenge personally a student who read little of the Bible. 'If you were as well acquainted with the Bible as you are with *The Baptist Handbook*,' Spurgeon exhorted, 'you would make a good minister.' Certainly in class he was not afraid to challenge publicly his students. 'There are many persons, they do not know what is in the Bible; they could tell you what is in *The Churchman's Magazine*, or *The Wesleyan Magazine*, or *The Baptist Magazine*, or *The Evangelical Magazine*, but there is one old magazine,' Spurgeon said, 'A magazine of arms, a magazine of wealth that they have forgotten to read – that old-fashioned Book called the Bible.'[8]

The Mighty Seer of Geneva

Returning to the 'old truth' for Spurgeon meant a Biblical and Christward turn to the Reformation within the theological heritage of John Calvin.[9] After all, one's commitment to the inspiration of Scripture and the infallibility of 'the Great Teacher' of the Word does not nullify the need to learn from others. 'It seems odd,' Spurgeon mused, 'that certain men who talk so much of what the Holy Spirit reveals to themselves, should think so little of what he has revealed to others.'[10]

In subordination to the Scriptures, preachers can learn from others who have walked with Christ. Theodore Nelson notes that Spurgeon believed himself to preach 'substantially what Calvin preached.'[11] Nelson's assertion seems correct. Spurgeon believed that what Calvin taught in the main was flowing directly from the Bible. 'That doctrine which is called Calvinism,' he says, 'did not spring from Calvin; we believe that it sprang from the great founder of all truth.'[12] Therefore, when Spurgeon recollects preaching in Calvin's church in Geneva, Spurgeon declared, 'there has not risen a greater than John Calvin.'[13] Calvin is the 'chief and prince, and king of all uninspired teachers, the mighty seer of Geneva, filled with the Spirit of God...a God-sent angel of the churches.'[14] It is not surprising then that during his inaugural sermon at the Metropolitan Tabernacle, Spurgeon would declare, 'I am never ashamed to avow myself a Calvinist.'[15]

The Grand Name

But, the term 'Puritan' also describes Spurgeon's view of the 'old truth.' 'Puritan' is a 'grand name,' Spurgeon felt.[16] Phrases such as 'an old Puritan says' or 'an old Puritan puts it' dot the pages of Spurgeon's sermons. Amid nineteenth-century views of truth and the Spirit, the 'old truth' as Spurgeon saw it flowed from the ocean of the Scripture into the rivers of Calvinism and into the streams and creeks of Puritanism. Spurgeon made this connection when defending himself against the derision he regularly and sometimes cruelly received from those whom he sometimes referred to as 'ultra-Calvinists.'

> I do feel so grieved at many of our Calvinistic brethren, they know nothing about Calvinism I am sorry to say, for never was any man more caricatured by his professed followers than John Calvin. Many of them are afraid to preach from Peter's text, 'Repent and be baptized, every one of you.' When I do it, they say, 'He is unsound.' Well, if I am unsound on this point, I have all the Puritans

with me, – the whole of them almost without a single exception.[17]

Similarly, when criticized from clergy on the other theological side for publicly and earnestly teaching the doctrine of election, Spurgeon defends himself by asking, 'You who love the old Puritans, you have no right to quarrel with me, for where will you find a Puritan who was not a strong Calvinist?'[18] Of both the ultra-Calvinists and his Arminian brothers, Spurgeon would write to a friend, 'What on earth are other preachers up to, when, with ten times the talent, they are snoring along with prosy sermons and sending the world away?' Spurgeon then gives his candid reason for pulpit ineffectiveness. 'They are afraid of real gospel Calvinism and therefore the Lord does not own them.'[19] Some will no doubt take issue with Spurgeon's strong statement. Important for us is to note that his conviction was for a gospel-driven Calvinism preached without prosy sermons. Following Calvin, Spurgeon felt that this kind of gospel-Calvinism was found in the Puritan tradition.

Spurgeon learned of the Puritans from his family, especially his grandfather and mother. He recommended these 'old writers' because of their depth of Scriptural understanding, their pastoral communication, and their godly example. Of their depth of scriptural insight he said, their books 'have more sense in one line than there is in a page of our new books.'[20] But he also felt that their theology was accessible to people. 'The reason why the old puritan preachers could get congregations was this,' he said. 'They did not give their hearers dry theology. They illustrated it; they had an anecdote from this and a quaint passage from that classic author; here a verse of poetry; here and there even a quip or pun.'[21] Their example also stirred Spurgeon's imagination. '"Now," said the Puritans, during the great plague of London, when the hireling parish priests had fled from their churches – "now is our time to preach."' Spurgeon then describes that 'all through that terrible time, when the carts, filled with the dead, went through the streets overgrown with grass, these strong-minded Puritans occupied the pulpits, and boldly preached the word of God.'[22] Such a scene then grounds the exhortation from Spurgeon to his hearers, to seize the times for preaching the gospel.

Central to his Puritan affection is John Bunyan. When Charles was five he happened upon a copy of *Pilgrim's Progress* in the attic of the Stambourne manse. Spurgeon declared that he had read that book over 100 times since then. Throughout Spurgeon's sermons one will find 'John Bunyan said' or 'John Bunyan put it.'

This Puritan stream of theological mentoring is most readily identified in the Catechism that Spurgeon compiled and gave to his Park Street Congregation when he was just twenty-one years old. 'Compiled from the Westminster Assembly's and Baptist catechisms,' Spurgeon believed that 'a good catechism' would be a 'great safeguard against the increasing errors of the times.' Importantly, Spurgeon called it *A Puritan Catechism* and just below his name, near this title, was written, 'Heir of the Puritans.'[23] Through it, the preacher learns, among other things, how Spurgeon understood the person and work of the Holy Spirit. These catechism answers form beginning implications for Spurgeon's ministry of the Word.

First, Christ is living and presently reveals Himself to men by His 'Word and Spirit,' revealing 'the will of God for our salvation.' The ministry therefore is Christ's. The ministry of the Word is Christ's present means for revealing the Father's will; and this is done by the power of the Spirit. Because it is the Spirit that presently 'communicates to us the benefits of Christ's redemption' through the 'outward and ordinary means' of the Word (by which souls are begotten to spiritual life) and sacrament, preachers must learn that it is 'The Spirit of God' and not us, that 'makes the reading, but especially the preaching of the Word, an effectual means of convicting and converting sinners, and of building them up in holiness and in comfort through faith to salvation.'

Second, the reason that Christ presently reveals the Father's will by His Spirit through the especial means of the preached Word is that the redemption 'purchased by Christ' is made ours only by 'the effectual application of it to us by His Holy Spirit.'

Third, any good that the preacher desires for his hearers in the Christian life, whether understanding the Scripture, experiencing true conviction of sin, embracing Christ and growing in holiness, all of this is impossible apart from the present and active ministry of the Holy Spirit, no matter how skilled, forceful or eloquent the preacher is.

It is 'the Spirit' that 'applies what Christ purchased' by 'working faith in us and by uniting us to Christ in our effectual calling.' 'Effectual calling' refers to the new birth. It identifies that divine enablement and human embrace of the call to repentance and faith in Christ. For Spurgeon, 'effectual calling is the work of God's Spirit.' He is the one who 'convinces us of our sin and misery,' and who 'enlightens our minds in the knowledge of Christ' and who renews 'our wills.' As we will explore further in our next chapter, the Spirit then is preaching through the preacher's use of the outward means, to 'persuade and enable us to embrace Jesus Christ freely offered' in the gospel.

Consequently, Spurgeon clarified elsewhere, 'no systems of divinity' or 'schemes of theology' or 'commentators' or the 'most learned' are the 'authoritative oracle.' The only 'infallible teacher' of the Bible is the Holy Spirit whom Christ has given 'to explain the Scripture.' This Spirit 'shall be the authoritative oracle of God, who shall make all dark things light,' 'untwist all knots of revelation,' and make us 'by his influence' to understand the old truth that we could not attain by ourselves.[24] Even the Confession which described the Spirit's connection to the ministry of the Word, must surrender authority to that Spirit and that Word of which it speaks.

Spurgeon's Puritan theology of the Spirit joins his gospel Calvinism and sets the stage for Spurgeon's theology of preaching. But, first, Spurgeon adds one more mentor to his team of Calvin and Bunyan.

Life, Fire, Wing and Force
The final tributary for 'old truth' flows into the ponds and lakes of spiritual awakening. Quoting Habakkuk 3:2, Spurgeon beckoned, 'We need to pray earnestly, "O Lord, revive Thy work."' When speaking of revival, Spurgeon often referred to 'a great awakening' taking place in a land or location among God's people in history or in the present. An 'awakening' is 'God pouring out His good Spirit,' by which the ordinary means of the preached Word is accompanied by

an extraordinary effect such that 'the name of our God shall be glorified and His church shall be greatly increased.'[25] Here, the analogy of 'kindled fire' is most profoundly set forth. Spurgeon described 'awakening' in this way:

> 'A bruised reed shall He not break, and smoking flax shall He not quench.' He carefully takes the flax, and blows it with His own sweet breath; and when one spark appears, He gently bloweth it until there is another, and at last the flame becomes bright, and strong, and mighty. So may it be with each of us in our own hearts, in the hidden man of the soul![26]

Spurgeon described the result of the divine breath kindling preachers and hearers.

> Have you ever seen an assembly listening to an orator all unmoved and stolid? Suddenly, the Holy Ghost has fallen on the speaker, and the King Himself has been visibly set forth among them in the midst of the assembly, and all have felt as if they could leap to their feet and cry, 'Hallelujah, Hallelujah!' Then hearts beat fast, and souls leap high; for where Jesus is found His presence fills the place with delight.[27]

With this definition of awakening in mind, Spurgeon was leery of a 'professional' or 'got-up' revival. 'This kind of revivalism,' Spurgeon urged, 'does no good.'[28] 'It is ours to use all right means, methods, and instrumentalities,' he said, 'but it must be also ours to recollect that all the strength, and all the might, and all the success, must come from on high, even from God the Holy Spirit.'[29]

Often, his pursuit of an awakening of Christianity focused on the First Great Awakening – or as Spurgeon said it, those 'old revivals in America a hundred years ago.'[30]As his *Puritan Catechism* would suggest, Spurgeon connects such awakenings to the ministry of the Spirit by the preached Word. 'There comes, every now and then, a mighty stir in our churches,' he says. 'God sends a George Whitefield, or a John Wesley, and a great wave seems to arise upon the surface of the Church, and it rolls over the sands of man's indifference.'[31] Regarding the Reformation, Spurgeon would speak highly of Luther but pre-eminently of Calvin. So Spurgeon will highly extol Wesley but will claim Whitefield as his mentor. 'Whitefield was all life, fire, wing, force,' Spurgeon said. 'My own model, if I may have such a thing in due subordination to my Lord, is George Whitefield; but with unequal footsteps must I follow in his glorious track.'[32]

Spurgeon commended Whitefield as an imperfect but genuine picture of what the Spirit of God is willing to do among His preachers for His people. In so doing, Spurgeon called his students beyond a mere second-hand walk with God. 'If you would be like Whitefield, I would say *be* Whitefield,' he exhorted. 'Let the fire be kindled by the Holy Ghost, and not by animal passion, the desire of honour, emulation of others, or the excitement of attending meetings.'[33]

By 1858, Spurgeon would taste first-hand what he had publicly longed for and privately prayed for since the beginning of his ministry. Speaking of the Chapel at Park Street, Spurgeon testified:

> More than once we were all so awe-struck with the solemnity of the meeting that we sat silent for some moments while the Lord's Power appeared to overshadow us; and all I could do on such occasions was to pronounce the benediction, and say, 'Dear friends, we have had the Spirit of God here very manifestly tonight; let us go home and take care not to lose His gracious influence.' Then down came the blessing; the house was filled with hearers, and many souls were saved.[34]

Conclusion

A preacher's mentors help him learn how to define and seek 'kindled fire.' Charles Spurgeon called his generation to tenaciously adhere to the old truth of the gospel. For him this meant a return to a Biblical authority placed in the active hands of God the Spirit. Such a return for Spurgeon was viewed from the hills of a Calvinistic, Puritan and Great Awakening landscape. From these forests, Spurgeon emerges holding kindling for a fire in the night, asking the Spirit of God to draw near and blow again with the sweet ignitions of His divine breath. These foundations form the beginning theology of Spiritual preaching that chapter four will explore. But first, Spurgeon asks us to pray:

> I ask you to pray that it may be so – that God will bring to the front the old gospel, the doctrines of Whitefield and Calvin and Paul, the old gospel of Christ, and once for all by a supernatural working of the Holy Spirit give an answer to those who, in this age of blasphemy and of rebuke, are reviling the gospel of the living God, and would have us cast it behind our backs.[35]

Questions for Learning and Discussion:

1. What strikes you most when you read this chapter?

2. What is your conviction regarding the power of the 'old truth' of the Bible? What does it mean to adjust the age to the Bible rather than the Bible to the age?

3. Preaching and preachers pre-date and outlast us. On whose shoulders are you standing as you approach preaching in your generation? What mentors can you turn to in history?

4. What are some of the Baptist, Reformed or Evangelical magazines in your life that could distract you from the Word of God?

Part Two:

The Preacher's Practice

Key Points to Look for in Chapters Four through Seven:

- God more than Aristotle or Cicero, and the Bible more than *The Art of Rhetoric* or *De Oratore* are the primary teachers of preaching. God has not only offered content by means of His Word. He has also shown the preacher the divine style of communicating Himself to people.

- Preachers not only explain, illustrate and apply. They also 'testify'.

- Preachers do with people what is usually reserved only for the closest of friends.

- The Bible demonstrates a form of speaking that is true, familiar, imaginative and emotional.

- God's world and God's Word form a comprehensive and living arena for illustrating truth.

- Three kinds of emotions vie for the preacher's attention – those that are natural, those that are made-to-order, and those that are sacred.

- Preachers must not shy away from the hard truths of the Bible.

- God's mercy and grace form the central motivation for Christian obedience.

Overview for Part Two

The preacher needs God to teach him how to preach. When the preacher remembers that God is a preacher and that the Bible is an expression of God's communication to people, God becomes the model preacher and the Bible becomes the primary manual for preaching. With God and His Word serving as the preacher's models, the preacher learns to preach in a Christ-oriented way, with a familiar and plain style that is both fully imaginative and filled with truthful feeling. The preacher also learns from the divine model to testify personally and to speak in everyday language, stooping so as to help others understand. Undergirding this approach is a willingness to speak honestly about reality, without avoiding difficult issues or hard sayings. At the same time, the preacher seeks to motivate himself and his hearers to holy living in the manner that God Himself does. Motivation for obedience therefore takes into account the condition and circumstances of the person and magnifies the mercy of God as the primary mover toward holiness. 'Kindled fire' awakens preachers to pattern their preaching after God's own example.

4

A Scripture Manner:
Examining our Sermon Delivery

...this preacher looks to the many thousands who attend his services as if they were a number of friends, around a family hearth, with whom he is to talk for an hour. He is not a great orator, perhaps, but he is a great talker....[1]

Whether Spurgeon was a great talker rather than a great orator is a debated point. Some, like David Lloyd George, the Prime Minister of Great Britain in 1923, thought of Spurgeon as a 'giant,' a 'great orator' with 'perfect elocution.'[2] Others felt that 'Spurgeon's oratory was unequal and clumsy,' worthy of contempt by his audience and expressive of a 'spoiled boy with abilities not more than mediocre.'[3] Important for preachers is to learn that Spurgeon's own assessment of his preaching style indicates an intentional preference for being a great talker rather than a great orator. 'If I speak aright,' he said, 'you might think that we were in a parlour rather than in the Tabernacle. I am not speaking as some great orator might, but as a brother declaring the Father's name as best I know it....'[4]

This plain style finds its origins in what Spurgeon saw as the plain style of the Bible. He sought in his preaching to 'talk in Scriptural language' and to fashion his style 'upon Scriptural models.'[5] Lewis Brastow, who was not overly impressed with Charles Spurgeon, nonetheless noticed this practice, which he called Spurgeon's 'biblical diction.' Brastow observed Spurgeon's written sermons.

Biblical expressions are found on almost every page...
his rhetoric has been nurtured from these sources, and
by Christian hymns, and especially by the Old Puritan
writers...one fancies that his use of figurative language,
in which the metaphor, apostrophe, and interrogation
abound and which contribute to the qualities of style...
was the result, to a considerable extent, of his familiarity
with the language of the Bible.[6]

To construct a preaching style by imitating the style of the
Bible meant essentially that when Spurgeon approached
preaching, he not only asked what the text meant, but
he also observed how the text said what it meant. The result of this approach surfaced a conviction that Spurgeon
passed on to his students. 'Teachers of Scripture,' he said,
'cannot do better than instruct their fellows after the manner of the Scriptures.'[7] A Scripture manner was the goal
Spurgeon sought for his preaching style, a style which one
observer described as that 'strange medley of woe, blood,
despair, tears, laughter, rapture, and profanity.'[8] Such a
'Bible diction,' not surprisingly, is imitative of the Puritan
John Bunyan whom Spurgeon so esteemed. Spurgeon once
remarked concerning Bunyan: 'Read anything of his, and
you will see that it is almost like reading the Bible itself.'[9]
Charles Spurgeon intentionally sought this same goal.

A Plain Eloquence
To speak in a Scripture manner did not mean that Spurgeon merely memorized and quoted verses. By Scripture's
manner, Spurgeon referred to the way in which the Bible
presented itself to the reader. To observe the way the Bible
presents itself is to recognize the manner in which God has
spoken to people. For Spurgeon, the preacher can do no
better than to preach to people the way God did.

Spurgeon noticed, for example, that the Bible uses familiar language. It often uses the kind of content and manner that is usually reserved for only the closest of friends.
Only such friends would speak so candidly about personal
matters of sin, error, hopes and dreams. In this regard,
Spurgeon tried to distance himself from the rhetorical eloquence of the Victorian pulpit by describing his pulpit-work

as more of a conversation than a grand lecture. Preaching ought not to imitate a formal grand lecture, he felt. So, at times Spurgeon would say to his hearers, 'I am hardly going to preach to-night, but just to talk familiarly to you, and I want you to let your hearts talk.'[10] Or, he could step to the pulpit and say: 'Let us talk familiarly with one another on this theme.'[11] Speaking 'familiarly' meant speaking from the pulpit in a familiar manner, less like what one would expect from a public lecture hall and more like what one would expect among close friends in one's home. Spurgeon said, 'I wish to lay the formalities of the pulpit aside and talk to you, as if you were in your own houses.'[12]

While Spurgeon preached with great passion and enough volume to enable 6,000 people to hear him comfortably without the aid of a microphone, he was perceived by his audiences as speaking conversationally. As one described it: He 'stood erect, or, when reaching after his audience, bent over the desk...he stood there in perfect simplicity and talked in a free, familiar, conversational manner, as if he were intent upon taking his audience into his confidence...[he] spoke to the people as one talking in a simple, colloquial manner, without oratorical effort.'[13] Spurgeon's maxim of a Scripture manner led him to conclude that a pulpit-style of 'plain speaking' would imitate the inspired biblical speech of the Holy Spirit. This is not surprising in light of Spurgeon's Puritan sympathies. John R. Knott, Jr. writes:

> Discussions of sermon style, particularly among Puritans, were conditioned by an influential passage from Paul's epistle to the Corinthians: 'And my speech and my preaching were not with enticing words of man's wisdom, but in demonstration of the Spirit and of power' (1 Cor. 2:4). Whatever area of agreement there might be about avoiding affected eloquence, Puritans were more likely than Anglicans to link plainness with power; in fact, 'plain and powerful' became a Puritan formula for describing effective preaching.[14]

Spurgeon seemed to agree with this Puritan formula. Plain and familiar preaching was the work of the Holy Spirit. 'Let me tell you,' he said, 'it is one of the blessed effects of the Holy Spirit to make ministers preach simply...may the Spirit of God be poured out to teach our ministers to preach plainly, to set our young men talking about Jesus Christ....'[15] Moreover, plain and familiar preaching was not only the work of the Spirit, but it was a means by which the Spirit would demonstrate His power in the sermon. Notice this connection in the following quotation. 'Dear friend,' he said, 'may the Holy Spirit come to your rescue *while I talk familiarly with you* in his name' [emphasis added]!'[16] While the preacher speaks familiarly, the Holy Spirit will work in the hearts of hearers.

For this reason, Spurgeon not only sought to preach familiarly, but he also urged his hearers to seek out this kind of preaching. 'When you attend a place of worship,' Spurgeon opined, 'it will not matter much to you whether the edifice is architecturally beautiful, or the preacher a learned man, and a great orator.' Rather than learning or great oratory, 'You want to know whether you can hear of Jesus in that place, and be likely to meet with him in that assembly.'[17] The idea that Spurgeon had was that Christ was virtually present in the preaching moment. To speak familiarly as a preacher to one's hearers is simply to imitate the personal meeting that the hearers are intended to have with Jesus. As will be shown in the next two chapters, to preach familiarly and conversationally did not imply the absence of vivid illustration or intense emotion. What it did mean was that the preacher would speak without the language or air of a formal presentation. Rather, the preacher would speak as one man to another conversing honestly about the real and personal matters of life.

Laying Aside the Grace of Oratory

When Spurgeon turned to the language of the Bible, he saw the Bible as the writing of God's Spirit. Therefore, Spurgeon desired to recognize the eloquence or the rhetorical practice evidenced by the manner or style of the biblical text. For example, when referring to the biblical words, 'My God!' Spurgeon declared, 'There is more eloquence in those two words than in all the orations of Demosthenes or Cicero.'[18] The biblical text introduced for Spurgeon an eloquence superior to that of the classical masters. 'I conceive that there was such a majesty about Jesus Christ,' says Spurgeon, that 'he spake on earth, as not Demosthenes, Cicero, nor Pericles, nor all the orators of ancient or modern times could ever approach...his was pathos that could break the stony heart.'[19]

In contrast to some of his nineteenth-century contemporaries who sought helpfully to recover a classical rhetoric familiarity for homiletics students, Spurgeon suggested that Jesus and not Cicero or Aristotle was the one who should serve as the preacher's model orator. Similiarly, the Bible, and not *De Oratore* or Aristotle's *Rhetoric*, was Spurgeon's primary manual for rhetorical principle and style.

Furthermore, though Spurgeon seems to have enjoyed music, musical instruments, good art and architecture, he nevertheless would speak of the vanity of these good things if they were looked to for a recovery of gospel power in a generation. 'It does seem impossible, does it not' he asks, 'that the mere preaching of Christ can do this [work with power]? And hence certain men must link to the preaching of Christ all the aids of music and architecture.'[20] Spurgeon therefore warned that if 'religion consists in putting on a certain dress,' and the preacher becomes a 'mere performer' by attracting people 'by the sweetness of music or the beauty of architecture,' then religion becomes vain. Why? Because such use of power was 'not so with Christ and his apostles; they were everywhere preaching the word and proclaiming that "faith cometh by hearing and hearing by the word of God".'[21]

Importantly, Spurgeon was accused of attracting audiences by performing. One critic recounted Spurgeon's 'melodramatic-attitudes' and the fact that 'he walked about on the platform just as if he had been treading the boards of the Drury Lane Theatre, while performing some exciting tragedy.'[22] Spurgeon's response near the end of his ministry would have included an appeal to the motive behind those crowds attending the Tabernacle.

We know that the greatest crowd in London has been held together these thirty years by nothing but the preaching of Christ crucified. Where is our music? Where is our oratory? Where is anything of attractive architecture, or beauty or ritual? 'A bare service,' they call it. Yes, but Christ makes up for all deficiencies.[23]

Spurgeon may have underestimated his own giftedness for communication. But his statement possesses some genuine merit. The largest crowds in London, and perhaps in the Western world at that time, flocked to services that were recognized as 'bare' because of their simplicity. They consisted in a prayer, congregational singing without an organ, and then a sermon. Spurgeon refers to the absence of an organ as testimony that something more than musical power can attract and change people. Spurgeon was not against organs. He called them 'that wonderful box of music with which men praise God with wind.' But lasting power he felt lay elsewhere. 'We have nothing but the plainest possible singing,' he recounted. 'I am certain that the crowds do not come to hear that; and as for the preaching, I have purposely laid aside all the graces of oratory.'[24]

Spurgeon's 'laying aside' the 'graces of oratory' may not be an exaggeration. On June 20, 1884, *The Freeman*, for example, 'tabulated the causes "contributing to the simplification of pulpit style" in the previous "fifty years." The causes consisted of the Reform Bill, anti-slavery agitation, the *Penny Magazine*, cheap postage, the Corn Law League, the telegraph, and Charles Haddon Spurgeon.'[25] 'God deserves the best oratory, the best logic, the best metaphysics, the best of everything,' Charles declared. 'But if ever rhetoric [or education or a natural gift] stands in the way of the instruction of the people, a curse be on [them]'!'[26]

God's Familiar Speech

Spurgeon taught his students to preach familiarly because he believed that God preached in this same way. In Isaiah 1:18, for example, the text says: 'Come now, and let us reason together, says the LORD: though your sins be as scarlet, they shall be as white as snow.' Spurgeon commented on this passage, noting that the God whose 'voice...shakes the earth with tempests' is the same God 'who speaks to us' and says, 'Come now, let us reason together.' Spurgeon points out that God the creator and judge lays aside His thunderous power, draws near to the sinner, and invites the sinner to converse with reason. It is as if God says, 'Tell me, what is your difficulty? I will lay aside my glory, and will come down, and talk familiarly with you that we may have this question settled.'[27]

How God approached people in Isaiah 1, Spurgeon saw demonstrated in the incarnation of Jesus. 'The Lord stoops down to us,' Spurgeon observed.[28] In contrast to the philosophers, kings, and nobles of the time, Jesus demonstrated a 'condescending tenderness' and spoke familiarly with ordinary sinners.[29] Jesus offers himself to us as a friend of sinners, 'for that is what he really is.' 'He does not stand upon a lofty height, and bid sinners ascend to him,' Spurgeon said. He comes down 'from the mountain, and mingles with them.' He 'draws them to himself by the magnetic force of his almighty love.'[30]

Spurgeon sought to imitate this divine approach. One of the ways in which Spurgeon sought to demonstrate this same 'stooping' manner when he preached was to express himself with a humble posture of familiar tenderness as he made appeals to his hearers. He spoke to them as he would to a friend. 'Oh, friend,' Spurgeon could say, 'consider what your obligations are!'[31] Or, yet again, 'Oh! Friend, I wish you would turn while God is smiting you gently.'[32] Or, 'Oh, friend, if this cry be your cry....'[33]

Similarly, Spurgeon often expressed this condescending tenderness of Scripture's manner by appealing to his hearers as 'dear heart': 'I am not going to blame you, dear heart; but I do deeply pity you....'[34] Or, he might say, 'Hearest thou this, dear heart? Thou art shrinking from thy God; thou art anxious to run away from him; but that is where the forgiveness is.'[35] Likewise, speaking directly with tenderness to sinners, he will urge the hearer, saying something like, 'Whenever you think of Jesus Christ and think highly of Him, dear heart, say to yourself, "all this is meant for needy sinners".'[36]

Spurgeon also makes direct appeals to his hearers as a friend without pretension. Spurgeon at times expresses this appeal with the phrase 'poor soul'. 'In all thine agony, poor soul, in all thy repentance for thy guilt, look unto Christ, and find pardon.'[37] Or, 'Ah! Poor soul, do not despair.'[38] Or, 'Ah, poor soul, all these suggestions are Satan's lies!'[39]

This kind of familiar preaching infuriated his critics. As one critic declared: 'We do not advocate the coarse jokes and vulgar familiarities, "How are your poor souls?" and the like; which seem so attractive at the Surrey Music Hall.'[40] But Spurgeon insisted that such direct familiarity reflected the Scripture's manner. For example, Isaiah 55:1 says, 'Ho! Everyone that thirsteth come ye to the waters. And he that hath no money, come ye buy and eat; yea come buy wine and milk without money and without price.' Spurgeon observed from this passage that God calls for the attention of sinners who, though He is eager for them, are not eager for Him. 'Men pass by with their ears full of the world's tumult; and God calleth, again and again, "Ho! Ho!" Be you rich or poor, learned or illiterate, if you are in need, and specially if you feel your need, "Ho, every one that thirsteth."'[41]

Likewise, it was Jesus in John 6:25-26 who said to his hearers, 'Verily, verily I say unto you. Ye seek me not because ye saw the miracles, but because ye did eat of the loaves and were filled.' At this, Spurgeon remarked:

> What very plain talk this is! Our Lord does not try to gain popularity by the concealment of truth, but he tells these people to their faces, 'You are only following me because of what you get out of me'; 'Oh!' some worldly-wise man would have said, 'that is a very imprudent speech; it will drive the people away'.... Our Lord's example should teach us to speak in his name nothing less and nothing more than the truth in all love and kindness.[42]

For these reasons, in spite of his critics, Spurgeon continued to preach often with the 'familiar' collage of a tender but plain directness. In the following example, Spurgeon appeals to the hearer directly as a sinner, a friend, and a brother. In addition, the lamenting 'Oh' found in the Bible is present, as well as Spurgeon's empathy with the hearers in light of his own personal experience:

> Look, sinner, – look unto him, and be saved.... I know you, my friend; I 'know the heart of a stranger;' for such was my heart.... Oh, the heaviness of a guilty conscience! Oh, the long, dark, dreary winter of the soul, when sin

blots out the sun, turns even mercy into misery, and
sorrow makes the day into night! Ah! I know you, my
brother; your self-righteousness is all gone.... The Lord
help you...![43]

Students of preaching would learn from Spurgeon that a
Scripture manner leads preachers to cross social barriers of
conversation to places of speech usually reserved, both in
content and intimacy, for only the closest of friends. Seeking the magnetic force of love, the preacher speaks directly,
tenderly and personally to his hearers as one friend would
speak to another.

Every Condition of Soul
To speak like a friend is to speak, not in formulaic terms
to a group, but with understanding of the individual and
the particular needs of differing people listening. Spurgeon
lamented the damage done when preachers forget to speak
familiarly to different conditions of soul. 'Every condition
of soul must be duly met by a watchful pastor,' noted
Spurgeon.[44] Such care for the soul meant that preaching
must make applications that correspond to these different
conditions. 'Ah! I fear, my brethren in the ministry, that we
have often rebuked where we ought to have comforted, and
perhaps our unwise speeches, when we did not mean to do
it, have been very hard blows to the afflicted in Zion.'[45] Familiar preaching meant that preachers ought not rebuke the
afflicted and comfort the hardened. Rather, as the preacher
recognizes how a given text will apply differently to differing
conditions of life, the hearers begin to feel that the preacher
is speaking directly to them personally and not simply to a
large group generically. Spurgeon exposed this idea when
preaching to his congregation. He said to them:

I wish not now to preach to you in the mass, but to each
man as an individual. You can each judge in your own
conscience how far what I say is applicable to you. If
the fear of God and the love of Jesus be in your hearts,
these accusations belong not to you; occupy yourself
with earnestly praying that the Word may go where the
reproof is needed; that the arrow may reach its mark. Ye

who have faith in Christ, lift up your souls and pray, 'O
Lord, send home thy arrow in the heart that is forgetful
of thee.'[46]

Probably following the Puritan heritage of plain-speaking
on this point, Spurgeon identified his congregations as
consisting of believers and unbelievers. There are, at least,
three main kinds of soul conditions that are experienced
by both the believing and unbelieving hearer. The first refers to the economic circumstances of the person in this
world, whether he be wealthy or poor. 'While those who are
prospering will kindly take note of the voice of God's word
to themselves,' says Spurgeon as he preaches from a text
addressed to the wealthy, 'those of you who are not prospering may be profited by becoming the more contented with
your lowly lot....'[47] Economic circumstances affect the way
one hears the meaning of a Scripture text, and this must
be accounted for.

A second kind of soul-condition refers to the emotional
state of the person in the world, whether happy or sad, content or discontent. 'Some of you may know,' he says, 'that,
when the body is in a low condition, the soul also sinks.
Quite involuntarily, unhappiness of mind, depression of
spirit, and sorrow of heart will come upon you.'[48] Similarly,
when there are 'twenty other things, all claiming to be done
at once, then is the anxious soul apt to be disquieted. We
are first wearied, and then worried.' But, 'to be perfectly
at peace amid the hurry-burly of invading cares is a very
blessed condition of soul....'[49] Emotional differences among
people as they hear a particular text are to be accounted
for as the text is applied.

A third kind of soul-condition refers more vertically to
the hearer's relational posture toward God – whether sad
or happy. For example, Spurgeon can appeal directly to
the unhumbled sinner who experiences only momentary
thoughts of God: 'this is not your abiding condition of soul,'
he says. 'Tis but a spasm; the spirit of your heart is not
adoration of his majesty, but forgetfulness of his glory.'[50] Or,
he can confront the backsliding elder or deacon with plain
familiarity: 'I do not know how to talk with you as I want to
do concerning this sad condition of soul...'[51] Spurgeon can

also appeal to the happy circumstance of a soul experiencing relational trust with Jesus.[52] The point is that Spurgeon
spoke openly about these varying conditions and how the
Scriptures would apply varyingly to them.

The Language of Daily Life

This meant that ordinary language would join familiarity
and direct soul-care in forming the preacher's style. Amid
the Victorian move toward higher class and societal standing, Spurgeon argued that his generation needed 'parlour
and kitchen and workshop preachers, who can talk the
natural speech of men.'[53] He felt that preachers must be
willing to intentionally disregard technical language for
the sake of being understood by one's hearers. He testified that he intentionally pursued this practice. 'There are
many high and sublime doctrines' that he 'would like to
speak of, and many deep and rapturous experiences that
he would like to describe.' Yet, he felt that he must often
leave these things, and keep in the pulpit 'to the much more
commonplace.'[54]

That Spurgeon intentionally sought the 'commonplace'
in preaching provides interesting information for those
who criticize Spurgeon for sermons barren of erudition
or scholarship. It was Spurgeon's view of eloquence and
preaching that actually made such a critique possible. As
mentioned above, the June 20 edition of a journal entitled
The Freeman, 'tabulated' in 1884, the causes 'contributing
to the simplification of pulpit style in the last fifty years.'
The index listed these causes: Reform Bill, anti-slavery leg-
islation, Penny Magazine, cheap postage, Corn Law league,
telegraphs, and 'Charles Haddon Spurgeon.'[55]

A ready example of this kind of simplifying through the
language of daily life is found in his book entitled *Faith's
Checkbook*. He says for example that 'A promise from God
may very instructively be compared to a check payable to
order....'[56] He likens the promises of God to a 'mine of wealth'
with 'secret veins' offering 'hidden treasures.' These promises are an 'armory,' a 'sacred arsenal.' They are a 'surgery'
offering 'all manner of restoratives and blessed elixirs' and
'ointment for every wound, a cordial for every faintness, a
remedy for every disease' offered from a 'heavenly phar-

macy.' They are a 'storehouse of food,' like 'granaries.' The promises of God 'are the Christian's Magna Charta of liberty.' They are the title deeds of his heavenly estate.' The promises are a 'jewel room,' a 'regalia,' like a 'king with the silver key that unlocks the strong room.'[57]

Criticisms from the 'Strong-Doctrine-Brother'

Spurgeon was strongly criticized for his plain and familiar approach. For example, in one sermon he mentions 'some strong-doctrine brother' saying, 'I do not like this.' Spurgeon was not delusional. He was regularly criticized by such brothers. For example, one brother described Spurgeon's preaching as 'that mixture of slang and blasphemy' which is 'the staple commodity' at New Park Street. The critic went on to refer to Spurgeon as one who preaches 'insufferable trash' who 'has the audacity to compare his style of preaching' to Jesus.[58]

These critics felt that Spurgeon's 'wooing' and pleading made God seem like a beggar to sinners. Spurgeon's response was that God had represented Himself this way in the Bible. 'It is in the Scripture,' he pointed out, that God 'represents Himself as crying like a chapman at a fair.' Spurgeon then quoted from Isaiah 55:1: 'Ho, everyone that thirsteth, come ye to the waters.' He concluded that if God 'had not so represented' Himself as pleading with sinners, then 'we dare not have done so'; but as God has said it, we do but follow his footsteps and quote his words.[59] Spurgeon's primary argument, in other words, was that since God pleads with men, it is no 'derogation' of God for His appointed preachers to do the same.

His critics countered this response by suggesting that Spurgeon was making God seem vulgar and profane by the familiar and pleading manner of preaching. For example, one critic acknowledged Spurgeon's point about Jesus' example but asserted a further complaint:

> That the Great Teacher used plain and familiar language in addressing the people, that He adopted the commonest forms of speech and the homeliest illustrations, we readily admit. But we deny most strongly that in the New Testament can be found a single line, nay, a single

phrase or word of indecency, vulgarity, or profanity, such as adorn almost every page of the *New Park Street Pulpit.*[60]

An example cited as the basis for this charge of 'vulgarity and profanity' by these critics is this excerpt from one of Spurgeon's sermons, which reads: 'Look here! – your soul is in pawn to the Devil; Christ has paid the redemption money; you can take your faith for the ticket, and get your soul out of pawn.' To this the critic says, 'We are not aware that Satan is represented as a pawnbroker in Scripture....'[61]

What the critic considered 'unsufferable trash' was for Spurgeon an imitation of Christ who he thought would certainly have stooped to the capacity of his lower-class hearers amid the education-impoverished and urban landscape of nineteenth-century London. Spurgeon's rationale for such kind and loving plainness was also personal. 'There was a time,' he once said to his congregation, 'when I should have been thankful to have heard such plain talk as this, rather than a fine sermon that would have been of no service to me in my sad condition.'[62]

The God Who Stoops

Spurgeon felt that any preacher would know that when God met him and saved him, he did so through ordinary language, in direct and heart-searching ways, amid the familiar. For Spurgeon, therefore, plain speaking not only results from the Scripture's manner as it presents itself to any person, but plain speaking also results from how the Scripture's manner is personally demonstrated for the preacher when he is encountered by God. In other words, the preacher speaks as one who has been 'stooped to,' and this he must never forget. The God whom the preacher proclaims to others is the God to whom the preacher personally looks, not as a criminal to a judge, but as a child to a Father. From this familiar relationship, one cannot help but speak of God in affectionate terms. And because of this relationship, the preacher cannot help but plead familiarly with others. After acknowledging the charge of being 'profane' in the pulpit by speaking as if he and God are on familiar terms, Spurgeon explained his point of view:

A child may say to his father what no one else may dare to say, and yet he has more reverence for him than anyone else.... Look at the judge on the bench, with that big wig, and those solemn robes; the prisoner at the bar, and the court and the jury must all be very respectful and distant, but I warrant you when his lordship reaches home his grandchild has no dread of grandpapa or his robes. Love gives boldness, and is yet most reverent: reverently familiar. Chilliness and coldness are not for the children of God; they are called to close intercourse with their heavenly Father, and the meeting place is not at Sinai, but at Calvary.[63]

A student of preaching can ask himself how he believes that God relates to him personally as a sinner. How the student answers the question will give an indication of how that student will approach sinners from the pulpit when preaching.

Moreover, how the preacher perceives the Bible in private will impact how he speaks of relationship with God in public. When referring to Proverbs 6:22, which says, 'When thou awakest it shall talk with thee,' Spurgeon instructed his hearers that the 'Holy Scripture is very familiar.' He identified its manner of speech in stark contrast to the formal orations commonly associated with the preaching of his day. Spurgeon felt that the concern over his use of pathetic and familiar language was also rooted in a misunderstanding of reverence.

Many persons have a high esteem for the book, but they look upon it as though it were some very elevated teacher speaking to them from a lofty tribunal, while they stand far below. I will not altogether condemn that reverence, but it were far better if they would understand the familiarity of God's word; it does not so much preach to us as *talk* to us.... And here let me remind you of the delightful familiarity of Scripture in this respect that *it speaks the language of men*. If God had written us a book in his own language, we could not have comprehended it.... As men conversing with babes use their broken speech, so doth the condescending word. It is not written in the celestial tongue, but in the *patois* of this lowland country, condescending to men of low estate.[64]

Reverence, for Spurgeon, is a familiar, deep and emotional thing. In light of what God has done for the preacher, Spurgeon believed that a preacher does not speak reverently when preaching with stoic tones. The preacher cannot speak reverently who does so with an affected and distanced discourse that is removed from the very places that God is presently seeking sinners.

Redemptive Transparency
This sense of having been 'stooped to' by God added another trait to the familiar conversation, the direct appeal, and the ordinary language of Spurgeon's preaching style. His style was also dialogical. That is to say, Spurgeon did not preach as an observer but as a participant, not as a formal presenter but as a real man who spoke out of his own real experience. Consequently, Spurgeon was not afraid to refer to himself in the pulpit. In fact, he believed that a Scripture manner demanded it. His critics strongly disagreed.

Spurgeon seemed 'egotistical' because his style was pursued 'so much in the form of direct appeals' that were in the first person singular. Referring to those who printed Spurgeon's sermons, one critic remarked that 'the printer' must often 'run out of capital 'I's.'[65] Another critic declared that Spurgeon's preaching 'indicated low views of Deity, and exalted views of self. Indeed,' he asserted, 'self is never out of sight.'[66] The critic's aversion to the personal pronoun was aptly summarized by Ian Maclaren during the Lyman Beecher Lectures on Preaching at Yale University in 1896.

If the minister desires to give a personal experience he can say 'one,' or 'a man,' and if his people suspect the identity it is no matter. They have been delivered from the perpetual 'I' which devastates some men's utterances, and from whose monotonous boom you never escape.[67]

One biographer sought to bring a more positive note from the first-person tone of Spurgeon's sermons:

Though he spoke often of himself, he can be rightly termed a master illustrator because he used illustrations from living a life in Christ to the full. But then, the Apostle Paul himself gloried in sharing his own personal testimony of conversion on the Damascus road. Furthermore, Paul's Epistles contain his own opinions of his spiritual pilgrimage and experiences. So in one sense of the word, Spurgeon preached in a Pauline apostolic tradition....[68]

Actually, the biographer was not alone in mentioning the Apostle Paul's example. Spurgeon specifically points to the apostle when referring to his own dialogical self-reference in the pulpit and its importance for plain speaking in preaching. Preachers had traditionally followed Augustine and Cicero in offering three categories for the preaching task. The preacher is to instruct (explain), to please (illustrate) and to move (apply) his hearers. From the Apostle Paul's method of preaching, Spurgeon saw a fourth category. Preachers must also testify. In the following reference to Paul, Spurgeon identifies 'expounding', 'testifying' and 'persuading' or moving as the task of the preacher. 'Our apostle was not satisfied,' Spurgeon said, 'simply to expound and testify, his heart was full of love to his countrymen; and, therefore, he persuaded them. He entreated, he besought, he implored his hearers to turn to the Lord Jesus Christ.' It was in this Pauline framework, this scriptural manner, as Spurgeon saw it, that Spurgeon stood in order to counter his critics' assertions that his frequent self-reference was a sign of egotism. Spurgeon argued in contrast that as preachers:

> We must also *testify*. We must bear witness to the effect which the gospel has had upon our heart and life. The telling out of our personal experience is a means of grace to our hearers. Paul was wont to describe his own conversion.... There is much force in such a personal testimony. Oh, that you and I, after having explained the gospel, may always be able to tell out something from our own experience which will prove it! (465)

Preaching as Testifying

Spurgeon's students would learn that the pulpit is, among other things, a place for witness. 'In this regard,' according to Spurgeon, a hearer must 'select his pastor, not for his eloquence, learning, amiability, or popularity, but for his clear and constant testimony to the Gospel of Christ.'[69] The preacher, therefore, stands with a posture before his hearers, not as a performer whose performance is offered for aesthetic critique, but as a witness whose testimony is offered to them and is therefore either true or false. Spurgeon challenged the former notion. 'Let us preach as we may, while we are regarded by you as mere orators to be criticized, and not as witnesses whose testimony is to be weighed.'[70] The preacher is a man who has personally encountered God and from these personal dealings and God's personal call, the preacher speaks to people about this God with whom he has had first-hand experience.

The pulpit as a place for witness corresponds to and flows from the witness of ordinary believers in their ordinary spheres of proclamation and demonstrates another kind of eloquence fit for its purposes. Referring to the woman at the well who testifies to her townsfolk of what Christ had done for her in John chapter 4, Spurgeon noted:

> Her simple talk did more than eloquence could accomplish, though it should be as mighty as that of Cicero or Demosthenes. Her heart was in the words she spoke. Her speech was simple; there was nothing to recommend it of beauty of verbiage, or gaudiness of oratory. She said what she did know, and testified what she had seen, with an earnest desire that others should know and see what she had learned.[71]

Spurgeon's personal testimonies in the pulpit are voluminous. Generally, the shape of these self-references concern his personal experiences with God or his experience as a pastor who has seen God deal with others. For example, Spurgeon will say in a sermon, 'I can bear personal witness that the simple statement of the gospel has often proved, in God's hand, enough to lead a soul into immediate peace.' He then testifies, 'I once met with a lady...' and then he tells the story.[72] Or, after making the point from the Bible that 'God gives good things to men according to his promises,' Spurgeon referred to himself as a 'personal witness' to this 'fact.' 'My experience,' he says, 'has been long, and my observation has been wide; but I have never yet met with a person who trusted God, and found the Lord's promise fail him.... All my observation points the other way, and confirms me in the persuasion that the Lord is faithful to all who rely upon him.'[73]

Spurgeon turns to several places in the Bible to establish the use of the phrase, 'I testify.' Jesus speaks with the words 'I testify' in John 7. Paul does so in Acts 20, as does John in his book of Revelation. Notice in the following passage how the exclamatory 'Oh' of the Scripture manner joins with dialogical and direct appeal to the soul's condition in the form of personal testimony:

> But I testify yet again, soul, that after thou hast once believed in Christ, and received thy pardon, thou wilt find him to be willing to keep thy soul from sin....We have seen it, and we testify it. O drunkard, he can make thee sober! Unchaste man, he can make thee virtuous! There is no lust which his arm cannot subdue....[74]

At times, Spurgeon 'testifies' regarding doctrinal clarity. For example, 'There may be some who hold unconditional reprobation,' he says. 'I stand not here as their defender, let them defend themselves as best they can; I hold God's election, but I testify just as clearly that if any man be lost he is lost for sin; and this has been the uniform statement of Calvinistic ministers.'[75]

At times Spurgeon recounts the testimony of others in the history of Christianity concerning their dealings with Christ. But centrally, Spurgeon recounts his own experiences with Christ, past and present, both as a sinner needing mercy and as a Christian following Him daily. One sample gives a taste of this kind of testifying in the pulpit. To illustrate the one who despises Christ, Spurgeon uses his own life.

> I, too, once despised Him. He knocked at the door of my heart, and I refused to open it, He came to me, times

without number, morning by morning, and night by night; He checked me in my conscience, and spoke to me by His Spirit, and when, at last, the thunders of the law prevailed in my conscience, I thought that Christ was cruel and unkind. Oh, I can never forgive myself that I should have thought so ill of Him! But what a loving reception did I have when I went to Him! I thought He would smite me, but His hand was not clenched in anger, but opened wide in mercy. I thought full sure that His eyes would dart lightning-flashes of wrath upon me; but, instead thereof, they were full of tears. He fell upon my neck, and kissed me; He took off my rags, and did clothe me with His righteousness, and caused my soul to sing aloud for joy; while in the house of my heart, and in the house of His Church, there was music and dancing, because His son that He had lost was found, and he that had been dead was made alive again.[76]

In sum, the 'testifying' to which Spurgeon called gospel preachers might well be termed a 'redemptive transparency.' The preacher becomes vulnerable or transparent regarding his own dealings with God because preaching at its heart flows from a first-hand witness of the things of God.

Conclusion
In an article from an observer of those preachers who were trained under Spurgeon in his Pastors' College, a description of this preaching was given. Referring to the alumni of Spurgeon's College, the author observed:

I cannot but say that even where the finer graces of style may be wanting – where there may be very little of eloquence, or ornament, or illustration – yet the wholesome plainness of sound doctrine, delivered with the accent of a heartfelt conviction, which I generally find among your students, has a grace and an eloquence all its own, and storms the human heart.'[77]

As the next chapter will show, if there was little illustration among Spurgeon's students, it was not because he hadn't taught them the art of illustrating. But if it was true that

Spurgeon's students had little eloquence or ornament but much plainness and heartfelt conviction, then Spurgeon would have been thankful to God and proud of his students. He believed that such preaching would be owned by God and truly storm the human heart. Kindled fire will result in a preaching that removes the hindrances of distance, vagueness, formality or performance from the pulpit. Preaching in a Scripture manner begins when a person comes as a friend to proclaim the glory of God for the needs of people out of a first-hand knowledge of what the Scripture says on a given subject. He imitates by his preaching style the manner in which God will meet with sinners in that moment.

Such convictions are perhaps best understood from an anecdote taken from Spurgeon's ministry. Upon hearing that one of his hearers had taken offense at him, Spurgeon remarked once in a letter,

> You may tell Mr. —— that I was so far from intending to insult him by what I said that I uttered the sentence in the purest love for his soul; and that I dare not be unfaithful to him any more than to anyone else in my congregation. God is my witness, how earnestly I long for the salvation of all my hearers, and I would far rather err by too great personality than by unfaithfulness. At the last great day, none of us will be offended with Christ's ministers for speaking plainly to us.[78]

And so spoke Charles Haddon Spurgeon.

Questions for Learning and Discussion

1. What did Spurgeon mean by a Scripture manner of preaching?

2. What are the elements of this manner of preaching according to Spurgeon?

3. What were the primary criticisms Spurgeon received in this regard? How do you respond to their critique and Spurgeon's answers?

4. What do you think about the role of personal testimony in preaching? Look again at the ways Spurgeon did this. What are the merits and cautions with this approach?

5. What connection did Spurgeon make between the familiar speaking of the preacher with people and the way God would personally meet with him in that moment?

6. What will you take with you from this chapter?

5

THE HOLY FANCY:

Engaging our Imagination

Awake my imagination, and dance to holy melody. Gather pictures from all worlds…until all his works in all places of his dominion bless the Lord.[1]

It was simply called 'Sermons in Candles.' It reminded the preacher that, for Spurgeon, plain and familiar preaching does not mean unimaginative preaching. In fact, plain preaching is, by its very nature, illustrative.

As the story goes, Spurgeon was lecturing to his Friday morning class on the importance of illustrations in sermons. After pointing out that Jesus 'had many *likes* in his discourses,' Spurgeon was saying that 'a sermon without illustrations is like a room without windows.' At this, one of the students raised a problem. He agreed with his professor's extended Christ-ward rationale for illustrations. But what the student challenged was the practicality of finding sufficient illustrations. Spurgeon agreed but challenged the class by proposing that this difficulty could be overcome if preachers would learn to go through the world as those who are awake rather than as those who are asleep. That was the moment when Spurgeon made the now famous statement: 'You could see nothing else in the world but a single tallow candle,' he said, and yet 'you might find enough illustrations in that [one] luminary to last you for six months.' At that, the students began to look at one another with smiles of doubt and draw their breath with the sighs of disbelief. Their body postures changed in their chairs and Spurgeon noticed that 'the men who were around' him 'at that particular moment' believed that he 'had made a sweeping assertion' and 'their countenances showed it.' 'Well,' he said to the class. 'I will prove my words.' As Spurgeon began in that moment to multiply illustrations of candles for biblical truth, students were amazed and their disbelief quieted.

The result produced the 'rudiments' of a lecture that would be requested for repetition for more than a quarter of a century and finally published in 1890. Charles Spurgeon was alive to illustration and he urged his ministerial students to learn to preach with imagination.

The Sin of All Sins and the Prudes of the Pulpit
If a student could afford access to Alexandre Vinet's *Homiletics*, Paxton Hood's *The Vocation of the Preacher* or John Broadus' *Treatise on the Preparation and Delivery of Sermons*, the role of imagination in preaching would have been readily discussed. Daniel Kidder's *Treatise on Homiletics* in 1866 had asserted that 'in a high and moral sense the preacher is a painter.'[2] But Spurgeon's seven lectures later collected into *The Art of Illustration* would have far surpassed these other texts by the sheer volume and practicality of his thoughts on the subject, not to mention the way Spurgeon modeled his teachings on illustrations by his pulpit practice.

While American professors of sacred rhetoric like Phelps or R. L. Dabney[3] made distinctions between the imagination and 'the fancy,' a student of Spurgeon's would soon conclude that Spurgeon did not bother with these distinctions. He used the two words interchangeably, such as the time when he hoped to encourage his students in class: 'You may never be able to develop any vast amount of imagination or fancy,' he said, 'but by diligent attention to this matter you may improve upon what [you have].'[4] Furthermore, Spurgeon did not seem to place 'fancy' in a category that was lesser than imagination as some of his contemporaries did. Or if he did, he saw the fancy as something redeemable by God and made useful for Him, for he exhorted his students to give themselves to a 'wise and healthy use of holy fancy.'[5] As a matter of fact, long before television and postmodern concerns, Charles Spurgeon urged his students for the ministry to make two resolutions regarding the imagination and preaching.

God Helping Me

First, his students must give themselves fully to preaching with imagination – specifically, the telling of stories and anecdotes. 'God helping me,' he vowed, 'I will teach the people by parables, by similes, by illustrations, by anything that will be helpful to them; and I will seek to be a thoroughly interesting preacher of the Word.'[6]

Second, his students must give themselves to a routine of imaginative practice. 'Try to make comparisons from the things round about you,' he said. 'I think it would be well, sometimes, to shut the door of your study and say to yourself, 'I will not go out of this room until I have made at least half-a-dozen good illustrations.'[7] In fact, Spurgeon believed that the use of imagination in preaching was so essential that he placed the cultivation of imagination in preaching among the primary qualifications for a preacher.[8]

Students would have quickly learned the criticisms and misunderstandings that would attend their ministry if they followed these resolutions. Their professor had acknowledged that 'The prudes of the pulpit' had defined illustrations as 'the sin of all sins.'[9] Spurgeon would have had sympathy with the intent of the so-called prudes whose aim included the protection of sound doctrine and the hindrance of turning preaching into mere entertainment. 'Strings of anecdotes instead of sound doctrines,' Spurgeon agreed, 'would be as evil a thing as if you offered to hungry men flowers instead of bread.' Ministers are 'not storytellers, but preachers of the gospel,' he continued. They do 'not aim at the entertainment of the people, but at their conversion.' But while Spurgeon agreed that preachers were not entertainers nor fabricaters of stories, he lamented those prudish preachers who would not 'stoop to tell a simple, homely story.'[10] But why? What was the reason for Spurgeon's lament?

Enlivening and Quickening Attention

To begin with a secondary reason, Spurgeon felt the value of illustrations because they gave aid in keeping one's attention on the truth at hand. In his lecture entitled, 'Illustrations in Preaching,' under the heading, 'Reasons for Using Illustrations,' the third reason that the professor gave for using illustrations was that 'illustrations help enliven and quicken attention of hearers.'

But why was sermon attention a problem? The answer can surprise students of a later generation who may naively assume that attention problems with sermons rarely existed prior to television. Inattention has its source in the human condition. According to Spurgeon, inattention first arises from an unwillingness to learn.

Second, listeners get distracted by their hopes and sorrows. 'A handful of golden earth, a puff of fame, a shout of applause, a thriving business, my house, my home, will affect me more than all the glories of the upper world,' he said, 'simply because earth is near and heaven is far way.'[11]

Third, the issues of life can weigh down the soul. 'Recollect,' Spurgeon said, 'some of our people...have through the week been borne down by the press of business cares.' As if anticipating the critique that such explanations are not legitimate reasons for inattention to preaching, Spurgeon mentioned the Bible verse which teaches followers of Jesus to turn their 'burdens to the Lord.' The professor then asked his students: 'Do *you* always do so? Do *you* always find it easy to escape from anxieties? Are *you* able to forget the sick wife and the ailing children at home? There is no doubt whatever that many come into the house of God loaded heavily with the thoughts of their daily avocations.'[12]

Fourth, in addition to these circumstances of the preacher's hearers, there is the fact that his hearers are naturally uninterested in the things of Christ. 'Man is by nature blind within.... Talk to him of the wonders of the creation...he is well able to see all these things; but talk to him of the wonders...of the person of the Redeemer, he is quite deaf to all your description.'[13]

Keeping attention, then, is a matter of wisdom as the preacher takes into account his hearer's capacity to listen. Losing attention to the things of God is something resident within the human condition. Therefore, Spurgeon acknowledges that 'it is possible to maintain profound and long-continued attention without the use of an illustration,' but the nature of one's audience may require the preacher to wisely tell them 'stories, similes and parables.'[14] When this occurs, the preacher need not hesitate to offer an illustration.

This lack of hesitation did not mean that Spurgeon was naïve concerning the imagination. He believed it was fallible. Consequently, preachers needed to learn to submit what they imagined to be true to what God has declared to be true in the Bible. The reason for this subordination resides with the broken nature and sinful tendency of a person's imagination. Spurgeon warns of 'pious minds, a little over-heated with imagination,'[15] and of imagination's contributions to 'lascivious expressions'[16] or 'evil'.[17] Furthermore, because it is finite, 'imagination's utmost stretch fails to grasp any true conception of what God is.'[18] One is able to imagine and therefore feel all manner of things about God and the world – but such fancies have no authority. What one imagines is true becomes true for them and they begin to live their lives on the basis of a fully experienced fiction. Preachers are not immune to this temptation and find they are profoundly able to pass their fictions on to those who listen.

With such cautions in mind, Spurgeon urged his students to learn a holy use of the imagination. But where? The answer to this question reveals Spurgeon's primary rationale for illustrative preaching. 'Teachers of Scripture cannot do better than instruct their fellows after the manner of the Scriptures.'[19]

For Spurgeon, God has demonstrated in the Bible that He preaches with illustrations. Imagination in preaching is firmly rooted in the creative and communicative practice of God Himself. The student can turn to the Bible to learn a holy use of imagination.

The Visual Language of the Bible

Spurgeon wanted his students to notice two things concerning the way God speaks in the Bible. First, he wanted them to notice the kinds of speech patterns that exist in the Bible. Look, he would say, 'The Bible itself abounds in metaphors, types, and symbols; it is a great picture book; there is scarcely a poetical figure, which may not be found in the law and the prophets, or in the words of Jesus and his apostles.' If, as the Bible says, 'The preacher is bidden to speak as the oracles of God,' then the preacher 'should imitate their illustrative method, and abound in emblems and parables.'[20]

Second, he might say, 'notice the kinds of literature that form the Bible.' God used these varying genres to communicate Himself to us. The Bible is filled with 'history' and 'biography' which are meant to instruct us as much as the more explicitly doctrinal sections of the Bible. Therefore, 'Our Bible contains doctrines, promises, and precepts; but these are not left alone, the whole book is vivified and illustrated by records of things said and done by God and by men.'[21] Spurgeon would also point his students to the sacrificial system or the prophets of the Old Testament. 'The whole of the typical ceremonies and sacrifices of the Jewish law are so many acted parables,' he instructed. 'The prophets constantly employed parables and emblems.'[22]

Third, Spurgeon would urge his students to study the preaching of Jesus. 'Our Saviour, who is the light of the world, took care to fill his speech with similitudes,' said Spurgeon, 'so that the common people heard him gladly.' The result is a biblical rationale for the use of illustrations when preaching. The example of Jesus 'stamps with high authority the practice of illuminating heavenly instruction with comparisons and similes.'[23]

Fourth, Spurgeon would ask his students to think about how the imaginative method of Jesus was sanctioned by the Holy Spirit: 'Our Lord Jesus Christ, the great teacher of teachers, did not disdain the use of anecdotes,' he pointed out. What Jesus 'did we need not be ashamed to do. That we may do it with all wisdom and prudence let us seek the guidance of the Divine Spirit which rested upon him continually.'[24] The implication is that because the Holy Spirit rested on Jesus, and Jesus spoke with similitudes, then Spurgeon could conclude that speaking with illustration is an activity sanctioned and practiced by the Holy Spirit and worthy of our practice.

Fifth, Spurgeon's rationale for story and illustration came from the Puritan theology he so loved. 'The reason why the old puritan preachers could get congregations was this,' Spurgeon asserted; 'they did not give their hearers dry theology. They illustrated it!'[25]

Finally, God has also created men and women with a natural propensity for word and image combinations in order to hear and understand God's Word. 'People will more readily receive the truth of revelation if you link it with some kindred truth in natural history, or anything that is visible to the eye, than if you give them a bare statement of the doctrine itself.'[26] In his lecture entitled, 'The Uses of Anecdotes and Illustrations,' Spurgeon likewise stated that 'the anecdote in the sermon answers the purpose of an engraving in a book. Everybody knows that people are attracted by volumes with pictures in them; and that, when a child gets a book although it may pass over the letter press without observation, it is quite sure to pause over the woodcuts.'[27]

In short, because word pictures and pictured words abound in the Bible, the preacher who expounds that Bible must give himself to its illustrative example.

The Book of Nature

Spurgeon rooted his rationale for the use of illustration not only in the Bible and the human need for attention, but also in nature. If the Bible is a 'difficult classic,' 'a volume of more profound instruction for persons of riper years and higher culture,' then the natural world and providence are like a 'book for children,' or a 'primer.'[28] Davies identifies delight in nature as a primary characteristic of preaching in the Victorian age.[29] Davies suggests that such attention to nature resulted from the enthusiasm of the Romantic poets and the living desire to taste more than the dust and soot of the industrial revolution. The latter reality would have touched the lives of Spurgeon's students acutely. From 1861 to 1873, while the College was conducted in the basement rooms of the Metropolitan Tabernacle, gas lamps were the only source of light amid the crowded buildings and dusty streets which made natural light a scarce commodity for the classrooms.[30] Spurgeon was a man of his generation, but his recognition of nature found a larger and more historic root in what the Bible said about the role of nature in the Christian's life.

For example, in Psalm 19 Spurgeon saw a parallel between the non-verbal speech of God's creatures mentioned in verses 1-7 and the verbal speech of God's written law mentioned in verse 8 and following. This parallel, he says, 'seems to imply that there is a likeness between the two revelations; that they are, in fact, two books of the same revelation or two parts of one great poem.'[31] Because these two languages from God form one great poem, 'The whole world is hung round by God with pictures,' Spurgeon said. 'The preacher has only to take [these pictures] down, one by one, and hold them up before his congregation and he will be sure to enlist their interest in the subject he is seeking to illustrate.'[32] The world in which men and women live out their callings and communicate the gospel is filled with the poetry of God; a language of creation and word; nonverbal and verbal expressions of God's character and presence among them and for them.

Centrally, this divine poem not only forms categories of language for the preacher but also provides resources for sermon invention. Spurgeon's book entitled *The Teaching of Nature in the Kingdom of Grace*, which was published shortly after his death, illustrates this fact. The preface identifies how Spurgeon constantly 'read the Book of Nature in a way that proved how he looked upon the works of God with a poet's eye.'[33]

Within this volume of biblical lessons from nature, Spurgeon exposes a rhetorical pattern in the Bible for what we might call 'creation-visuals.' For example, he turns to the Old Testament book of Proverbs 24:30-32, which says: 'I went by the field of the slothful, and by the vineyard of the man void of understanding; and, lo, it was all grown over with thorns, and nettles had covered the face there, and the stone wall thereof was broken down. Then I saw, and considered it well: I looked upon it, and received instruction.' From this pattern of observing God's creatures for instruction, Spurgeon called preachers to awaken to the world around them. 'There is a great difference between one man and another in the use of the mind's eye,' he said, and continued:

> Some people have eyes and see not, which is much the same as having no eyes; while others have quick eyes for spying out instruction. Some look only at the surface, while others see not only the outside shell, but the living

kernel of truth which is hidden in all outward things. We may find instruction everywhere. To a spiritual mind nettles have their use, and weeds have their doctrine. Are not all thorns and thistles meant to be teachers to sinful men.... You shall find books and sermons everywhere, in the land and in the sea, in the earth and in the skies, and you shall learn from every living beast, and bird, and fish, and insect, and from every useful or useless plant that springs out of the ground.[34]

Walking Abroad in the Garden and the Field
When the preacher's eyes are opened by the Word to the world of nature and providence, the effect upon sermon preparation and delivery is noticeable. To begin, Spurgeon points his students to the Bible itself as 'the most effective' method for 'illustrating and enforcing the truths of the gospel.'[35] But he doesn't stop there. In his collection entitled *The Bible and the Newspaper*, Spurgeon speaks of the mental habit of daily observation of the world which lies behind a preacher's ability to use imaginative language. In this way the preacher gives himself to daily observing and meditating on the word *and* the world of God. Spurgeon explained:

'I read the newspaper,' said John Newton, 'that I may see how my heavenly Father governs the world;' a very excellent reason indeed. We have read the newspaper during the last three months that we might find illustrations of the teaching of our heavenly Father's word; and we think we have not read in vain, for we have gathered instances in proof, and facts in explanation, which we have jotted down in these pages. The worlds of nature and of providence are full of parallels to things moral and spiritual, and serve as pictures to make the written book of inspiration more clear to the children of God.[36]

With this framework, sermon preparation expands beyond the preacher's library time – opening up all of life as an inventive sermon resource given by God. By means of the word in the world, the preacher presently meets with God, conversing with God daily in light of God's verbal and nonverbal speech. As a preacher's life awakens to the reality of God at work with daily pictures of Himself in the world, the preacher's congregation learns to follow such a life approach to God. Even Sunday school teachers, for example, will learn that their preparation for study is not limited to the hour at the desk. Spurgeon describes what he means in order to 'encourage' his listeners in 'the habit of looking for emblems and analogies' through their daily lives. 'It is a mental exercise as profitable as it is pleasant,' he says. 'Sunday-school teachers and all other servants of the great parable-making Master would find it an improving occupation to walk abroad in the garden and the field, and resolve to find some instructive similes before they returned home.'[37]

As hearers practice such a mental habit, the language of the pulpit begins to echo the language of the hearer's week as the verbal and non-verbal language of God is recognized amid the mundane and ordinary routines of the world. By this practice, both preacher and people make the present speaking of God in His verbal and non-verbal expressions a daily and sought-after endeavor, placing the pulpit event into an atmosphere of divine conversation amid the ordinary things of life.

Exploring the 'Histrionic'
Spurgeon's concern for the practice of illustration moved him to go so far as to introduce what he calls 'the histrionic' use of communication on the basis of this 'nonverbal and visual' language. By this term, Spurgeon referred to the practice of bringing visual aids into the pulpit. Such aids which the prophets 'made use of' help the preacher to 'bring truth to the eye as well as the ear.' 'If you were to take a flower into the pulpit,' he explains, 'and especially if you were to exhibit a pair of scales, as Matthew Wilks did, you would be pilloried in the newspapers for weeks; but the prophets were divinely commanded to act as they did, and therefore obeyed the Word of the Lord, whatever man might think or say of their action.'[38] Prior to postmodernism and television, though Spurgeon did not follow this practice himself, he urged the use of visual aids from time to time because of the help that a person's eyes can be to the preacher.

Spurgeon was not unaware of the challenge that such practices received in his day. Perhaps it was pointed out to him that the prophets performed their 'histrionics' as an act of judgment on a stubborn people and not as a means of accessible communication. Or maybe, the challenges came from those who were concerned to limit entertainment or to uphold the centrality of the Word in their proclamation. What is certain is that while Spurgeon upheld the validity of visual aids, he felt that their use was a sign of deterioration in the congregation or culture. Such aids were to be used when 'plain talk' failed. He explains in full:

> Though the prophet wept, and entreated, and persuaded, yet they regarded him not; but turned on their heel and went each one his own way, to his merchandise, to his idolatry, to his adultery, or to his oppression. Therefore the Lord bade his servants add to their speech certain symbols which the people would see with their eyes, which would be talked about as strange things, and so would excite attention and command consideration. Perhaps, by this means the Lord would extort from some of them a deeper thought, and bring them penitently to their knees. It is better for preachers to do odd things than for men to be lost. If plain talk fails we may even use emblems and signs, for we cannot let the careless ones perish without another attempt to get at them. Oh that by any means we might save some![39]

This context of hard-heartedness ought not hinder the preacher's use of a visual aid if, by its means, the hearer can be won back to God. What seemed 'odd' to the Victorian culture both exposed the deadness of it and offered a way back to life.

Regarding contemporary questions of drama and preaching, while Spurgeon would have found a precedent here for a preacher occasionally to use nonverbal 'histrionic' visuals in the pulpit, he would not have understood this prophetic example as a warrant for the use of a drama troupe or other arts as the hope for regained power for the gospel in his generation. He saw such a move as a 'danger'. Rather, Spurgeon sought to expand the work of the pulpit into the greater drama he felt the Scripture represented. The drama was the called man speaking the Bible with melting and wooing tones, pleading for the hearer with illustrative and heart-softening communication. 'Until I see that the Lord Jesus Christ has set up a theatre, or planned a miracle-play, I shall not think of emulating the stage or competing with the music hall.'[40]

Nevertheless, Spurgeon taught his students the value of the eye as a means of drawing hardened sinners to the word for the ear and the heart.

Quoting Anecdote after Anecdote

Transcending adornment, visual words can also form an argument, or prove a case being made. Spurgeon would marvel at 'how frequently a word is itself a picture.'[41] With these words that are pictures 'there is a kind of reasoning in anecdotes and illustrations.' Initially, Spurgeon seemed bothered with this fact, stating that the need for this kind of reasoning may be 'unfortunate'. Like his concern with visual aids, this kind of visual reasoning was required for objecting hearts that are hardened, unable, or unwilling to follow a proposition logically. Such concern, however, gave way to an exhortation regarding the need for his future preachers to reason imaginatively. Visual reasoning simply means that the preacher connects word pictures to other word pictures in order to argue a point. Spurgeon explains:

> Instances, when sufficiently multiplied...prove a point. Take the very important matter of answers to prayer. You can prove that God answers prayer by quoting anecdote after anecdote, that you know to be authentic, of instances in which God has really heard and answered prayer...all these stories will be to many people the very best kind of argument that you could possibly use with them...so, if you want to prove the power of the gospel, do not go on expending words to no purpose, but tell the stories of cases you have met with that illustrate the truth you are enforcing, for such anecdotes will convince your hearers as no other kind of reasoning can.[42]

Testimony and story are compelling proofs to one's point:

> Often when didactic speech fails to enlighten our hear-
> ers we may make them see our meaning by opening a
> window and letting in the pleasant light of analogy...you
> may build up laborious definitions and explanations and
> yet leave your hearers in the dark as to your meaning;
> but a thoroughly suitable metaphor will wonderfully clear
> the sense...abstract truth comes before us so much more
> vividly when a concrete example is given, or the doctrine
> itself is clothed in figurative language.[43]

Again, after identifying that illustrations and anecdotes
may be used for explanation, he states that these kinds of
imaginative language 'may, in fact, be the very best form of
exposition.' Spurgeon declares that if a person would

> give me a description of a piece of machinery, he would
> possibly fail to make me comprehend what it was like;
> but if he will have the goodness to let me see a drawing
> of the various sections, and then of the whole machine,
> I will, somehow or other, by hook or by crook, make out
> how it works. The pictorial representation of a thing is
> always a much more powerful means of instruction than
> any mere verbal description ever could be.[44]

Spurgeon's visual reasoning is instructive and forms a complex view of mental imagery. On the one hand, he likens
imaginative language to 'windows' shedding light into the
rooms of argument, but on the other hand, he recognizes
verbal images in themselves as a form of exposition or argument. This imaginative reasoning or argument is demonstrated most in Spurgeon's method of teaching imaginative
preaching to his students. In his lecture, 'Illustrations in
Preaching,' Spurgeon says:

> The topic now before us is the use of illustrations in our
> sermons. Perhaps we shall best subserve our purpose
> by working out an illustration in the present address;
> for there is no better way of teaching the art of pottery
> than by making a pot.[45]

This is exactly what Spurgeon does. Likening a sermon to a building under construction and imaginative imagery to windows, Spurgeon teaches the use and misuse of metaphor by the means of metaphor. He does this by identifying different sizes and types of windows and their purposes, relating these to imaginative dos and don'ts in preaching.

When warning his students regarding the dangers of using too many anecdotes, Spurgeon uses imaginative language as argument and instruction. He says:

> Gentlemen I must warn you against the danger of having too many anecdotes in any one sermon. You ought, perhaps to have a dish of salad on the table; but if you ask your friends to dinner, and give them nothing but salad, they will not fare very well, and will not come to your house again.[46]

Also common is Spurgeon's attaching image to image to demonstrate how to use simile, metaphor, analogy, illustration, anecdote and others. In his lecture entitled, 'Anecdotes from the Pulpit,' Spurgeon states the reason for this approach:

> I shall make up this present address by quoting the examples of great preachers, beginning with the era of the Reformation, and following on without any very rigid chronological order down to our own day. Examples are more powerful than precepts; hence I quote them.[47]

Spurgeon's imaginative reasoning also forms a method for instruction in his sermons. For example, in a sermon in 1861 entitled, 'Not Now, But Hereafter,' Spurgeon presents the doctrine of the coming judgment. To make clear his meaning, Spurgeon chooses a visual connection with an element of nature. That is, instead of a connective word such as 'but' or 'and' which would lead to further didactic propositions, Spurgeon chooses the word 'imagine' and 'argues' the doctrine of God's coming judgment with word-oriented visuals. He says to the congregation:

> Imagine yourselves voyagers, far out upon the sea. A black cloud darkens the sky, you say you fear not the

cloud because it is not at present pouring forth the rain-flood. But that is the reason why you should fear it, for the cloud is waiting until it grows and spreads, till under the wing of darkness the egg of cloud has been hatched into the black screaming eagle of the storm. See you, the clouds are hurrying from east and west, mustering for the strife! Mark you not the sea heaving heavily in sympathy with heaven's convulsions? Behold how all the dread artillery of heaven is gathering up for one tremendous shock. Fools! Do you say you will not fear because the thundercloud has not yet burst, because as yet the breath of wind has not transformed itself into the blast of hurricane?[48]

Another example can be found in 1858 when Spurgeon preached a sermon entitled 'The Blood.' Having made his argument for his first point, he seems to recognize that he is not being clear. Rather than adding more didactic reasoning, he chooses visually oriented words as his method of 'reasoning.' He says to those listening:

And yet I fear that I have not been able to make you think of the blood of Christ. I beseech you, then, just for a moment try to picture to yourself, Christ on the cross. Let your imagination figure the motley crew assembled round about that little hill of Calvary. Lift now your eyes, and see the three crosses put upon that rising knoll. See in the center the thorn-crowned brow of Christ. Do you see the hands that have always been full of blessing nailed fast to the accursed wood! See you his dear face, more marred than that of any other man? Do you see it now, as his head bows upon his bosom in the extreme agonies of death? He was a real man, remember. It was a real cross. Do not think of these things as figments, and fancies, and romances. There was such a being, and he died as I describe it. Let your imagination picture him, and then sit still a moment and think over this thought: 'The blood of that man, whom now I behold dying in agony, must be my redemption; and if I would be saved, I must put my only trust in what he suffered for me, when he himself did 'bear our sins in his own body on the tree.'[49]

Conclusion

Fire is kindled as the pictures of God's Word and world are discovered afresh in the pulpits of a generation. When nature and providence come alive within the authority of the Bible and when wise cautions of inappropriate imaginations are understood, preachers can learn to imitate their Lord who preached with a holy fancy. With God's speech patterns, the need for attention, and the help of word pictures in making one's case, preachers can begin to look at candles in a room in a whole new light and preach with God-given and cultivated imagination.

Questions for Learning and Discussion

1. What is Spurgeon's rationale for illustrative preaching? How do you respond to it?

2. Discuss how God's two picture books of the Bible and nature inform the way a preacher would approach his sermon preparation.

3. What is a histrionic? What do you think of Spurgeon's point?

4. What is visual reasoning? What do you think about Spurgeon's practice?

5. What is the difference between merely 'stringing anecdotes' together for storytelling and using visual reasoning for the purpose of explaining the Bible?

6. What would it look like for you to begin to notice nature and daily events as potential illustrations of biblical truth?

7. What will you take with you from this chapter?

6

THE SOUL RUNNING OVER
AT THE MOUTH:
Anchoring our Emotions

If our sermons were to hang like icicles around our lips, they would not be very likely to melt the ice in your minds…your testimony must be earnest, or it will be fruitless. There must be passion and there must be pathos. The soul must run over at the mouth, and the speech must be the outflowing lava of a heart that swells and heaves with inward fires.[1]

Spurgeon's students would learn from him that plain-speaking was not only illustrative but was also something that the preacher was to feel. 'We shall never do much good in preaching unless we feel what we utter,' Spurgeon counseled. The Bible was the source for his convictions on this matter. Appealing to 2 Corinthians 5:11, for example, Spurgeon highlighted the connection between Paul's inward experience and his persuasion of others. 'Knowing the terrors of the Lord,' Spurgeon noted of the verse, 'we persuade men.'[2]

As with his use of illustrations, Spurgeon was known for his pathos in the pulpit. One observer of his preaching noted, 'It is in pathos that he excels, though he does not seem to be aware of it.'[3] Another observed that 'Many parts of the sermon were distinguished by exceeding pathos and strength of imagination.' Others agreed: 'His pathos brought tears to all eyes.'[4] Like his rationale for illustrations, Spurgeon saw the speech of God as presented in the Bible as filled with holy passion. Because the Spirit inspired the Bible, Spurgeon reasoned that the Holy Spirit was the source of the passion found on its pages. Kindled fire would evidence itself in plain speaking filled with a holy fancy and fueled by 'an outflowing lava' from the heart. This chapter explores Spurgeon's rationale for emotion in preaching and how such a view informs the delivery style of the preacher.

The Pathos of God

To preach with passion is first to preach with an abiding love from the heart for people. Spurgeon derives this understanding from what he sees of God's communication style in the Bible. Spurgeon explains: 'Even thus doth God, with sacred pathos, with love welling up from the depth of his heart plead with every sinner before me, and he words the pleading thus: "Oh Israel, return unto the Lord thy God."'[5] For Spurgeon, God's pathos is most clearly demonstrated in His loving movements toward sinners. Spurgeon explains:

> Here is a text, 'Their sins and their iniquities will I remember no more forever,' that is God's own assertion. He knows his own memory and he has put it so. Let me repeat those words. They melt my own heart while I speak them, and therefore I hope every child of God will feel the sweetness of them. What inconceivable love! What force, what pathos, what grace there is in every syllable: 'and their sins and their iniquities will I remember no more forever.'[6]

Thus far, a student of Spurgeon's would learn that the content of God's declarations in the Bible, the effect they intend for the sinner, and the grace that is there illustrated, form the elements of a holy pathos. Pathos is an experience of genuine love in the heart of the preacher for God and people. The preacher's genuine love for God seeks to imitate how God expresses genuine love to people. The preacher sees that 'like a father pleading with a beloved but disobedient son who is ruining himself, God himself pleads, as if the tears stood in his eyes,' says Spurgeon.[7] Therefore, the preacher learns to participate in this Fatherly pleading.

But, God is not only a Father pleading for ruined children. He is also a God compassionately seeking the wanderer, who strives 'to get away from God and holy influences.' The preacher learns to preach to such wanderers by looking, not to a homiletics text, but by looking at God's ways in the Bible. The wanderer is demonstrating that he is an enemy of God:

> Yet the Lord follows him, and with a voice of touching love and tender compassion he calls to him, 'this is the way, walk ye in it.' The word of warning, instruction, and entreaty follows the wanderer, and with ever-increasing pathos beseeches him to run and live. Again and again the wise, earnest, personal, voice assails his ear, as if love resolved that he should not perish if wooing could win him to life. The wanderer seeks not God, but his God seeks him. Man turns from the God of love, but the love of God turns not away from him.[8]

Spurgeon would say that God is 'love' journeying 'to and fro among the sons of men, with the voice of trembling pathos, pleading with them to be reconciled.'[9] The student of preaching learns how to approach sinners by seeing how God approaches them.

Pathos, then, is the energy of divine love, as described in the language patterns of the Bible. Sacred pathos describes the content of love in the heart and the pursuit of sinners in the will. These patterns of divine pathos form the basis for the familiar and tender condescensions of dialogical appeal made by the preacher to his hearers.

The Wooing Mannerisms of Christ's Preaching

However, when viewed through Spurgeon's account of the person and work of Jesus Christ, pathos becomes identified more closely with the manner of one's preaching. Pathos is not just what one feels about sinners, and not just that preachers are to pursue sinners, but sacred pathos concerns how one delivers the sermon to sinners. Spurgeon points to the preaching of Jesus to describe what he means.

> For the most part, throughout his ministry, though masculine to the last degree, yet there is this softness, a

pathos of love...in the person of Christ...he is, as it were, both father and mother to the children of men, blending everything that is sweet in manhood and womanhood in one individuality, and showing it all in his style, which is forcible as a hero's energy in the day of battle, and yet gentle as a nurse with her children. All mannerisms of Christ are wooing....[10]

A preacher's delivery style must imitate the Savior and so demonstrate the gentle ferocity of His 'wooing' of sinners. The presence of this earnest manner, and the reasons for it in Christ, discovers a kind of eloquence distinct in object and expectation from ordinary oratory. The goal is not to feel. The goal is to glorify God and take His good news to men. When this object is pursued and set before the preacher's mind, he cannot help but feel. His feeling then is rooted, not in his own strivings, but in the beauty of the object set before him. When the preacher has the glory of God and the plight of sinners before him, his concerns move beyond the polish of rhetoric to the earnest demonstration of the glory that he sees in God. Such a great object in view drives out the 'affectations of self-adulation' and renders absurd the preacher who stands 'at the glass to arrange his beauties.' More than 'how he puts that poetic word or how he mouths that polished sentence,' the preacher's 'sole desire is to deliver the message.' His sole concentration is 'to impress men with the matter in hand.' Because of this focus, 'Earnestness' will carry the preacher 'beyond the orator's rules of self-display; his rhetoric is melted down by his enthusiasm.'[11] This melting is what takes place as the preacher beholds the glory of God in the moment of preaching. He cannot help but preach with some measure of pathos according to the facilities of his personality and frame. He cannot help but feel for people in their condition of sin and misery apart from the reconciling movements of God in Christ. This feeling leads him to reach out to others in the manner of Christ.

By No Means a Stoic

Consequently, pathos describes the content of divine love swelling in the preacher's heart, and the manner of divine love demonstrated in the preacher's delivery. This heart overflowing into one's manner of speaking disrupts any hint of stoicism's distaste for unreality in Christian preaching. While rootless or manipulated emotion is to be avoided, so is a preaching of divine things which has no resulting emotion appropriate to what those things mean. Spurgeon turns again to the Bible for instruction on this point. Referring to Jeremiah, Spurgeon describes 'the weeping prophet' who 'sorrows over the desolation of his land, in words that have seldom been surpassed for sublime sympathy and pathos.'[12] Spurgeon then laments his inadequacies in comparison. To his hearers, he says: 'I wish that I had power to plead with you with the pathetic earnestness of Jeremiah. I fall short of that, but I can at least speak with all his sincerity.'[13] Here again, Spurgeon does not establish a certain measure of pathos that is a rule for all people. But within the personality and gifts of an individual preacher, he expected some analogy to the pathos exemplified in the Bible. The preacher cannot match Jeremiah, but he can learn from Jeremiah and pursue such preaching.

Another example of a disrupted stoicism from the Bible is the Apostle Paul. 'Oh with what pathos did he preach to the ungodly,' says Spurgeon.[14] He points out that Paul 'was by no means a stoic.' Nor, said Spurgeon, was Paul 'an invulnerable man in armor.'[15] Spurgeon called upon his hearers to hear the voice of grace in Paul and then, 'speak in tones of strong emotion like those of Paul.'[16]

Pathos refers then to feeling the truth and to delivering the truth feelingly. It is the substance of divine love warming the heart. In practice it runs over into a manner of speaking and relating that imitates the passion of God in Christ and is exemplified in those preachers whom the Bible describes. Such sacred emotion honors God and disrupts any stoic tendency among God's preachers.

The Tones of Jesus' Praying

Furthermore, Spurgeon would teach his students that the pathos of Christ is not limited to his preaching but is found especially in his prayers. Speaking of Judas the betrayer in the garden of Gethsemane, Spurgeon stated that Judas, 'Knew the tones of his [Jesus'] voice, the pathos of his pleading, the intense agony of that great heart of love when it was poured out in prayer.'[17] Interestingly, in this light of pathetic prayer, Spurgeon was known as 'a glowing-hearted "remembrancer" of God'.[18] Mrs. Spurgeon would remember these tones of voice and prayerful pleading from her husband on Saturday evenings. She recalls:

> At the tea-table, the conversation was bright, witty, and always interesting; and after the meal was over, an adjournment was made to the study for family worship, and it was at these seasons that my beloved's prayers were remarkable for their tender child-likeness, their spiritual pathos, and their intense devotion.[19]

Spurgeon would teach his students that authentic feeling begins for preachers as it did in their Savior. The Savior's experience of the object set before Him moved Him in praying and living and gave a passionate context in which He preached. With some overstatement to drive home this point, Spurgeon would say emphatically to his people:

> No wonder that you have not any peace, if you have been bringing before God your cold prayers. Heat them red-hot in the furnace of desire, or think not they will ever burn their way upwards to heaven.... It is he who concentrates his soul in every word, and flings the violence of his being into every sentence, that wins his way through the gates of heaven.[20]

As we will discuss in chapter twelve, Spurgeon was not dismissing the trials of men and women, nor was he identifying a certain measure of feeling that must accompany a good prayer. His point was to challenge the consistent pattern of life among followers of Christ who rarely seemed to feel the things Christ felt. Spurgeon felt that some measure of feeling was reasonable to expect because of what prayer is by its very nature. Spurgeon asks, 'What does praying a prayer mean? It means first, that you present it to God with fervency. Pray as if you meant it, throw your whole soul into the petition.'[21]

Pathos is rooted in the great object of God's glory. It follows the manner of Christ's pleading for sinners, wooing them to forgiveness and restoration. It is the content of one's love overflowing for God and people in the moment of preaching.

Logic Set on Fire
Holy emotion in preaching and prayer not only derives its validity from the character of God in Christ and the manner of the Scriptures, but it also stems from the very nature of what it means to know divine truth. The very nature of the truth itself was, for Spurgeon, a thing that warranted and produced certain feeling in the soul. In this sense, truth is by its nature experiential, or 'experimental' as Spurgeon's herit-age would have deemed it. In other words, to know the truth is to know more than its bare facts. Speaking to preachers in his own Calvinistic heritage, Spurgeon warns:

> You do not know the truth, my brother, because you have read...any...classic of our faith. You do not know the truth, my brother, merely because you accept the Westminster Assembly's Confession, and have studied it perfectly. No, we know nothing till we are taught of the Holy Ghost, who speaks to the heart rather than to the ear. (33)

In the classroom, therefore, his students heard him urge them to use a 'heart-argument' in the pulpit, which he described as 'logic set on fire.' If knowing the truth re-quires that we feel in some measure those feelings which are warranted in light of what the truth means, then we must communicate that truth with its appropriate feelings attached. As an example, consider how Spurgeon speaks about the wrath of God to his assembly. As you read his words, notice how he is longing for a greater capacity to describe the wrath of God with the emotions that such a doctrine warrants.

> I would that I could speak upon this dreadful subject in a proper manner. Whitefield had tones and emotions which were fitting for such a subject. He would cry out, 'Oh, the wrath to come! The wrath to come! The wrath to come!' He would cry, I say, until all his hearers responded

with, 'What must we do to be saved?' And good Baxter, trembling lest he should be guilty of men's blood, while he delivered the message as a dying man to dying men, knew the terrors of the law, and right earnestly he persuaded men to escape for their lives. O sirs, if I saw you in a burning house, there were not half so much need of earnestness as when I see you in the midst of a mass of sin and corruption which must be consumed by God's anger, and you with it. Sinner, why wilt thou die?[22]

For Spurgeon, therefore, when encountering the doctrines of God as God relates to sinners, stoicism was no option. To simply describe God's wrath with bare logic, in his mind, was to betray the meaning of the truth. Knowing the truth about God's wrath meant that its logic would set ablaze in the soul of the preacher and those listening. This did not mean that Spurgeon would challenge the natural force of 'Cold logic'. But he did believe that another kind of argument more fully represented the character and manner of God and was therefore more suited to preaching. Bare logic, he taught his students, must be 'made red hot with affection.' The preacher therefore must 'argue as a mother pleads with her boy...quickened...by the living warmth of love.'[23]

Painted Fire
In this context, there is a caution, however. As the student approaches emotion in the pulpit, he must not be naive. Preachers must learn that certain kinds and sources of emotion are inappropriate for the sermon. Logic must be set ablaze by a certain kind of fire. Feeling must be of a certain kind. It must originate with the kindling of the Holy Spirit. Preachers do not want the kind of passion that is aroused from our 'animal' passions or base desires. Neither must preachers seek that emotion which stems from 'the desire of honour,' the affected 'emulation of others,' or the natural 'excitement of attending meetings.' Emotion from any of these sources, and for any of these reasons, is not an evidence of the Spirit's work. Therefore, though each of these sources possesses its own ability to promote mental power, these are not to be trusted for a sure work from God. In fact, to possess these kinds of emotions for these kinds

of reasons, is to possess nothing more in the pulpit than the study of rhetoric has to offer.

Rather, wisdom requires that the student of preaching must learn to recognize at least three kinds of emotion available to him in the pulpit: the natural, the manufactured and the sacred. Such distinctions in emotion will uncover four kinds of preaching. First is the kind of preaching that is without pathos. As already noted above, Spurgeon believed that such emotion-deficient preaching actually betrays the example embedded in the language and descriptions of the Bible.

Second, there is the kind of speaking in which pathos is made-to-order and acted for the moment. 'Nothing is more to be despised than a mere painted fire,' Spurgeon said. Such 'painted fire' is nothing more than a 'simulation of earnestness.'[24] Preachers are to desire true rather than simulated emotion.

Third, there is the kind of speaking that is rich with natural pathos. Natural pathos refers to those emotions that are common to any human being. Such pathos must be carefully watched. 'I do not think it does anybody any good spiritually,' Spurgeon warned, 'when tears are excited simply by the description of a funeral, or by being reminded of one's childhood, or of one's parents. Some preachers appeal much to the passions, and think when the congregation is weeping, good is being done.'[25]

Natural emotions in the pulpit may move an audience, but this kind of movement cannot be equated with doing the hearers spiritual good. Such emotions, though real and genuine are, in themselves, no evidence of the Holy Spirit. Spurgeon does not deny the place of such emotions. But such emotions left by themselves deceive both the preacher and hearer who believe that God is working among them when in fact, what is happening arises from the common technique of rhetoric or the human bond between the preacher and people. The preacher must move from these kinds of emotions on to another kind.

When the preacher can make these natural emotions a platform upon which to stand and work upon the conscience, then it is well and good, but if he has only succeeded in drawing briny tears from mortal eyes, they may flow until the floor be watered with them without any salutary result.[26]

But why? Why are natural emotions not enough for the aim of the Christian pulpit? Spurgeon answers by pointing to the source of the feeling. 'Men may weep to the tragic muse in a theater as well as to the prophetic strains in a chapel,' Spurgeon observed. 'Their creature passions may be impressed through the acting of the stage as well as by the utterance of God's own servants.'[27] The source of the emotion is not rooted in a response to God's character and truth, but is a response to the realities of the human condition which bring feeling into our souls. This kind of feeling is good, but 'there is something more that is wanted,' without which 'all preaching' will be null and void. Preachers need the 'mysterious power of the Holy Ghost' going with the emotions.[28] They need *kindled fire* because of the inability of natural emotion. Even if 'the gospel itself' should come to hearers with 'a sort of power' that is sourced only in the 'pathos of the preacher, or the eloquent manner of his speech,' then the power needed for eternal issues remains absent.[29]

The inability of a preaching which depends merely on natural emotions lies behind Spurgeon's aversion to a certain kind of manuscript preaching. 'I have heard of a minister who put in the margin of his manuscript sermons, "Cry here"; and in another place, "here lift up your eyes." It must be very dreadful preaching when the emotion is made to order.'[30]

Spurgeon even questions his own degree of sacred pathos. He notes that 'God gifts certain speakers with the power of moving the natural feelings...there is a pathos about them... so manifest that for the heart of the hearer to be touched is a natural consequence.'[31] Now as Spurgeon seems to apply this truth to himself, he longs that his preaching may be more than this for his hearers' sake:

Now, I dread lest any of you should be so moved by myself when I preach that your feeling should arise from my tone or mannerism, or because you have an Affection or esteem for me...a temporary cause cannot produce an everlasting change.... Everything about the preacher's choice words, or musical tone, though proper enough as an accessory, if it becomes the principle and the power that moves you, will end in failure.[32]

Going Deeper than the Eye

The need for more than mental power in feeling leads the preacher finally to the fourth kind of speaking which is rich in 'sacred pathos.' This kind of passion is the fruit of an inward burning that results from having 'been in solemn fellowship with the Lord.'[33] Sacred emotion involves but transcends common human emotions. The difference lies with the reason for the feeling. Spurgeon explains: 'We must go deeper than the eye; we want to make the heart weep; we want tears of penitence for sin, not tears of regret for departed husbands and wives.'[34] The reason for the sacred emotion is a response to the truth as God has revealed it. The preacher must ask whether his hearers are feeling because the preacher told a moving story or whether his hearers are feeling because they have been gripped by the meaning of that truth which the preacher is proclaiming from the Bible.

'If the gospel be indeed the gospel of God to us, it will exalt God in our estimation.'[35] This understanding of an emotion rooted in a truth which raises the estimation of God in the hearer's eyes, is found for example in Psalm 19:8: 'The Law of the Lord is perfect, converting the soul. The statutes of the Lord are right, rejoicing the heart.' Spurgeon commented on this passage, pointing to the direct correlation between knowing the truth and a rejoicing response. This correlation, he believed, distinguished 'earthborn mirth' from 'heavenly delights.' 'As a physician gives the right medicine and a counselor the right advice,' he said, 'so the Book of God' gives 'the truth which' gives 'joy to the right heart.' 'Free grace brings heart-joy. Earthborn mirth dwells on the hip and flushes the bodily powers; but heavenly delights satisfy the inner nature....'[36]

In contemporary terms, a response of tears to a television commercial may become suspect as the impetus for the tears asserts that 'cotton is the thread of life.' So, a preacher and people must inquire as to the object upon which their passions rest and the source from which their passions flow. Spurgeon explained:

We want you to know the truth so as to feel its power, till it dominates your entire nature, sways the scepter of your soul, and becomes a resident monarch within you. Then will you be able to stand alone, and you will not need a crowd about you, and a flaming orator to hold you in your place; you will know whom you have believed, and be persuaded that he is able to keep that which you have committed to him.[37]

Sacred emotion is described by the experience of truth in the soul. It is divine logic set on fire with the warmth of love and the greater estimation of the worth of God and overflowing the human heart into a passionate manner of speech.

Conclusion

For Spurgeon, 'your heart can never palpitate with life divine, except through the Spirit; You are not capable of the smallest degree of spiritual emotion, much less spiritual action, apart from the Holy Ghost.'[38] But when such spiritual emotion is ignited in the heart by the Holy Ghost and when the estimation of God is raised by an authentic experience of what is true and what that truth warrants, then 'the tears roll down [the preacher's] cheeks, and he begins to plead with all the pathos of his nature, while he begs souls to come to Christ.'[39] Such 'begging' with 'all the pathos of his nature' is not only a rejection of stoicism and an imitation of the divine manner, it is an expression of reverence from a child to his Father. Therefore Spurgeon pleaded to God for his hearers:

Oh! Who shall give me tears? Who shall teach me to speak with pathos? How shall I reach your conscience and stir your hearts? Eternal Spirit, do thou this mighty work, and win this night to thyself.[40]

Questions for Learning and Discussion

1. What does Spurgeon mean by pathos in the pulpit?

2. Where does Spurgeon turn in order to explain the need for pathos in preaching?

3. What does it mean to 'know' the truth?

4. How do you interact with Spurgeon's critics and Spurgeon's reasoning regarding the familiar ways and language of God with sinners?

5. What do you think about Spurgeon's description of God as one who stoops?

6. What do you think about Spurgeon's understanding of reverence?

7. Describe painted fire. How does one discern the difference between emotion that is natural, painted, or genuine from God?

8. Why does Spurgeon reject stoic preaching?

9. What do you make of Spurgeon's concern that logic must be set on fire? What did Spurgeon mean by this statement? What did he not mean?

7

OPENING MERCY'S DOOR:

Motivating our Hearers

I suppose that when religion is painted as a dark and black thing there may be some hearts that are attracted by it, but I believe there are more flies caught with honey than with vinegar, and that there are more people led to think about their souls by grateful Christians than by the murmuring of believers.[1]

Spurgeon recounts a memory that he had of his brother James, who when he was a child 'suffered from weak ankles.' As a consequence of these weak ankles, Spurgeon remembered that his brother 'frequently fell down,' and because of it, he often 'got into trouble at home.' Their father believed that the cause of the frequent falling 'was only carelessness.' With this diagnosis in mind, their father soon grew impatient with such 'carelessness' and sought to correct the behavior. The way the elder Spurgeon sought to motivate young James to keep from falling was to threaten him. Every time the boy fell, he would be whipped. Years later, Charles and his father had a conversation about these childhood moments. Upon remembering his strategy for motivating the behavior change in James, the elder Mr. Spurgeon was quite happy. He recalled that his son had stopped falling. The threatening had worked and the boy was 'completely cured from that time' on. 'Ah!' Charles answered his father. 'So you thought. Yet it was not so, for he had many a tumble afterwards.' At this, his father was surprised. Perhaps he looked inquisitively to Charles, who then answered the new-found question in his father's eyes.

'I always managed to wash his knees, and to brush his clothes,' Charles confessed to his father, 'so as to remove all traces of his falls.'[2]

This anecdote offers students of preaching a clue as to how Spurgeon sought to motivate behavior change among his listeners. For him, God's grace and love more than God's threatening and frowning would form the primary motives that sinners need in order to turn and follow God. 'While the winds and tornadoes of the Law may sometimes tear away a [sinner's] cloak,' Spurgeon observed, 'far oftener they make him hug his sins, and bind his self-righteousness more tightly around him.' Therefore, Spurgeon felt that, as a rule, 'the gentleness and love of Jesus Christ' could better 'disarm the man, and make him cast away both his sins and his self-righteousness.'[3]

This rule is rooted in the nature of the gospel message itself. At the heart of this message is 'the story' of Jesus' love. The preacher's power for motivating his hearers is more firmly found when he learns to 'open mercy's door' for sinners, and when thereby he endeavors 'to attract' them to the story of God's unmerited love.[4] Consequently, as we will explore in this chapter, Spurgeon would teach his students that the demands of God's law are best proclaimed in the context of the merits of God's love.

These Terrible Themes

That Spurgeon preferred the merit of God's love for motivating obedience among his hearers does not mean that he sought to minimize the 'threatening' found in the Bible. On the contrary, Spurgeon readily acknowledged the 'sharp warfare' that went on as he and other preachers wrestled with the hard sayings of the Bible. 'A voice whispers in my ear' Spurgeon admits. It says to me that 'that threatening of God is too severe: that sentence of Scripture is too harsh.'

When this warfare took place, Spurgeon counseled preachers not to 'rub down the rough texts' with their 'pumice-stone' in order to meet the terrors of God with a 'larger hope.' Rather, preachers must make it their commitment, when they find their minds 'quarrelling with a line of Scripture,' to say to their souls, it is better to school one's heart and bow 'before the thunder of divine judgment' than to 'alter the Scripture.'[5] The doctrines of God's judgment, wrath and eternal punishment are to be bowed to and not softened or avoided. The good character of God is to be trusted to sort out rightly what seems harsh to our minds.

Consequently, Spurgeon did not avoid or soften such Bible themes. In fact, some of the most moving sections of his sermons are his descriptions of the Day of Judgment. Using all the skill of his familiar, direct, pleading, imaginative and passionate way, the hearer feels as if the Day has come. Spurgeon often describes the Day by imagining his hearers gathered there and asking them to do the same. 'I think I see that day of fire, that day of wrath,' he'd begin. Then he'd say to his hearers, 'You are gathered as a great multitude before the eternal throne.' Then, after describing the happy condition of those among his hearers who have believed and followed Jesus, he'd turn to imagine the condition of those who had been self-righteous in their religious practice, believing that their goodness was enough to merit God's favor. 'Come forward, come forward – you who said you had been a good citizen, had fed the hungry, and clothed the naked – come forward now, and claim the reward. What! What! Is your face turned to whiteness? Is there an ashy paleness on your cheek?' Then he'd turn to those who had mocked and resisted Jesus throughout their lives. 'Oh! I see you, I see you, you are not boasting now; but you, the best of you, are crying,' as you face him who sits upon the throne with no place to hide. 'Why, why such a coward? Come, face it out before your Maker.' Then Spurgeon would directly speak to the atheist and to those who had demanded that their preachers resist the Bible's teaching. 'Come up, infidel, now, tell God there is no God. Come, while hell is flaming in your nostrils; come, and say there is no hell; or tell the Almighty that you never could bear to hear a hell-fire sermon preached. Come now, and accuse the minister of cruelty, or say that we love to talk on these terrible themes.' A section of a sermon like this might end by magnifying in the imagination the sounds of the damned as they contemplated their end after having mocked the mercy of God all their lives. 'Hark below,' he'd say. 'If you could descend with them, you would hear their doleful groans, and hollow moans as they now feel that the

God omnipotent was right and just, and wise, and tender, when he bade them forsake their righteousness, and flee to Christ, and lay hold on him that can save to the uttermost them that come unto God by him.[6]

Students of Spurgeon would learn to let the hard truths of the Bible stand in their full expression. He would teach them not to round the edges to soften them. The same measure of skill must be given to elucidating these terrible themes as is given to more appealing themes. Rightly motivating the hearer does not come from removing or changing doctrines. Right motivation comes by placing those doctrines into the larger context of their relationship to God's provided mercy in Jesus Christ. How could Spurgeon speak so terribly and descriptively of these awful themes and still intend to motivate his hearers by grace? To answer this question, the student of preaching requires a brief exploration into how Spurgeon viewed the role of the law in relation to Christian life and preaching.

The Two Covenants
The judgment, wrath and eternal punishment of God are each related to the requirements of God's law not being met. For Spurgeon, however, this fact was not the only news that the Bible addresses, nor was it the only news that preachers are to bring to their hearers. This was Spurgeon's problem with how his father had tried to handle James. Spiritually speaking, threatening and whipping have their place, but they are incomplete when separated from the grace and mercy of God. Furthermore, the law is incapable of bringing the kind of change in behavior that God requires in the Bible. Charles felt that his brother James needed someone to help him stand again and to graciously clean his knees, if James were to work through and overcome his problem. Threatening and whipping without such compassion, closeness, help and grace were incompatible with the power the boy needed for change.

Spurgeon was equally concerned with those not tempted to soften the harder themes, who seemed to delight in the harshness of those themes and who tended to make God only a bearer of bad tidings. This latter concern was apparent as preachers handled the law of God in preaching. Trying to motivate behavior change, they relied on the threatening and the whipping of the law to spiritually upbraid people. Spurgeon believed that this approach was faulty.

The first fault of such preaching involves forgetting or ignoring the covenantal context of God's law. Following his Puritan theological heritage, Spurgeon began his discussion of God's law in the Garden of Eden. In his book, *The Covenant of Grace*, he explained that God had made a 'Covenant of Works' with Adam, 'our first father.' This covenant by its nature was 'not first in purpose,' for another covenant would be revealed. But this covenant in the garden was revealed first in time. The terms of this covenant were that Adam would live happily as long as he kept the law that God had revealed to him. Spurgeon pictured God saying in essence to Adam and his posterity, 'To test your obedience to me, there is a certain tree; if you let that alone, you shall live: if you touch it, you shall die, and they shall die whom you represent.' When Adam 'snatched greedily the forbidden fruit,' Spurgeon continued, the result was at least four-fold. First, 'all of us fell down' with Adam in sin and misery. Second, 'it was proven once for all that, by works of law no man can be justified; for if perfect Adam broke the law so readily,' Spurgeon said, 'depend upon it, you and I would break any law that God had ever made.' Third, there is 'no hope of happiness for any of us by a covenant which contained an "if" in it.' Fourth, this covenant can only bring a curse for us now and so our hope depends upon a merciful provision from God. Spurgeon's point is that such a provision has been made!

This merciful context for the law of God has been provided for by a covenant of 'pure grace and nothing else but grace.' The mediator of this covenant is Jesus, who stands before God as 'the second Adam.' In contrast to the first Adam, Jesus fulfills all of God's requirements and satisfies the demands of God's justice completely. Consequently, it was on the basis of this finished work of Christ, that Spurgeon asked:

> Do you see why it is that the covenant [of grace], as I have read it, stands so absolutely without 'ifs', 'buts', and 'peradventures', and runs only on 'shalls' and ' wills'? It is because the one side of it that did look uncertain was

committed into the hand of Christ, who cannot fail or be discouraged. He has completed his part of it and now it stands fast, and must stand fast for ever and ever.[7]

For this reason of Christ's merit, Spurgeon exhorted that 'no man attempt to mix up works with it, or anything of human merit.' Through this fulfilled covenant of grace in Christ, 'God saves now because he chooses to save.' Preachers must learn that God will not save people because they get good enough for grace. Rather, the reason anyone can be saved and accepted by God is because Jesus has been good enough and He stands as our representative where our first representative had failed. Students of preaching would learn from Spurgeon that when 'God observes us' He considers us 'all lost and ruined.' But, because of this new covenant, He 'in his infinite mercy' now 'comes with absolute promises of grace to those whom he hath given to his Son Jesus.'[8] The commands of God's law and the results of disobeying them are not rightly proclaimed if left to stand alone. Listeners must hear preachers place these commands and their terrible consequences for disobedience into the context of mercy's hope in Christ's merit. The effect of this understanding undergirds how Spurgeon understood that a sinner can be made right with God. Rightness can only come by 'free grace' on the basis of Christ's righteousness alone and by faith alone. In his *Puritan Catechism*, Spurgeon asks 'What is justification?' He then answers, 'Justification is an act of God's free grace, wherein he pardons all our sins (Romans 3:24; Ephesians 1:7), and accepts us as righteous in his sight (2 Corinthians 5:21) only for the righteousness of Christ imputed to us (Romans 5:19), and received by faith alone.'[9] The law must be placed into the context of God's covenant of grace so that hearers learn from preachers that their hope for acceptance with God relies not on their works but on Christ's work.

The Law at the Feet of the Gospel
A second fault arises, then, when preachers use the law of God for a purpose that God did not intend. Spurgeon had implied this earlier, when he said that the covenant of works was first, not in purpose, but in time. When preachers try

to use the commands of God as a means of converting their hearers, Spurgeon believed that they were mistaken.

'Neither the Jewish law of ten commands, nor its law of ceremonies was ever intended to save anybody,' Spurgeon observes. 'It was not the intent of the ceremonial law in itself to effect the redemption of the soul.' What then is the purpose of God's law? Spurgeon answered by explaining that as 'by a set of pictures,' the law sets 'forth the way of salvation, but it was not itself the way. It was a map, not a country, a model of the road, not the road itself.'[10] Therefore, as it relates to trying to gain acceptance with God, and being cursed by our inability to keep God's law, 'We are not under the yoke of Moses, but we are the subjects of King Jesus, whose yoke is easy and whose burden is light. Consequently, 'we have entered upon another kingdom, in which the ruling principle is not law, but love....'[11]

This does not mean that God's law is unimportant. Nor as already mentioned does it mean that the commands and consequences of the law are to be softened or avoided. Rather, the law must be preached in the context of the covenant of grace and according to its intended purpose. Its intended purpose is to point the hearer to the beauty of Christ's fulfillment of those commands and their need to rely on Him as their savior from their disobedience to those same commands. 'See here an instructive sight,' Spurgeon says. '[Set] the law at the feet of the gospel. This is the place for the law; the best work the law can do is to bring us to the feet of Jesus.'[12]

In this regard, the preacher must recognize the different conditions of souls among his hearers. The law is for the self-righteous, to humble their pride; the gospel is for the lost, to remove their despair.[13] How does the preacher take the self-righteous to the law and still keep the law at the feet of the gospel? Spurgeon describes what this is like.

The preacher first magnifies the beautiful declarations of God in light of the promises resulting from mercy's effects. 'I will be their God,' he promises.

But in response to these promises, some hard-hearted sinner cries, 'Oh! I will not have thee for a God.'

'Wilt thou not?' asks the preacher. Then the preacher gives the hardened man 'over to the hand of Moses; Moses takes him a little and applies the club of the law, drags him to Sinai, where the mountain totters over his head, the lightnings flash, and thunders bellow.'

The hardened softens. Then he cries, 'O God, save me!' 'Ah!' says the preacher. 'I thought thou wouldst not have' the Lord 'for a God?'

'O Lord, thou shalt be my God,' says the poor trembling sinner, 'I have put away my ornaments from me; O Lord, what wilt thou do unto me? Save me! I will give myself to thee. Oh! take me!'

'Ay,' the preacher says and then speaks what God Himself would say, 'I knew it, I said that I will be their God, and I have made thee willing in the day of my power.' 'I will be their God, and they shall be my people.'[14] 'This day I have made you my own.'

When preachers use the law as a means of acceptance and salvation with God, they are misinformed regarding its purpose. Only Christ and not the law has the power to save. Therefore, the law exposes the need for acceptance but it does not then offer itself as the means or the power for this acceptance. Neither must the preacher do so.

When God says, 'I will love them freely,' He means that no prayers, no tears, no good works, no almsgivings are an inducement to Him to love men. In fact, Spurgeon said, not only can there exist 'nothing in themselves,' but also there is 'nothing anywhere else' that explains 'the cause of his love to them.' Startlingly, Spurgeon even said that the blood, groaning and tears of Christ the beloved Son, while these are *the fruits* of God's love, they do not explain *the cause* of God's love for sinners. Then Spurgeon made the profound and central point of the covenant of grace. God 'does not love because Christ died, but Christ died because the Father loved.'[15] Thus, the law of God is 'the rule which God revealed to man for his obedience.'[16] But it is neither the means of God's acceptance of sinners nor is it the power God has given sinners for obedience. The preacher must bring the news of Christ in His fullness as the means and power for acceptance with God because of His righteous fulfillment of the covenant.

The Same God

Finally, to the gracious context and purpose for the law, Spurgeon adds a third faulty way of speaking about the law – speaking as if the God of the Old and New Testaments are two differing beings, or as if one Testament is mean and harsh and the other nice and sweet. Spurgeon explains that 'under the New Testament God is not an atom less severe than under the old; and under the covenant of grace the Lord is not a particle less righteous than under the law.' Spurgeon's point is that the covenant of grace does not mean the absence of God's holiness. Rather, the extension of grace from God to sinners is a further expression of that holiness. Therefore, far from excusing one's disobedience, grace actually solidifies and empowers one's need for holiness. 'We are so saved by mercy that no sin goes unpunished: the law is as much honored under the gospel as under the law,' Spurgeon says. This means that 'the substitution of Jesus as much displays the wrath of God against sin as even the flames of hell would do.'

> While the Lord is merciful, infinitely so, and his name is love; yet still our God is a consuming fire, and sin shall not live in his sight. If your offering and mine be evil, it will be an abomination unto him. He is of purer eyes than to behold iniquity; if our worship and service are mingled with hypocrisy and pride, he will not endure them.[17]

To speak of grace in separation from holiness, or holiness in separation from grace, is to misunderstand them both. They are, according to Spurgeon, intricately related; the one explains the other. The one fuels the other. Far from diminishing motivation for good deeds, then, Spurgeon believed that a view of this unearned love of God must form a central motivation and enablement for his listeners' salvation and edification. Holy lives flow from gratitude to God for unearned love. He explains: 'let deeds of holy consecration mark the whole of our lives, for with such sacrifices God is well-pleased, when they are not brought as a price to purchase merit, but as a love-token and tribute to His grace.'[18] Obedience is not offered in order to obtain God's love. Obedience is offered in response to the love that God

has already given. Doing something for God therefore is
not only a tribute to grace that has been already shown,
but it is also a matter of the heart that 'is prompted by
gratitude.'[19]

In sum, Spurgeon believed that service to God, which he
identified in preaching as promoting 'salvation' and 'edification,' stemmed from gratitude in the heart after having comprehended the gracious love of God. This context, purpose
and continuity for the law created a maxim that Spurgeon
hoped his students and fellow-workers would learn: 'It is
love that wins the heart.'[20]

Consequently, when the preacher calls for conversion
or obedience, he must seek to 'open mercy's door' from the
pulpit. As Spurgeon's Catechism states, repentance comes
not only from 'a true sense' of one's sins, but also from 'an
apprehension of the mercy of God in Christ.'[21]

For this reason, preachers need two tools from Spurgeon's workshop to help them in their quest honestly to
engage the demands of the law within the context of the
merit of Christ. These two tools are 'the Love-Token' and
'the Two Hands.'

The Love-Token as Man's Obedience

The idea of the love-token arises from Spurgeon's Puritan
theological heritage, which said that obedience from 'the
heart is prompted by gratitude to think of doing something
for God. As an old Puritan says,' Spurgeon observed, 'we
give for love-tokens a cracked sixpence, or a flower that
soon fades.' By the metaphors 'cracked sixpence' and the
fading flower, Spurgeon referred to a person's obedience
to God. A Christian's obedience is like a cracked coin or a
fading flower to God. But such imperfect acts of obedience
are 'accepted as a love-token,' not for their 'intrinsic value,
but as an emblem of what our heart feels, and would do
if it could.' In Christ, God looks upon our obedience born
out of gratitude to His love and mercy and, though they are
'trifles,' He 'makes much of them.'[22]

A love-token, first, describes the hearers' obedient response to God. The direction for their response to God is
the commands of Jesus Christ. The fuel for that response
is love and affection for God's mercy in Christ. The strength

for such a loving response of service to God is God's own mercy to count what is intrinsically imperfect as acceptable in His sight. Consequently, the follower of Christ by grace must understand that obedience to Christ is not an option. 'Brethren,' says Spurgeon, remember that 'if you would serve Christ personally you must obey him.' Spurgeon then anticipates the objection. 'Oh,' say you, 'I did not think that would be a very choice way of serving him.' Spurgeon counters by reminding the person of the words of Jesus. 'Listen! If you love me, keep my commandments.' Spurgeon speaks of the presence of these commands, as well as Jesus' instruction concerning them and his hearers' submission to them, as a divinely appointed token and pledge of love. 'Jesus has chosen obedience,' Spurgeon continues, 'as the special pledge and token of our love. You have said, "I wish I could build a chapel, or support a minister or missionary out of my own purse." I wish you could,' Spurgeon says, 'but still Jesus has not selected that as the love token.' Rather, Jesus has said, 'If you love me, keep my commandments.' Thus, seeking to obey Christ is the sign of something deeper in the heart. Obedience surfaces the love and gratitude that exist in one's heart for God. Because of this, to seek a 'complete, prayerful, habitual obedience to Christ is the very choicest pledge of affection which we can present to our Lord.' Then Spurgeon draws the listener's attention back to mercy's door for the strength needed to put such love into action. 'May infinite mercy help us to present it.'[23]

In this sequence, Spurgeon is applying strands of his Catechism at this point. While the moral law of God is the revealed rule of our obedience, the sum of that law is love from the whole heart, mind and strength.[24] Obedience is a token of love rooted in the strengthening mercy of God. Obedience is not an act to merit God's favor but an expression of love for God and His favor already given. While the law has the power to expose the character of God and the penalty for mistreating that character, Christ as the law's fulfillment has the power to enable new obedience. Spurgeon wanted his hearers to know that they must seek to love God, not in order to gain His love, but because He has already loved them. Spurgeon explains:

It is necessary to believe in Christ in order to be capable of true virtue of the highest order. It is necessary to trust Jesus, and to be yourself fully saved, before there is any value in your feeding the hungry or clothing the naked. God give you grace to go to my Master wounded yonder, and to rest in the precious atonement which he has made for human sin; and when you have done that, being loved at such a rate, show that you love in return; being purchased so dearly, live for him that bought you; and among the actions by which you prove it, let these gleam and glisten like God-given jewels, the visiting of the sick, the comforting of the needy, the relieving of the distressed, and the helping of the weak.[25]

The Love-Token as God's Provision

But Spurgeon motivated obedience, not only by identifying good works as love-tokens, but also by magnifying the provisions of God for sinners as love-tokens. In this way, both a believer's obedience and God's provisions are rooted in love.

In his sermon entitled, 'The Sacred Love-Token,' Spurgeon called upon the listener to contemplate the blood shed by Jesus as a token of love from God. 'The blood is a love-token. The blood is a token of *ancient love*...the Lord has given thee an ancient token which sets forth his great love.'

Spurgeon places the doctrine of God's election into this framework of love for the hearer. 'Before thou wast born the blood was poured forth which is to-day the ensign and pledge of everlasting love. It is a token of *intense love*, for it is a pledge taken from the heart of Christ, and denotes not the love of the lip, not love which begins and ends with outward deeds of mercy, but a love which wells up from the essence of the Redeemer's being.'

The blood of Christ, the election of Christ, and the perfect obedience of Christ are a 'token of *mighty love*,' for these testify that He who gave them 'possessed a conquering flame of love, which many waters could not quench nor death itself destroy.'

These tokens of Christ also point to the character of God. These are tokens of 'a *wise all seeing love*...when he gives us the blood he does as much declare, "my child, I am aware of the evil which is in thee, for I have suffered its penalty; I know thy sin but thou shalt know it no more, for I have carried it away, and cast it into the depths of the sea...."[26]

A fuller outworking of the maxim that 'love wins the heart' is demonstrated in Spurgeon's sermon entitled, 'Do You Know Him.' Spurgeon begins by addressing the imaginations of his hearers with the fragrances of love.

Suppose that as you wake up one morning, you find lying up on your pillow a precious love-token from your unknown friend, a ring sparkling with jewels and engraved with a tender inscription, a bouquet of flowers bound about with a love-motto! Your curiosity knows no bounds. But you are informed that this wondrous being has not only done for you what you have seen, but a thousand deeds of love which you did not see, which were higher and greater still as proofs of his affection.

After bringing to the listener's mind a picture of an unknown initiator of love, Spurgeon next depicts the thoughts and actions of this loving initiator toward the listener. Spurgeon continues with an allusion to Christ and His suffering:

You are told that he was wounded, and imprisoned, and scourged for your sake, for he had a love to you so great, that death itself could not overcome it: you are informed that he is every moment occupied in your interests, because he has sworn by himself that where he is there you shall be; his honors you shall share, and of his happiness you shall be the crown.

Now Spurgeon envisions the response of love aroused in the receiver by the initiative of the unknown lover. He characterizes this love-response on the part of the receiver by moving the scene from the second and third person description to the first person voice. He continues:

Why, methinks you would say, 'tell me, men and women, any of you who know him, tell me who he is and what he is;' and if they said, 'But it is enough for you to know

that he loves you, and to have daily proofs of his goodness,' you would say, 'No, these love-tokens increase my
thirst. If ye see him, tell him I am sick of love...the love-
tokens which he gives me, they stay for awhile with the
assurance of his affection but they impel me onward with
the more unconquerable desire that I may know him. I
must know him; I cannot live without knowing him. His
goodness makes me thirst, and pant, and faint and even
die, that I may know him.[27]

This sermon illustrates Spurgeon's strategy of opening
'mercy's door' so that the listener may behold God's love
for him in Jesus Christ. Spurgeon believed that such an
apprehension of merciful love will cause the heart to thirst
and respond, not with mere disinterest, not with mere outward show, but with heart-felt love toward God.

Offering the Two Hands
Spurgeon's theology of the covenants of works and grace,
which led to Christ-merited obedience rooted in love and
gratitude, formed a preaching practice which Spurgeon
called the 'two-fold ministry' of 'warning' and 'invitation.'
'Blend the two in wise proportion,' Spurgeon counseled, and
then 'set both on fire!' Spurgeon explained:

Tell of Christ's coming to judgment, and then invite men
to come to Christ for mercy. Warn them that he is on the
way; but tell them that he waits to be gracious, and that
while he lingers they have space for repentance. You will
thus both drive and draw, both convince and comfort,
and your testimony will have two hands with which to
bear men to their Savior.[28]

Spurgeon finds this twofold ministry in the preaching style
of Jesus. Jesus 'threatens as well as entreats,' Spurgeon
observed. 'He warns you, "if ye turn not, he will whet his
sword; he hath bent his bow and made it ready." He declares
that the despisers shall wonder and perish. He asks, "how
shall we escape if we neglect so great a salvation?"' 'And
yet,' Spurgeon continues, 'the Lord does more than command, he graciously invites; with tenderness he bids sinners

come to his banquet of mercy, for all things are ready.' As an example, Spurgeon points again to Isaiah 55:1. Where God could command, he instead cries, 'Ho, every one that thirsteth, come ye to the waters.'[29]

These two hands can, at times, form the overall structure of Spurgeon's sermons. For example, in a sermon entitled, 'Satan's Banquet,' Spurgeon begins:

> This morning...I am about to introduce you to two houses of feasting. First, I shall bid you look within the doors of the devil's house...having bidden you look there and tremble, and take heed to the warning, I shall then attempt to enter with you into the banqueting house of our beloved Lord and Master Jesus Christ, and of him we shall be able to say, as the governor of the feast said to the bridegroom, 'thou hast kept the good wine until now.'[30]

Spurgeon sums up his communicative methods by lamenting death as the enemy of these warnings and invitations of love. Spurgeon states that when death comes, '[I will no longer be able to] set mercy's door before you...then I can never warn you, nor invite you; never again depict the agonies of my Lord and Master and endeavor to attract you by the story of his love, his dying, bleeding love.'[31] Opening mercy's door magnifies the story of God's dying bleeding love and gives warnings and invitations in light of the person and work of Jesus.

The Two Hands Pastorally Applied

After learning the method for opening mercy's door, the student of preaching must learn from Spurgeon to pastorally apply these warnings and invitations concerning the story of God's love. He must first consider the conditions of believers.

For example, the heart that struggles with neglect of reading the Bible and praying to God hears Spurgeon warn and invite in the context of the love-token. Growth in these spiritual disciplines is not enabled by merely pronouncing condemnation. Rather, the warning is placed into the context of love in order to arouse a loving response of gratitude

and to empower greater care for the disciplines. Spurgeon
says to such a person:

> He [God] gave us a book as a love-token, and he desired
> us to read it, for it was full of love to us; and we have
> kept it fast closed till the very spiders have spun their
> cobwebs over the leaves. He opened a house of prayer
> and bade us go there, and there would he meet with us
> and speak to us from off the mercy seat; but we have
> often preferred the theater to God's house and have been
> found listening to any sound rather than the voice which
> speaketh from heaven.[32]

Similarly, on another occasion he would say of the Bible,
'This is thy Father's love-token; let it never be shut up and
covered with dust.'[33] The Bible is a love-token because it is
'a book of promises for every believer.' Every believer is a
'welcome guest at' its table of 'promises.' It is a 'never fail-
ing treasury filled with boundless stores of grace.' It is the
Father's 'love-token' and believers are 'free to it at all times'
just as they are 'free to the throne of grace.'[34]

Spurgeon also considered those believers who are afflicted or needing assurance. When peace is lost on the
troubled seas of thought, he said, 'Whatever there was to
trouble the son, the father gave him a kiss to set it all right;
and in like manner, our God has a love-token for every time
of doubt and dismay which may come to his reconciled
sons.'[35] Such assurances clothe the doctrine of election as
a comfort for the struggling conscience. Those who belong
to Jesus 'belonged to the Father' and were given to Jesus
by the Father 'as a love token.' Now, Spurgeon counsels,
'our Lord pleads that because they were the Father's gift to
him he should have them with him.' Spurgeon concludes
that on the basis of this present intercession of Christ for
the downcast, that they have a seal of the Father's favor.
'Nobody can have such a right to your wedding ring, good
sister, as you have yourself. And are not Christ's saints, as
it were, a signet upon his finger, a token which his Father
gave him of his good pleasure in him?'[36]

The conditions of unbelievers were also to find consid-
eration and application. In every sermon Spurgeon believed

that the preacher ought to labor to remove prejudices, to resolve doubts, to conquer objections, and to drive the sinner out of his hiding places.[37] The love-token and the two hands formed a strategy which Spurgeon employed to this end. For example, the absence of felt love-tokens from God ought to cause a discomfort in the sinner, moving him to earnest prayer. 'If I have no love-token,' Spurgeon warned, 'then so much the worse for me, and so much the more reason why I should never be happy till I get one. If he has not invited me, then I will cry to him for an invitation.'[38] Spurgeon felt that an absence of such prayer signified a contentment to live without the love of God manifested in one's life. Such a state is dangerous for the soul, and in the professing Christian is called backsliding. For the unbeliever, it designates the corrupted priority of one's heart. Spurgeon warns and invites: 'you were wont to mourn like doves if you had no word from your Master in the morning, and without a love-token before you went to rest, you tossed uneasily on your bed; but now you are carnal and worldly, and careless, and quite content to have it so.... O may God be pleased to arouse you from this lethargy.'[39] Such an arousal was to be found in God's power in the context of a reminder of His love.

In short, the two hands of invitation and warning are meant, in the context of love, to find pastoral application to differing conditions and situations that believers and unbelievers find themselves in.

Conclusion
To conclude, Spurgeon's strategy of 'opening mercy's door' and revealing the 'story of Christ's love' by depiction, warning and invitation, demonstrates for students of preaching how to motivate obedience to God. One is reminded again, regardless of whether one agrees with Spurgeon's theological heritage, that Spurgeon's preaching practice was thoroughly informed by his theology. In fact, on this point, as on so many others, it seems that Spurgeon's sermons are simply applied theology. In this case, preachers proclaim the law in the context of grace, the purpose of Christ, and the power of God's unearned love for sinners. Upon these foundations, the preacher can say with Spurgeon:

Let me say to thee, sinner, yield thy heart to the goadings of divine love.... Oh! Think not that the Savior's blood will be unable to cleanse thee. Not thy worthiness, but thine unworthiness attracts His attention; not thy strength, but thy weakness; not thy riches, but thy poverty. He came to save just such as thou art. Lost one, but loved one, trust Him![40]

Questions for Learning and Discussion

1. How does Spurgeon's conversation with his father, in the opening paragraphs of this chapter, illustrate Spurgeon's approach to correcting behavior?

2. What are the two Covenants? How does recognizing the first and second Adams, in relation to God, impact our preaching?

3. What do you think about Spurgeon's concerns that preachers soften the terrible themes of the Bible? What do you think about Spurgeon's concerns for how preachers can misuse the law of God?

4. Describe the limitations of the law in terms of motivating one's obedience. What is the proper role of the law?

5. Describe how Spurgeon understood the role of holiness and grace for obedience.

6. What do you think of Spurgeon's 'love-token' idea? What about the two hands?

7. What will you take with you from this chapter?

PART THREE:

The Preacher's Power

Key Points to Look For in Chapters Eight through Eleven

- There are at least two kinds of power available to the preacher; only one of these has the capacity to accomplish the preacher's purpose.

- Biblical truth requires the active ministry of the Holy Spirit to be effectual.

- The triune God presently preaches to the hearer's soul as the preacher speaks to the human ears. The ear hears the preacher's voice but the soul hears the voice of God.

- The Spirit exalts Christ in preaching for the glory of the Father.

- The Spirit uses favored instruments by which He demonstrates His power in preaching. Trust of the Spirit is tested according to the measure by which a preacher surrenders to and utilizes these means.

- When the preacher gives his sermon, he is participating in a spiritual war.

- The Spirit of God has a free will. Though He works by appointed means, He is not obligated to accomplish our desires through those means. The preacher must learn to surrender to the Spirit's purposes, utilizing the Spirit's means out of love and obedience rather than out of a strategy to get what the preacher wants.

- Yet, the preacher cannot expect the Spirit to demonstrate His power when the preacher gives himself to means other than those appointed by the Spirit.

- Preachers need to learn what it means to grieve, quench and walk in the Spirit. Gaining biblical convictions concerning the ministry and fellowship of the Spirit is vital for the preacher.

- Preachers need fresh empowerments from the Spirit for their calling each day.

Overview for Part Three
God is the preacher. He draws near through the instrumentality of His called man and He Himself preaches with power in the preaching event. The preacher must look to God's resources and appointed guides for preaching. Through these resources, within the weaknesses of the preacher, the Spirit of God intends to demonstrate His attendant power in the moment of preaching. God drawing near and virtually preaching alongside of the human minister is descriptive of 'kindled fire'. Truth is made effective by the Christ-exalting Spirit and what was once lifeless and cold is made alive and warm again. Preachers must learn what it means to walk in the Spirit.

8

THE LORD'S WAYS:

Trusting the Spirit's Appointed Means

There are certain persons in the world who do not believe in instrumentalities....
Our Savior was not of their mind.... He believed in his Father's omnipotence,
but he also believed that the Lord would work by means....[1]

Now that the student of preaching has encountered Spurgeon's thoughts on the practices of preaching, a question might arise in his mind. Why must a preacher pursue a scriptural manner and view his style, delivery, illustration, emotion and motivation in light of that manner? Spurgeon would answer these good questions by taking us back to the Holy Spirit. The preacher must minister the Lord's Word in the Lord's way. By this, Spurgeon meant that the Spirit of God has ordained certain means by which He will demonstrate His power.

The Spirit's Favored Places
The Lord's ways are discovered when the preacher realizes that 'The Holy Ghost uses means.'[2] By the term 'means', Spurgeon referred to what he called the 'appointed ways' of the Spirit. The word 'way' refers to a path or a road on which to get from one place to another. Or, it can refer to a method or strategy by which a thing can be accomplished. Thus, an 'appointed way' refers to a path or strategy which the Spirit of God has specifically chosen, by which He will normally accomplish His purposes. Preachers and people find both a rationale for their existence and a direction for their work

when they learn that the Spirit who appointed them has also appointed certain ways of fulfilling their calling. One may throw leaves and aluminum cans into the smoldering heat of long-burned wood. But only smoke and darkened aluminum will result. Kindling a fire back into a full blaze of light and heat requires certain resources and ways.

The Spirit of God knows the best ways to kindle the gospel of Christ in the human soul. Therefore, Spurgeon believed that rather than blessing any means attempted by a preacher who is seeking God's power, the Spirit of God has 'his favoured places for displaying his might.' 'There are things congruous to the Spirit, and things contrary to his mind,' he said. 'Things congruous to the Spirit' means that the Spirit will attend those things which do not contradict His character and work. Though He is the 'free Spirit of God', the Holy Spirit 'is by no means capricious in his operations.'[3] He will not adorn that which counters His nature. What then are the Spirit's favored means and places for kindling fire among His preachers and people?

Our Nearer Tools

First, it is 'by human agency' that Spurgeon believed 'God ordinarily works out his designs.'[4] Though 'flaming seraphim would surely have been majestic golden lamps with which to illuminate the nations,' God nonetheless 'has purposes with regard to himself to be answered by using men as his agents.'[5] Central to this God-ordained human agency among the community of Christians is the preacher.

Because the Spirit of God uses people to display God's power, the preacher must take a conscientious look at the tools available to him for ministry. Spurgeon believed that the preacher had two sets of tools for which he had a divinely given responsibility. These tools he identified as the preacher's 'near-tools' and 'remote-tools.' The illustrations, books, study constructs, supplies and programs so useful to the preacher are considered his 'remote-tools.' But a preacher requires a tool nearer than these in order to be a useful agent in the hands of the Spirit. 'It will be in vain for me,' Spurgeon says, 'to stock my library, or organize societies, or project schemes, if I neglect the culture of myself; for books, and agencies, and systems, are only remotely the instruments of my holy calling; my own spirit, soul, and body, are my nearest machinery for sacred service.'[6] Therefore, preachers must recognize that 'we are, in a certain sense our own tools, and therefore must keep ourselves in order':

> If I want to preach the gospel, I can only use my own voice; therefore I must train my vocal powers. I can only think with my own brains, and feel with my own heart, and therefore I must educate my intellectual and emotional faculties. I can only weep and agonize for souls in my own renewed nature, therefore must I watchfully maintain the tenderness, which was in Christ Jesus.[7]

The preacher, because the Spirit displays His power through him, must take care with his own body and soul as he gives himself to preaching. He must watchfully maintain the tenderness of Christ in his ministry. Perhaps Paul's instruction to Timothy in the New Testament comes to mind. 'Do not neglect your gift...be diligent in these matters...watch your life and doctrine closely. Persevere in them,' and 'you will save both yourselves and your hearers' (1 Timothy 4:14-16). Spurgeon's words expose a tendency among preachers to concentrate on 'remote tools' as the primary answer for powerlessness in their generation. He reminds preachers that the primary instrument by which God works is personal and relational. Our hearts before God, if cold and dull toward Him, will deaden preaching no matter how easy our access or how competent our skill with remote tools. 'There are certain things about Christian ministers which God blesses and certain other things' which 'hinder success.'[8] The preacher must recognize that he is able, as is every person, to grieve the Holy Spirit. What grieves the Spirit is 'anything that would have disqualified' a preacher as 'an ordinary Christian for communion with God.' These will also disqualify him from 'feeling the extraordinary power of the Holy Spirit as a minister.' For his students, Spurgeon listed and explained six 'special hindrances' to the workings of the Spirit in the preacher's ministry. Each of these involved the preacher's 'nearer tools.'

1. A want of sensitiveness to the presence and movements of the Spirit
2. A want of truthfulness
3. A general scantiness of grace
4. Pride
5. Laziness
6. The neglect of prayer[9]

A preacher's personal and first-hand communion with the Lord is a means which God uses to display His power through the human agency of the preacher. When there is powerlessness in the pulpit, a preacher must examine his own heart and the hearts of those to whom he ministers. Is there a measure, albeit small, of genuine fellowship with the living God and a resulting pursuit of His character? If grieving the Spirit means to affirming that character which the Spirit would resist, then is there a need for the preacher's repentance and renewed conformity to the Spirit's holy character in Christ?

This Great and Piercing Instrument
Another 'favoured place' 'congruous to the Spirit' is the Bible. 'The word, as we have it printed in the Bible,' Spurgeon says, 'is the great instrument in the hand of the Spirit for leading the children of God in the right way.'[10] The Word of God is uniquely fit for the rough terrain of the human heart. In light of Hebrews 4:12, Spurgeon states: 'The difficulty with some men's hearts is to get at them. In fact, there is no spiritually penetrating the heart of any natural man except by this piercing instrument, the Word of God.'[11] The Spirit of God who wrote the Bible is the same one who wields it like a sword overcoming hostility and bringing stability to the human soul (Ephesians 6:17). A ministry apart from the Spirit's book will find it impossible to display the true power of God, because 'The Spirit speaks to people by means of the Word of God.'[12]

It is not the Bible itself, however, but the Bible in the hands of the Spirit that instrumentally demonstrates the power of God. Spurgeon here follows Calvin, who states: 'without the illumination of the Holy Spirit, the Word can do nothing.'[13] 'But when the Spirit of God goes with the Word,'

Spurgeon concurs, 'then the Word becomes the instrument of the conversion of the souls of men.'[14]

Spurgeon believed that the idea of the Bible as an instrument in the Spirit's hands most ably accorded with the free agency of human beings: 'For a word is a suitable instrument by which to rule a free agent.... The way to make blocks of timber move would be to drag them, and if we wish to shape them we must hew them with the axe, or cut them with a saw; but the way to deal with men is to speak with them. That is how Jesus operates.'[15] Unlike other words, therefore, and when 'perfumed' by the 'unction' of the Holy Spirit, 'the Word of God deals with us as no word of man ever did or could....' This is so, because the penetrating power of the Bible resides not only with its nature as God's Word but also with its purpose in God's hands. The Bible 'is not merely an instrument of good,' notes Spurgeon, 'but the Holy Spirit makes it an active energy within the soul to purge the heart from the sin....'[16]

Therefore, the particular sermon form that preachers choose – whether doctrinal, practical or experimental – can be good in its season and ought not generally to cause friction among brethren as long as the preacher is expounding what the Bible says. Spurgeon recounts:

> I have heard of doctrinal preachers who hated the very sound of the word 'duty'; I have also heard the practical brother declare that 'election' he detested; while the experimental brother has affirmed that the doctrinal preacher was merely 'a dead letter man.' Oh, what naughty words for God's children to use to one another.[17]

The preacher's personal style is therefore of lesser concern than whether or not in his style he preaches the Bible. Spurgeon urges that 'The sublime and commanding style of Isaiah should not put us out of patience with the plaintive tones of Jeremiah, nor with the homeliness of Hosea, or the abruptness of Haggai.'[18] Consequently, different settings join personal styles and lead preachers to different sermon structures that should not concern us. For example, for his Monday evening prayer meetings Spurgeon intentionally refrained from 'studying or preparing anything,' and from choosing difficult 'expository topics' in order rather to give himself to an extemporaneous preaching approach.[19] What is primary for the preacher, then, is not what particular sermon structure he may use on this or that occasion, nor what personality style he may tend towards, but that in each of these cases he must strive to 'keep close to the Scriptures.'

This conviction of 'Scripture-closeness,' however, led Spurgeon to recognize that other legitimate styles of preaching ought to be careful not to push 'proper expository preaching out of place.'[20] Feeling that an absence of expository preaching was taking place in his time, Spurgeon asserted that 'there is more necessity for our commenting during the time of our reading the Scriptures.' Because people had little time or resources to learn the meaning of the Bible in the course of their ordinary days of family and work, Spurgeon could not see how the preacher could counter this lack of Bible understanding and offer 'such spiritual assistance except through the regular practice of exposition.'[21] Ezra, the Old Testament priest and scribe, served as a model for Spurgeon in this regard.

> Many of our ministers think that, in the public service, they must read a certain quantity of the Scriptures; and they take, perhaps, three long chapters out of Ezekiel, and not a soul in the congregation knows the meaning of what they are reading.... Instead of reading, as Ezra did, and expounding the meaning to the people....[22]

Spurgeon then connects public Scripture reading with the necessity of the Holy Spirit's working in order to form his rationale for expounding the meaning of what one reads. 'One sentence of the Bible prayed over, and bedewed with the Spirit,' he says, 'though it be only a short sentence of six words, will profit you more than a hundred chapters without the Spirit.'[23] The Spirit, he assumes, will display the power of God through the human agency of Scripture explained.

Added to these expository comments during the public reading of the Bible, Spurgeon believed that while other methods of sermons are valuable and have their proper place, 'no preaching will last so long, or build up a church so well, as the expository.' 'I cannot too earnestly assure you,' he says, 'that, if your ministries are to be lastingly useful, you must be expositors.' Being an expositor meant for Spurgeon that the preacher by his sermon was 'mighty in expounding the Scriptures.'[24] For Spurgeon, as for his American contemporary, John Broadus, to say that a message was 'expository' could have a variety of definitions. According to Broadus, the general definition of an expository sermon 'is one which is occupied mainly with the exposition of Scripture...it is a sermon which draws its division and the exploration of those divisions from the text.'[25] And 'while the expository sermon is frequently from a longer passage, an expository sermon may be based on a single verse or even on one word.'

For example, on a cold Thursday evening in early February in 1881, Spurgeon says, 'My discourse this evening will scarcely be a sermon – it will be expository rather of the life and experience of Jacob upon one point.'[26] Whether preaching on the life of Jacob or preaching from a word or phrase in a passage, Spurgeon sought to preach in an expository manner, and those who described his preaching often recognized this feature of his preaching. In 1854, for instance, those who heard him preach for the Young Men's Christian Association characterized his 'deeply impressive sermon' as an 'expository effort' of much value to all.[27]

While some may critique how well Spurgeon expounded some passages of Scripture in his sermons, his 'expository effort' cannot be denied and finds its rationale when locating his explanation of the Bible as the Spirit's appointed way. Spurgeon summarizes the impact of this appointed means on sermon structure in this way:

We should not unite in any indiscriminate censuring of hortatory addresses, or topical sermons, nor should we agree with the demand that every discourse should be limited to the range of its text, nor even that it should have a text at all; but we should heartily subscribe to the declaration, that more expository preaching is greatly needed, and that all preachers would be the better if they were more able expounders of the inspired Word.[28]

Thus Spurgeon lamented his generation's search for sermon power when pulpits were sometimes given to oral presentations which displayed little of the meaning of God's Word. Spurgeon understood why a preacher may be so tempted. Sometimes the weapons that God has given for the war upon the soul feel inadequate. The preacher must yield, stand in front of people with his own reputation exposed, and say with love what God has said. Spurgeon is fully mindful of the searching questions that such a point raises and yet fully adamant in his convictions. What one preaches demonstrates the degree to which he is relying on mental or spiritual power.

> My brethren, the method by which Jesus proposes to subdue all things unto himself appears to be utterly inadequate. To teach, to make disciples, to baptize these disciples, and to instruct them further in the faith! Good Master, are these the weapons of our warfare? Are these thy battleaxe and weapons of war? Not thus do the princes of this world contemplate conquest, for they rely on monster guns, ironclads, and engines of death-doing power. Yet what are these but proofs of their weakness? Had they all power in themselves they would not need such instruments. Only he who has all power can work his bidding by a word, and dispense with all force but that of love.[29]

The absence of God's Word meant for Spurgeon that powers other than those which belonged to God would be on display. 'How many there are of God's people who go up to houses of prayer, so-called, where...all the isms and fancies of man are preached, instead of the truth of God, in all its...power.'[30] In contrast to isms and fancies, to preach the Bible is to follow the manner of Jesus and His Apostles. 'Though quite able to speak of himself,' observes Spurgeon, 'our Lord continually referred to Holy Scripture...so did his apostles.'[31] The Bible is a favored place for the Lord to demonstrate His power and the preacher must therefore locate this place and expound its meaning. To do so is to expound that which is congruent to the Spirit and to display the power of God.

The London Road

The Spirit powerfully attends that preacher who looks to the Bible primarily to see Jesus. Spurgeon cried out, 'Blessed Spirit, help me ever to glorify the Lord Jesus Christ!'[32] Spurgeon's reasons for this perspective reside in his view of the Holy Spirit's nature as constant with that of Christ. 'Let me warn you,' he said, 'of the great sin...of putting the Holy Spirit into contrast or rivalry with Jesus Christ.' Then referring to the words of Jesus as recorded in the Gospel of John, Spurgeon observed: 'The testimony of Jesus is the testimony of the Holy Spirit; and when the Holy Spirit works in men he works with the things of Christ, not with any new things. He takes the things of Christ, and shows them unto us.'[33] For this cause, Spurgeon believed that the experience of power peculiar to the Holy Spirit will only result from a particular kind of biblical exposition; mainly, the prayerful preaching of what the Bible says in a manner that exalts the person and work of Christ. According to Spurgeon, if preachers do 'not glorify Christ, they are not of the Holy Ghost.'[34] Likewise, Spurgeon elsewhere warned: 'the Spirit of God bears no witness to Christ-less sermons. Leave Jesus out of your preaching, and the Holy Spirit will never come upon you.'[35] Bible preaching, as a means of demonstrating the Spirit's power, will have nothing more than human effect, unless Christ is exalted from its pages. Spurgeon offered an illustration:

> I have found, wherever I have been during the last month, that though there might not be a road to this place or that, there was sure to be a London road. Now, if your sermon does not happen to have the doctrine of election, or the doctrine of final perseverance in it, let it always have Christ in it. Have a road to London, a road to Christ in every sermon.[36]

This conviction that every sermon requires a 'London Road' stems from the sentiments of Paul, who declared that he

preached 'Christ crucified.' Spurgeon agreed with the implication. 'We preach Christ;' so do a great many more: but,
'*we* preach Christ *crucified*,' so, alas! do not so many more.'[37]
The connection of Christ with crucifixion means that the
preacher not only glories in the person of Jesus – His ethi-
cal teachings, His integrity of leadership, His fulfillment of
prophecy, His nature with God – but the preacher also must
concern himself with the Lord and 'His cross, His blood, His
death.'[38] 'Christ Crucified' must therefore form the 'general
summary' of the preacher's ministry.[39] This summary forms
the favored place and the proper materials for kindled fire.
Spurgeon not only laments the 'guilty' minister who makes
no place in his preaching for the 'blood' or 'atoning sacrifice
of the great Redeemer,' but he also pleads earnestly with
Sunday school teachers to consider their own task and look
to the agency of the Holy Spirit with regard to it. 'To stand
up in a Sunday-school and say, "Now, be good boys and
girls and God will love you," is telling lies,' Spurgeon warned.
'Dear teachers of the school, whatever you do not know, do
know your Lord...and do make it a matter of prayer that
you may get a knowledge of Christ and his atoning blood
into their young hearts by the Holy Ghost.'[40]

Preaching Christ also informs the preacher's method of
looking at Scripture passages for sermons. For example,
the preacher should explore Old and New Testament con-
nections when explicitly 'pointed to' by the text. Wherever
'I find our Lord Jesus Christ, or any of his apostles, referring to an incident in the Old Testament,' says Spurgeon,
'I always think it is our business to look at that event to
which they refer.'[41]

This means that even the Old Testament is meant to
point the preacher and his hearers to Christ. Referring to
the Apostle Paul, Spurgeon notes, 'He had come by way of
Old Testament history to Christ, and by way of John the
Baptist to Christ; and that is how the preacher of the gospel
should travel. On whatever road he journeys, his terminus
must be Christ.'[42] This means that an Old Testament text
should yield a New Testament sermon. Referring again
to the example of Paul, Spurgeon said, 'He takes his text
from the Old Testament, but he gives us a New Testament
sermon upon it.'[43] These convictions stem from Spurgeon's

belief that the Old and New Testaments establish a gospel continuity culminating in the person and work of Jesus.

He explained it this way:

> As for us, the Old Testament is prized by us as much as the New. We do not preach Jesus as a fresh arrival, the inventor of a new religion, the founder of a novel way of salvation. No; we preach the Messiah of the Old Testament, whose gospel is set forth in the types and in the teachings of Moses and the prophets.... Do not imagine that the religion of Abraham was one thing and ours another: ours is but the continuation of that gospel which was revealed to all the faithful from the days of righteous Abel until now.[44]

The preacher must expound the biblical text and from it exalt Christ from both the Old and New Testaments. This means is favored by the Holy Spirit, because 'the Spirit of God is not in it if it does not glorify Christ.'[45] Consequently, the preacher must own the conviction that 'To spread the faith, is to bring men, through the agency of God's Spirit, to feel their need of Christ, to seek Christ, to believe in Christ, to love Christ, and then to live for Christ.'[46]

The Rhetoric of the Heart

'Of course,' Spurgeon asserted, 'the preacher is above all others distinguished as a man of prayer.'[47] This fact resides among other things in the preacher's weakness. 'What can you and I alone do?' reminds Spurgeon. 'If I am to be an instrument...my very first action must be to fall on my knees and pray.'[48] Prayer forms another means of the attending power of the Spirit. Preachers often fall into the temptation of believing that prayer 'is second to preaching.' The preacher must never doubt, however, that 'prayer in the Christian church is as precious as the utterance of the gospel.'[49] Indeed, many believed Spurgeon's prayers to equal, or even to transcend in effectiveness, his own sermons.[50]

The preacher's prayer begins in private and directly impacts the authenticity of his sermon delivery. 'A truly pathetic delivery, in which there is no affectation, but much affection, can only be the offspring of prayer,' he explains.

'There is no rhetoric like that of the heart.'[51] Therefore, the preacher takes the apostles' convictions as his own: 'We will give our attention to prayer and the ministry of the Word' (Acts 6:4). Likewise, the preacher, as an agent in the hands of God, turns to prayer as a means by which his nearer tools are kept ready for use. Meeting personally with God in prayer is meant to become a way of life for the preacher. How can one display God's power publicly when he is little acquainted with it privately? 'Habitual communion with God must be maintained, or our public prayers will be vapid or formal...private prayer is the drill ground for our more public exercises, neither can we long neglect it without being out of order when before the people.'[52] Authentic and effective public prayer and preaching is directly related to the preacher's personal communion with God.

This communion includes how one approaches sermon preparation. 'How dare we pray in the battle if we never cried to the Lord while buckling on the harness,' Spurgeon asked. 'The remembrance of his wrestlings at home comforts the fettered preacher when in the pulpit.'[53] When conscience is assailed or eyes are sleepy, the preacher in the moment of delivery draws upon the ministry of God to his own soul as he cries out for these sleepy ones.

The content of such prayers for sermon preparation first concerns the illumination of the Spirit as to the meaning of the biblical text. 'Do not let us take up the Bible and imagine that we shall at once understand it as we do another book.' The preacher sits before the open Bible, and counts prayer as his primary nearer tool, among the other remote tools, by which God will 'give grace to know its meaning and feel its power.' Consequently, the preacher must 'breathe the prayer' to God.[54] The preacher also prays for God to draw near in the moment of preaching. He prays for authenticity and freedom from pretended fire and affectation. 'May the Holy Spirit make my words to be full of force and holy fire,' Spurgeon cried. Furthermore, the preacher asks for God Himself to preach. 'May it not merely be the voice of man that speaks to you; but may it be clear that God has commissioned his servant to speak to your hearts, and that by my sermon God himself expostulates with you even as he expostulated with Cain in those ancient times!'[55]

Plain and Heartfelt

Public prayer joins private prayer as the calling of the preacher. These public prayers often occur prior to the sermon. These must be 'earnest, full of fire, vehemence, and prevalence.' They are to be 'plain and heartfelt' so that 'while the people may sometimes feel that the sermon was below the mark, may they also feel that the prayer compensated for all.'[56] Again, such 'fire' cannot find authentic kindling outside of private praying.

According to Spurgeon's example, the preacher may also occasionally pray publicly during his sermon. Openly, Spurgeon publicly longs for the Spirit of God: 'Spirit of the Living God, I want thee. Thou art life, the soul; thou art the source of thy people's success; without thee they can do nothing, with thee they can do everything.'[57] He could be heard praying by stopping in the midst of his discourse, 'O heavenly light, shine now into the soul of all who hear or read this sermon!'[58] He declares in the midst of another sermon, 'let us pray the blessed Spirit to put an edge on our preaching, lest we say much and accomplish little. Hear us in this thing, O blessed One!'[59] His hearers heard him pray amid the proclamation, 'may the Spirit of God give his own unction and power!'[60] and 'O Spirit of God, apply the Word!'[61]and 'may the Spirit of God seal this sermon upon the hearts of his people, for Christ's sake! Amen!'[62]

One wonders if Spurgeon learned this seemingly rare pulpit-practice from George Herbert, whose poems Spurgeon would quote in his sermons and whose works he often enjoyed on Sunday evenings with his wife. When speaking of the holy character of the sermon, Herbert instructed his readers:

> By turning often, and making many apostrophes to God, as 'Oh Lord, bless my people and teach them this point'; or 'Oh my Master, on whose errand I come, let me hold my peace and do though speak thyself....' Some such irradiations scatteringly in the sermon carry great holiness in them. The prophets were admirable in this, So Isaiah 64, 'O that thou wouldst rend the heavens, that thou wouldst come down!' &c; and Jeremiah 10, after he had complained of the desolation of Israel, turns to

God suddenly, 'Oh Lord, I know that the way of man is not in himself, &c.'[63]

Prayer, even during the sermon, is meant to demonstrate that the preacher is in direct conversation with God and that the people are hearing the sermon in the very presence of the living God. The holiness of the moment is made apparent when one prays as if God is actually there and listening in order to act on the preacher's behalf.

Prayer Will Keep

Importantly, the potential efficacy of this 'most essential thing' transcends the time of its actual practice and the preacher must not underestimate its value to the fruit of his ministry. Spurgeon states:

> There was a mother, perhaps, [now] in heaven, who had prayed for the man forty years before, for prayer will keep, and be fragrant many a year. And let me say that, if neither father nor mother ever prayed for that conversion, perhaps a grandfather did, for prayer has power for hundreds of years; and a great-grandfather's prayers may be the instrumentality of the conversion of his great grandchildren. There is no end to the efficacy of prayer.[64]

The conversion which results in the context of the preacher's sermon may have its roots in something which radically pre-dates the preacher's work. Conversely, the preacher's fruit may surface later than anticipated. The Spirit of God may bring the content of the message, which seems at the time it was delivered to have had little effect, back to the mind of the hearer in a not-too-distant moment of need. Prayer outlasts the moment for which it was intended and this brings hope to the preacher as he surrenders to the purposes of the Holy Spirit's timing with regard to the efficacy of his preaching.

Heart Bleeding Preachers

The Spirit's appointed ways therefore redefine how a preacher evaluates his strength and his weakness in the pulpit. Strength begins when the preacher submits himself to the Spirit's appointed means. Weakness is evaluated on the basis of whether or not those same means are disregarded. What results is an instrumental measure of pulpit strength and weakness, such that a preacher may rightly and emotionally feel the limits of his own power. Yet, if he is giving himself to the appointed means he is strong, in spite of what he feels, because he is looking to definitions of pulpit-strength as God has appointed. The converse is equally true. A preacher who feels strong with evidences and effects of human power, actually steps to the pulpit in weakness when he avoids or pays little attention to the Spirit's appointed means.

What results is a pattern for strength which corresponds to the Biblical descriptions of strength and weakness. A gospel preacher, though disregarded by multitudes, may nonetheless be strong before the eyes of God, while those preachers who are loved by multitudes for speaking what their itching ears want to hear may actually be weak before the eyes of God. True strength and power, therefore, are not tied to immediate results or large crowds. Though such crowds can designate the fruit of genuine spiritual power, the gospel preacher puts his trust in deeper and more established divine measures for determining strength and weakness. Amid a powerless age, therefore, the preacher must maintain his consistency in the appointed means, both because *kindled fire* comes by the Spirit through these means and because the preacher may underestimate or overestimate what is actually strong and weak in his generation apart from these means.

Consequently, the preacher who longs for God to display His power in a generation can first ask himself, 'To what degree am I giving myself to God's appointed means for strength?' Spurgeon contrasts two preachers to make this point. The first preacher we might identify as the automated or non-trembling preacher. This preacher is, based upon cultural appearances, very strong. He believes that having a sermon completed and memorized is equal to being ready to preach. He approaches readiness accordingly, with no felt need for the power of God to attend his way. According to Spurgeon, this preacher is actually weak. 'His sermon is in his pocket; there cannot happen any mischief to it unless a thief should steal it; he has rehearsed all his action, he is as safe as an automaton. He does not need to pray for the Spirit of God to help him in his preaching...the notion of trembling is far from him, he is not so weak.'[65]

In contrast, Spurgeon describes the trembling or heart-bleeding preacher who is strong, even though on cultural appearances he seems weak. His sermon is ready, but he knows that he still has the preaching to attend to. He knows that his sermon has no power to change his or anyone's heart. He has done his work and has thoroughly and faithfully prepared. But he feels that if God does not attend his way then no lasting good will come of his labors. Spurgeon observes:

> Yonder is a poor brother, who has been tugging away with his brains, wrestling on his knees, and bleeding at his heart; he is half-afraid that he may break down in the sermon, and he is fearful that he will not reach the hearts of the people; but he means to try what can be done by the help of God. Be you sure that he will get at the people, and God will give him converts. He is looking up to God, for he feels so feeble in himself.[66]

Spurgeon then comments: 'You know which of the two preachers you would sooner hear, and you know who is the really strong man of the two; the weak man is strong, and the strong man is weak.'[67]

The Weak Man's Strong Preaching
According to Spurgeon, in the midst of the preacher's weaknesses, the Lord's ways lead him to:

- *Depend entirely upon the Spirit of God*, 'Should we not in preaching give more scope for his operation?'
- *Preach Christ and Him crucified*, 'Where Jesus is exalted souls are attracted.'
- *Teach the depravity of human nature*, 'Show men that sin is not an accident, but the genuine outcome of their corrupt hearts.'[68]
- *Preach the necessity of the Holy Ghost's divine operations*, 'Dire necessity requires divine interposition.'

- *Preach the certainty that every transgression will be punished,* 'We rob the gospel of its power if we leave out its threatenings of punishment.'

- *Preach the doctrine of atonement,* 'This is the great net of gospel fishermen; the fish are drawn or driven in the right direction by other truths, but this is the net itself.'

- *Preach justification by faith,* 'I once heard a sermon upon "They that sow in tears shall reap in joy," of which the English was, "Be good, very good, and though you will have to suffer in consequence, God will reward you in the end." The preacher, no doubt, believed in justification by faith, but he very distinctly preached the opposite doctrine. Many do this when addressing children, and I notice that they generally speak to the little ones about loving Jesus, and not upon believing in him. This must leave a mischievous impression upon youthful minds and take them off from the true way of peace.'

- *Preach earnestly the love of God in Christ Jesus and magnify the abounding mercy of God,* 'Regard love in the high theological sense, in which, like a golden circle, it holds within itself all the divine attributes.'[69]

Conclusion

According to Charles Spurgeon, the Lord has appointed particular ways 'congruent' with His character and work, by which He intends to display His power in preaching. These ways include the preacher, the Bible and prayer. Spurgeon reminds us that the means one chooses for preaching effectively must correspond to the character, work and Word of the Spirit of God. The Spirit is the authority for our preaching. Thus, as the preacher gives himself in faith to the 'appointed ways' of the Spirit, he demonstrates definitions of strength and weakness that imitate biblical truth and yield to God's designated avenues for displaying His glory.

Questions for Learning and Discussion

1. What strikes you most when you read this chapter?

2. What do you think about Spurgeon's idea that God uses instruments to display His glory? What does it mean to you that preachers must learn to submit themselves to instruments which are congruent to God's character, work and Word?

3. Describe strength and weakness in preaching as Spurgeon sees it.

4. What role does the Bible play in your preaching? What sermon structures and approaches do you use in order to expose more of what God is saying through His word?

5. What do you think about Spurgeon's idea that private prayer fuels public prayer and sermon delivery? How would God have you grow in prayer with preaching?

6. What will you take with you from this chapter?

9

LIPS TOUCHED BY THE LIVE COAL:

Seeking the Spirit's Attendant Power

...while preaching, the power of God came upon the people.[1]

Instrumentalities from the Spirit offer paths for the preacher to walk on in order to find those favored places in the woods where the Spirit likes to dwell. To trust such paths indicates a core belief in the preacher that the means for preaching require the Spirit's activity in order to be useful and effective. Spurgeon agreed. The old truth must be preached, he asserted, 'by men whose lips are touched as with a live coal from off the altar.'[2] This picture of 'the live coal,' an allusion to Isaiah 6, continues Spurgeon's 'kindled fire' metaphor. There, the prophet Isaiah had his mouth touched by the live coal from the altar of God. Spurgeon used this biblical event to picture the nature of the truth as the preacher encounters it. Truth must have an attendant fire that is alive and coming from the very presence of God. Old truth with its practices and instrumentalities is lifeless apart from the living presence of the Holy Spirit.

When Truth Becomes an Iceberg

Spurgeon believed that an 'experimental acquaintance' within the soul 'is the best [kind] of knowledge.'[3] A preacher seeks this experimental knowing of the truth because, as Spurgeon explained, 'when divine truth' is 'merely heard' with the ear, it 'takes no effect upon the mind.' But when divine truth is enlivened by 'the Spirit of God' it then 'becomes a quickening force.' The Spirit enlivens divine truth by making it real to the soul so as to affect the heart.[4]

A preaching student might ask at this point why the Spirit should be needed for an experience of the truth. Isn't it enough to say what the text says? Spurgeon would answer this good question by saying that without the Spirit attending the truth, the truth itself 'becomes an iceberg.' Consequently, 'frozen and lifeless' are the terms that describe the truth brought to the soul without the Spirit.[5]

'Distance' is the reason for lifeless truth without the Spirit. The human heart is naturally disengaged from the character and truth of God. The preacher needs God, because only God can 'annihilate' this distance.[6] The truth by itself does not cross the barriers of the human condition. Only the Spirit can do this. When God annihilates the distance between Himself and a person, the Spirit does not 'merely show the truth,' Spurgeon explains. He 'leads us into it, so that we stand within it, and rejoice in the hid treasure which it contains.'[7] The distance is annihilated when preachers and hearers not only get the information of the truth, but also experience its meaning. Spurgeon explained that 'God the Holy Spirit vivifies the letter with his presence, and then it is to us a living word indeed.'[8] Therefore, it is one thing to rightly answer the question, 'What is repentance?' It is another thing, however, to actually repent. To answer such a question without actually experiencing the answer is to receive the truth frozen and lifeless.

When a preacher gains this conviction that God intends His truth for information *and experience*, a preacher endeavors to preach so that his hearers feel the Word of God. A preacher will do so because he understands that 'to understand the Word is not enough.' Hearers are meant to experience the power of what the truth is saying and such power can only arise from the Holy Ghost.[9]

God Coming Upon the Scene
Because the power of the sermon originates with the Holy Ghost, therefore, a preacher possesses a particular longing when prayering. The preaching moment is not merely mundane or natural. Supernatural things are hoped for. God intends to visit and kindle fire. 'Oh,' Spurgeon beck-

ons, 'that some of you, who have never known the Spirit of God may feel his power coming upon you at this moment.'[10] Such preaching annihilates the distance between God and man.

Spurgeon referred to this 'true power of the gospel' drawing near in the moment of preaching the old truth, as 'the attendant power of the Spirit of God.'[11] An 'attendant power' identifies a close power or an 'alongside of' power. According to Spurgeon, the 'attendant power of the Spirit of God' refers to that 'secret something' which 'goes along with' the preacher's 'pleadings'. When the preacher preaches, two voices are being heard – the preacher's voice and God's voice alongside it, such that 'the voice of man' is made 'to be the voice of the Holy Ghost.'[12] Accordingly, the preacher assumes that any true power in preaching depends upon 'God himself' who 'must come upon the scene' and kindle the fire of the truth.[13]

Spurgeon's conclusion is striking. Where the message of Jesus 'is honestly and truthfully delivered with the Spirit of God, Jesus Christ himself is virtually present, speaking through the lips of his servants.'[14] In other words, both the preacher and the hearers are met by the present and living Jesus, and He Himself speaks presently to them by means of His Spirit, attending the preacher's sermon with power.

Commenting on 1 Thessalonians 1:5, which says: 'our gospel came to you not only in word, but also in power and in the Holy Spirit,' Spurgeon asked:

> Do you sometimes, after hearing a sermon feel...as if God himself had been there, you did not know what else it could be. It could not have been the speaker nor the words he uttered, but the very God did come and look into your eyes, and searched the thoughts of your mind, and turned your heart upside down, and then filled it full again with his love and with his light, with his truth and with his joy, with his peace and with his desire after holiness?[15]

According to John 16:8, Spurgeon said that the Spirit is the 'special pleader' with people concerning their sin. Spurgeon describes this work of the Spirit in the preaching moment.

While the minister preached, 'Did not the Holy Spirit come?'
he asked.

> Did he not stand and tell you that your works were filthy
> rags? And when you had well-nigh still refused to listen to
> his voice, did he not fetch hell's drum and make it sound
> about your ears, bidding you look through the vista of
> future years and see the throne set, and the books open,
> and the sword brandished, and hell burning, and fiends
> howling, and the damned shrieking for ever? And did he
> not thus convince you of the judgment to come? He is a
> mighty advocate when he pleads in the soul – of sin, of
> righteousness, and of the judgment to come.[16]

With attendant power, the Spirit as the 'special pleader'
will also advocate comfort for the broken soul during the
preacher's words. 'O my soul, thou art ready to burst
within me!' the hearer says to himself. 'O my heart, thou
art swelled with grief!' he laments. Then Spurgeon asks,
'Do you know who can utter that groaning, who can understand it and speak it so Christ can hear it? Oh! Yes; it
is God the Holy Spirit; he advocates our cause with Christ
and then Christ advocates it with his Father. He is the
advocate, who maketh intercession for us, with groanings
that cannot be uttered.'[17]

Spurgeon's conviction on this point informed his prayers
and at times led him to plead to God publicly from the pulpit,
'Oh,' he at times cried, 'that the Spirit of God may give the
sermon!'[18] It also informed the way he sometimes applied
the truths of his sermons to his hearers. For example, when
speaking to the point of forgiving love, Charles preached
as if Jesus were actually living and present to minister to
his hearers in that very moment. He spoke as though his
hearers were meant to leave him and go to Jesus directly
for healing. 'Your Lord himself stands before you,' Spurgeon declared. 'You remember how he forgave you all your
trespasses and I am sure you will give earnest heed to his
exhortation to forgive.' Spurgeon then called publicly upon
the present Spirit of God to apply Christ's message, saying:
'May the dove-like Spirit now brood over this assembly, and
create love in all our bosoms.'[19]

Spurgeon was merely following his theological heritage with this view of the Spirit's attendant power when preaching the Bible. John Calvin, for example, had noted that 'In the preaching of the Word, the external minister holds forth the vocal word, and it is received by the ears.' But alongside the vocal word of the external minister, there is 'the internal minister, the Holy Spirit, truly' communicating 'the thing proclaimed through the Word, that is Christ....'[20] The purpose of preaching then is this, Calvin said: 'A man preaches so that God may speak to us.'[21]

Spurgeon believed that God speaks during the sermon and annihilates the distance that exists between God, the preacher and the listeners. Preaching then becomes more than a speech, a lecture or a seminar for education. Preaching is the means by which God draws near and presently speaks to His people. Preaching is a meeting with God.

Marred by a Thousand Imperfections
By saying these things, Spurgeon did not believe that the preacher speaks infallibly. Spurgeon maintained that the tongue of the preacher is a 'feeble instrument,' and 'marred by a thousand imperfections.' Yet, God makes the bearer of His words able to speak by His blessing.[22]

Preachers are also not passive in their preaching as if God simply took over their minds. Rather, God by His Spirit illumines the meaning of the text and the matter for the moment and grants preachers and/or their hearers an awareness of God's presence with them in Christ. 'Our minds are active and have a personal existence while the mind of the Spirit is acting upon them,' Spurgeon said. 'Our infirmities are apparent as well as His wisdom.' In fact, the attendant power of God speaking to the souls of men and women alongside the preacher's feeble speech greatly sobers and humbles the preacher. He fears his own 'ignorance or error' which is 'manifested at the same time' and therefore he longs more genuinely for the mercy and blessing of God.[23] With this in mind, Spurgeon counsels his hearers: 'Remember...you must not expect every time' you preach or hear preaching 'that God will speak with you; in fact, the preacher himself fails often, and is painfully conscious of it.' Spurgeon then asks: 'How shall one man always speak without sometimes feeling that he himself is not in a fit frame to be God's mouthpiece?'[24]

A Sacred Longing after God
Though a called man remains naturally unfit to deliver God's Word, his inadequacies do not disqualify him for the work. A preacher's longing directed in his weakness to the strength of God is a powerful thing. Spurgeon describes it:

> Did you never note the all-subduing power of a great desire? When God makes the heart tender, and sets it longing after Jesus, it forgets its own feebleness, and ceases to be alarmed by that which once distressed it. A longing soul would break through angels and through devils, through heaven and through earth, to reach Jesus. We must have him. We must behold the Well-beloved. Our soul is all on fire for him, it cannot be restrained, it will burn its way to him as the flame makes its way across the prairie. We want Jesus, and we will not be content with anything short of him.[25]

God in Christ has paid for and bears with the called man's infirmities. Examining the object of his own longing, Spurgeon changed the direction of his prayers. 'Sometimes I breathe as I walk along, this prayer, that God would raise up more ministers to preach the gospel with power; there is so much feeble preaching, mere twaddling, and so little declaration of the gospel with power.' But as Charles learned to lift his longing even higher, his prayers changed and therefore, so did the amount of power he longed for. Rather than praying for more preachers, he determined to pray:

> 'Lord, send thy Spirit upon the churches!' then will come the ministers, then will come the earnest workers. The Spirit of God will touch their tongues with fire, and they will say, 'Here am I, send me'.... The Spirit of God is the power of the church, and speaks with might in her.[26]

Attendant versus Mental Power
Why should preachers look for this attendant power? First, the Spirit of God is the 'author of the sacred Word,'[27] and

therefore gives authority to its contents. 'The Holy Ghost has made this Book himself,' Spurgeon explains. 'Every portion of it bears his initial and impress.'[28]

Second, Spurgeon wanted preachers to recognize that two kinds of power are at their disposal. Both kinds of power possess the ability to produce effects. But as Spurgeon explained: 'The sort of power of which we feel the need, will be determined by our view of our work and the amount of power that we shall long for will also very much depend upon our idea of how that work should be done.'[29] The preacher needs a 'sort of power' which has the capacity to perform what preaching is meant to do.

Spurgeon hints at these two distinct kinds of power when he states that 'it is extraordinary grace, not talent, that wins the day; extraordinary spiritual power, not extraordinary mental power', is our hope.[30] Note in this statement that natural talent is connected to 'mental power' in contrast to the grace from God which describes the substance of 'spiritual power.'

'Mental power' refers to that energy, creativity and force which derives from human ingenuity and human strength. This kind of power is both noble and desirable. The preacher must labor and spend energy to think, reflect, preach and love his hearers. Spurgeon does not denigrate mental power. 'We want to have such mental vigor as God pleases to give us,' Spurgeon said. His point is that if the work of preaching is to annihilate the distance between God and His people, then mental power will prove insufficient to accomplish the preacher's work.[31] 'The world is not going to be saved by worldly wisdom or by fine oratory; brilliant speeches and poetic periods win not souls for Christ.'[32] A 'brilliant speech,' in other words, even though it is desirable, does not possess the kind of power necessary to 'win' a 'soul for Christ.' We must 'remember that text,' he said, 'Not by might, nor by power, but by my Spirit, saith the Lord.'

Spurgeon believed therefore that 'mental power' cannot stand alone in preaching. It must be accompanied by 'spiritual might.' 'Mental power may fill a chapel,' Spurgeon warned, 'But spiritual power fills the Church. Mental power may gather a congregation, but spiritual power will save souls.' His conclusion? 'We want spiritual power.'[33]

For this reason, Spurgeon seems at times to denigrate reliance on rhetorical study. Edwin Paxton Hood suggested that Spurgeon was, most likely, 'ignorant of it.'[34] But Spurgeon's disinclination toward rhetorical practice was not due to ignorance. According to Spurgeon, Socrates and Aristotle were 'great teachers' and 'rare among men.'[35] Spurgeon could reference the 'eloquence of such men as Demosthenes and Cicero,'[36] and could even critique the 'polished nullities of Blair.'[37]

Spurgeon was not ignorant of rhetoric. He simply felt its good practice was insufficient for the preacher's task. Spurgeon was concerned that preachers would mistakenly assume that rhetorical and spiritual power were identical and thus rely only on rhetorical skill. 'When the Spirit of God is gone,' he warned 'then all the ministers become exceedingly learned, for not having the Spirit they need to supply the emptiness his absence has left.'[38]

Spurgeon therefore urged preachers: 'It is better to be taught of the Holy Spirit than to learn eloquence from the rules of oratory, or at the feet of masters of rhetoric.'[39] 'Moral suasion, explanations and arguments' will have no true effect unless they are attended by 'a power much stronger than' these. Without this stronger power Spurgeon felt that the preacher was 'sure of defeat.' Rhetoric must be seen for what it is with its strengths and limitations. Non-Christian orators can rely on oratorical skill for temporal change or persuasion to a cause. But for Christian preachers, the goal of their work requires more. 'Except the Lord endow us with power from on high, our labor must be in vain, and our hopes must end in disappointment.'[40]

With such statements, Spurgeon seemed to allow for the disturbing possibility that powerful and successful pulpit oratory could build congregations without possessing or requiring a saving presence of the Holy Spirit in the souls of the excited and affected hearers. He posits a kind of preaching with merely mental power in which God has not come upon the scene nor actually spoken. In this scenario, a generation of preachers is considered successful because of changed minds, or moral reforms. Yet, changed minds and moral reforms can be accomplished with mental power alone. Only God's power can thoroughly change the sin-sick soul. 'Oh,' Spurgeon exclaimed, 'let the Church feel that her power is not mental power, but spiritual power.'[41]

The Limits of Mental Power
Spurgeon was not against rhetoric, but he was convinced that mental power was limited in its capacity to fulfill the goals of preaching. The first limit of mental power results from sin. Divine power can go into and overcome areas of sin that mental power cannot. A look into his *Puritan Catechism* tellingly discloses the picture of the soul's fallen condition as it sits in the audience before the preacher:

16. Q. Into what estate did the fall bring mankind?
    A. The fall brought mankind into a state of sin and misery (Romans 5:18).

17. Q. Wherein consists the sinfulness of that state where-unto man fell?
    A. The sinfulness of that state whereunto man fell, con-sists in the guilt of Adam's first sin (Romans 5:19), the want of original righteousness (Romans 3:10), and the corruption of his whole nature, which is commonly called original sin (Ephesians 2:1; Psalm 51:5), together with all actual transgressions which proceed from it (Matthew 15:19).

18. Q. What is the misery of that state whereunto man fell?
    A. All mankind, by their fall, lost communion with God (Genesis 3:8, 24), are under his wrath and curse (Ephesians 2:3; Galatians 3:10), and so made li-able to all the miseries in this life, to death itself, and to the pains of hell for ever (Romans 6:23; Matthew 25:41).[42]

Spurgeon found a metaphor in the Old Testament book of Ezekiel to describe the condition of sinners. Each has a heart of stone. Such a heart is impenetrable by merely mental power. 'Without God,' Spurgeon believed, 'the turning of a heart of stone into flesh would surely be impossible.'[43] The preacher's theology of people and of sin will necessarily determine the kind of power a preacher seeks and where the preacher will turn to find it.

The limits of mental power are revealed, however, not only by the anthropology of the hearer and preacher, but also by the position of the preacher as one whose very oratory engages him in a 'heavenly warfare.'[44] The preacher must not only 'contend with sin, but with the spirit which foments and suggests sin.' Preachers 'must resist the secret spirit of evil as well as its outward acts.'[45] 'Come fair or come foul, the pulpit is our watch-tower, and the ministry our warfare,' Spurgeon said.[46] Gospel preaching, as an act of spiritual warfare, reminds the preacher that misunderstanding of truth is not simply the result of 'noise' or natural reasons. The gospel orator must ask himself, 'Where does this noise come from? Why is there noise to begin with?' Natural noise is not the preacher's only difficulty. What rhetoric does not take into account must remain of primary concern to the preacher. The souls of his hearers are under spiritual attack – both by sin and by Satan.

The Road to Strength
The preacher's inability to overcome the power of sin and Satan creates in him a lingering feeling of vulnerability. After all, what Spurgeon is actually saying is that the gospel preacher is called to a task that he has no native power to accomplish. Furthermore, the reality of sin and Satan in the preacher's own heart requires that he counter these in a profound way by depending upon a power beyond himself. Far from discouraging the preacher, however, this felt vulnerability was meant to offer the preacher hope. 'I pray you, do not despair,' Spurgeon urges. 'The painful discovery of your own insufficiency ought to be the means of leading you to the Lord, and so of girding you with new strength.'[47]

When a preacher feels that he has the capacity to change a soul by his perfected skill and force of personality, then his preparation and delivery of sermons will reflect this belief. He will turn mostly to himself each week to find the power needed to preach his sermons and teach his studies. The preacher will believe that he is ready to preach once he has the power of a story, the force of an argument, the creativity of language, and the form of the structure in place.

In contrast, the preacher who feels that only God has the kind of power requisite for changing a soul will turn with a felt vulnerability to a preparation and delivery of sermons which includes more than mental energy and ingenuity. Regular and constant conversation with God for insight, for help, for intervention will become typical. The preacher needs a force larger than his personality and a power that goes beyond the intrinsic value of a good story. 'Make up by spiritual force what you lack in natural ability,' Spurgeon urges. 'If you lack talent,' by which Spurgeon meant, 'mental power,' then, 'get all the more grace, and you will be no loser.... It is spiritual power, not mental power, which avails in conversion.'[48] In other words, if a preacher has a choice between more talent or more grace, Spurgeon would bid him to ask for more grace.

Such a posture makes the preacher feel humbled and even miserably weak, as he must step up to the pulpit in front of hearers who may naturally prize mental power. He is tempted to offer what is merely naturally uplifting. He is tempted to offer a sin-and-misery-avoiding speech in the pulpit. He is tempted to offer personality and skill alone. Spurgeon recognized this temptation. 'Our responsibilities, when they are thoroughly felt, crush us, and then are we weak indeed.' But an irony exists in this weakened condition. 'This weakness is the road to strength,' he said. Quoting the Apostle Paul, Spurgeon declared: 'When I am weak, then am I strong...when God makes us feel that our work is impossible to us without His aid, then are we driven to His strength.'[49]

For Spurgeon, therefore, spiritual power is synonymous with the actual and present strength of God exerting itself in the preacher's favor in the moment of preaching. Confidence is not tied, then, to one's level of rhetorical skill, as important as this skill is. More pointedly, the preacher's goal is not to work up a strategy for feeling confident in his skills before speaking. Rather, the preacher must thank God for his skills but embrace the sorrow of their impotence apart from Him. This leads the preacher to longingly appeal to God, rather than to avoid such felt weakness. It is as if Christ's words, which He reserved for the church of Laodicea, could apply to the preacher, who, as he steps to the pulpit, turns inward to his skills, his preparation, and his anecdotes in order to forge a sense of felt confidence for the preaching moment:

> You say, I am rich, I have prospered, and I need nothing, not realizing that you are wretched, pitiable, poor, blind, and naked. I counsel you to buy from me gold refined by fire, so that you may be rich, and white garments so that you may clothe yourself and the shame of your nakedness may not be seen, and salve to anoint your eyes, so that you may see....[50]

In light of biblical definitions of strength and weakness, the gospel orator begins to learn that, 'weakness, fear, and much trembling' do not exclude the possibility of the 'power of God' and the 'demonstration of the Spirit' in the preaching event.[51] Consequently, when a preacher seeks the touch from the live coal, his preaching begins to aim at a lasting impression for the glory of God.

The Lasting Impression

The momentary or merely moral effects of mental power lead the preacher to a new goal. He longs for a lasting impression. He desires his hearers to have an experience of the truth by means of the attendant power that can enable them to live according to God no matter what may come in their lives. Hear the lament and longing in Spurgeon's voice as he came to the end of one of his sermons:

> And now I have this mournful reflection that, though I have tried to put the way of salvation before you, this audience will all be scattered in a few minutes north and south and east and west, and with it every word that I have said will be scattered and forgotten too, save where, here and there, God's Spirit shall be pleased to make a lasting impression. I do pray it may be so, in many of your souls.[52]

Though the hearers of Spurgeon's sermons were sometimes known to laugh or cry, Spurgeon clarified that seeking a lasting impression means more than the ready responses a preacher can evoke in his hearers.

We have heard a good deal about crowds weeping, but we had rather see one individual believing.... I aim rather at preaching Christ crucified, so as to beget faith, than to paint pathetic pictures of death-beds and dying mothers, which things work on the emotions but have small tendency to lead to faith.[53]

This lasting impression was identified by Spurgeon as 'saving faith' or 'conversion.' The need for conversion explains the virtual preaching of Christ in the power of the Holy Spirit during the preaching moment. 'As a rule,' Spurgeon noted, 'God has sent us to preach in order that through the gospel of Jesus Christ the sons of men may be reconciled to him.'[54] For Spurgeon, reconciliation between men and God through Christ begins by directing the preacher to 'edify' those who are already converted by setting Christ before them in such a way that they are sustained and nourished in their saving faith. 'It is a noble work to instruct the people of God,' Spurgeon continued, 'and to build them up in their most holy faith.' If the presence of saving faith requires nourishment, then the absence of saving faith requires conversion. 'Our great object of glorifying God,' Spurgeon declared, 'is to be mainly achieved by the winning of souls. We *must* see souls born unto God.'[55] Because saving faith can only come from God himself, Spurgeon asked: 'Should it not be our aim to find men out, and make them feel that at the present moment they are themselves addressed; that there is a message from God to the soul?'[56]

God, the Great One to be Extolled
If God is present, such that Christ intends to presently preach through the feeble means of the preacher with an attendant power of truth for the soul, then preaching must aim at hallowing that present glory of God.

My firm conviction is, that in proportion as we have more regard for the sacred godhead, the wondrous Trinity in Unity, shall we see a greater display of God's power, and a more glorious manifestation of his might in our churches...may God send us a Christ-exalting, Spirit-loving ministry.[57]

Spurgeon called his generation to preach more about God and to preach more about those things which extolled the Great God rather than 'those things which look [merely] at the creature to be saved.' What resulted is an idea that preaching is, at its core, a proclamation of the Trinity. Each person of the One God is meant to be extolled in all of His character, work, ways and words in the course of one's preaching. For this reason, whenever Spurgeon meant to extol one person of the Godhead, he almost always began by setting the character and work of that person in the context of the other two. Spurgeon urged preachers to proclaim the triune God in all of His offices. Preachers are meant to 'extol God the Savior as the author and finisher of our faith.' They are not to neglect the 'Great God, the Father of his people, who, before all worlds, elected us in Christ his Son, justified us through his righteousness and will inevitably preserve us and gather us together in one, in the consummation at the last great day.' Finally, the preacher is meant to 'proclaim God the Holy Ghost in all his offices.'[58]

All matters of the text, therefore, including all practical issues of living and salvation, are meant to find their context in the character and majestic power of God. In other words, because the Bible has God as its hero, and because the Bible preached is God's means of displaying His attendant power, every sermon must somehow extol this hero as He comes to speak, nourish and change hearts. Therefore, 'preaching is not the great end of the Sabbath-day' nor is 'listening to sermons.' The goal of preaching and of meeting on Sunday is for us to glorify God, and this in service and the singing of praises.[59]

This means that a preacher must work 'as though he meant it.' He must seek to preach 'his best sermon every time he mounts the pulpit.'[60] This means that he aims his sermon at God's glory 'by seeking the edification of saints and the salvation of sinners.'[61] Such an aim will require weighty words which are intended for more than a momentary impression. Such a noble goal will require more than mental power and will lead the preacher to feel his weakness and, from there, to cry out for the attendant strength of God. And this God intends to come upon the scene and speak powerfully to the soul while the preacher speaks feebly to the ear.

Conclusion

Spurgeon testified to his hearers that they themselves had often known such attendant visits from God. 'We have known that Jesus himself drew near,' he said to his congregation. 'We have heard the words of the Holy Scripture as though they fell fresh from his lips. Thus they have, by the power of the Holy Spirit, burned in our hearts and made our hearts to burn like coals of juniper, which have a most vehement flame.'[62]

The next four chapters explore the implications of attendant power on the practice of Spurgeon's preaching. Spurgeon sought to see the preacher's sermon style, delivery, illustration, emotion and application through the lens of God's attendant power. In doing so, Spurgeon leads the preacher to pray for his hearers: 'Oh, may God, in his infinite mercy, bring the gospel with something more than this common power to your souls! May it come with "the Holy Ghost" as well as with power.'[63]

Questions for Learning and Discussion

1. What strikes you most when you read this chapter?

2. What is the purpose of preaching? How does God's glory inform your approach to preaching?

3. What is mental and attendant power? What are the differences between temporary and lasting impressions made on hearers by preaching?

4. Describe how your views of sin, Satan, Spiritual warfare and your own inward conflicts shape the kind of power you long for in preaching.

5. What do you think about Spurgeon's conception of God speaking presently and alongside of the preacher's feeble speech? What difference would this truth make for the way you approach preaching?

6. Do you long for God to come with power in the churches by His Spirit? Do you pray that God will raise up a

generation of preachers who possess more than mental power? Why or why not?

7. What will your next step be?

10

The Free Spirit:

Bowing before the Spirit's Mysteries

There is an arbitrariness about the wind, it does just as it pleases, and the laws which regulate its changes are to man unknown. "Free as the wind," we say, —"the wild winds." So is the mighty working of God.[1]

Spurgeon labored to say that the Spirit of God for preaching must be sought among those instruments which most manifest the Spirit's character and purpose. With probable reference to his hyper-Calvinist critics, Spurgeon answered those who challenged why a preacher must use means for gospel ministry when God, after all, 'can do his own work.' To such challenges, Spurgeon pointed out that these 'appointed ways' to which the preacher is to surrender, find their foundations first in Christ himself. Though Jesus is 'the light of the world,' he does not fulfill his purposes 'without instrumentalities.'[2] Moreover, in the 'apostolic example' Paul, like his Master, 'did not expect' things 'to happen apart from the ordained methods and ordinary institutions of grace.'[3] Spurgeon was concerned that preachers trust the sufficiency of God-ordained means for securing relevance and power to meet the challenges of a generation. He felt that some preachers harbored no responsibility for the working of the Spirit in their ministries. Their doctrine of God's sovereignty enabled them to approach preaching without concern. Regardless of what they did, God would work. Spurgeon sought to challenge this idea.

On the other hand, some preachers were turning to means other than those appointed by the Spirit for the effective preaching of the gospel. Rhetoric, music, architecture and force of personality, though good in themselves, were veiling the true need of the hour. As we have seen, Spurgeon passionately urged men to trust the means of the Spirit and thereby to give themselves to a power that was more than merely mental in origin and capacity.

Having established the necessity of appointed means, to counter these two views, Spurgeon equally cautioned those who believed that these Spirit-appointed instruments possessed intrinsic power to procure pulpit effectiveness by their mere use: 'The Holy Ghost uses means, which are adapted to the end designed,' he agreed. 'Yet my trust is not in the Word itself,' he clarified, 'but in the quickening Spirit who works by it.'[4] Spurgeon warned preachers of this temptation: 'We have tried to propagate the truth in a certain way, and the Lord has blessed us in it, and therefore we venerate the mode and the plan, and forget that the Holy Spirit is a free Spirit.'[5]

The Free Spirit

By a 'free Spirit,' Spurgeon meant that the Spirit has no obligation to use His appointed instruments in the way that preachers and people demand. That preachers and people would give themselves to the Spirit's means is a matter of duty and delight and is a blessing to them, quite apart from the things they hope will come to pass as a result. In his sermon, 'The Holy Spirit Compared to the Wind,' Spurgeon cites John 3:8, in which Jesus teaches Nicodemus concerning the sovereignty of the Spirit. From this passage, Spurgeon declared that there is mystery to the Holy Spirit's operations which transcend the use of means.

'The various motions of the air remain a mystery to all but the infinite Jehovah. My brethren, the like mystery is observed in the work of the Spirit of God. His person and work are not to be comprehended by the mind of man. He may be here to-night, but you cannot see him: he speaks to one heart, but others cannot hear his voice.[6]'

Because the Spirit has a free will, and because giving oneself to the Spirit's means is the duty and delight of the preacher, the preacher must surrender to the fact that the Spirit will work through us for His own grand purposes. Therefore, the preacher cannot use the means of the Spirit in a manipulative fashion as if offering a trade. The preacher may say to himself, 'I am doing what he said to do, therefore I want this and that to happen.' And when 'this and that' do not happen, the preacher may feel indignant and feel that the Spirit has not kept His end of the bargain. Spurgeon reminds preachers, however, that using the means of the Spirit has never been a matter of keeping a bargain. It has always been a matter of obedience and surrender. Therefore, the preacher must learn to trust the Spirit's purposes for his sermon. The Spirit, and not the preacher, is the one who determines the purposes of that week's sermons. For example, when referring to one of his sermons which he felt was less than effective, Spurgeon acknowledged that the first place to look is to his responsibility with the *nearer* and *remote* tools and the appointed ways of the Spirit. But upon examination, if the preacher in good conscience can honestly say that he was faithful to his responsibilities, and the sermon still seemed less than effective, then the preacher must surrender to the purposes of the free Spirit.

> The simple fact is this, 'the wind bloweth where it listeth;' and sometimes the winds themselves are still.... Therefore if I rest on the Spirit, I cannot expect that I should always feel His power alike...in the one case the Holy Spirit went with the Word; and in the other case He did not. All the heavenly result of preaching is owing to the Divine Spirit sent from above.[7]

'All the heavenly result of preaching' resides not with the preacher but with 'the Divine Spirit sent from above.' Assuming that one's nearer tools are fit and ready, Spurgeon will acknowledge that 'At times, the Spirit gives or withholds his blessings connected with ourselves.' At other times 'the Spirit of God blesses one preacher more than another and the reason cannot be such that any man could congratulate himself.'[8]

In sum, while the preacher is responsible for faithfulness, and while lack of faithfulness may grieve the Spirit and render preaching ineffective, it is also the case that a preacher's proper faithfulness is not the cause of effective preaching nor does it guarantee it. The preacher needs both the appointed instrument and the attendant power alongside that instrument in the sermon moment in order to pursue that spiritual strength and power which is competent for the lasting needs of the human soul.

This paradox brought Spurgeon into conflict with hyper-Calvinists, who challenged aspects of responsible instrumentality, as well as with the 'new measures' of others, who were tempted to trust solely, instrumentality for pulpit power. Spurgeon therefore challenged both an adherence to Victorian decorum on the one hand and a lust after innovative novelty on the other.

Exploring the Paradox
This paradox in Spurgeon's theory and practice of preaching has exposed him to the charge of being 'inconsistent.' According to Nelson, 'herein lay the great inconsistency of Spurgeon's theology – that he insisted on man's responsibility for accepting or rejecting redemption, while at the same time he preached the doctrine of predestination.'[9] Long before Nelson, however, Spurgeon himself anticipated this charge of inconsistency. In light of his conviction that God must work on the preacher's behalf, he says, '[Somebody may perhaps ask] "why, then, do you preach to these people?"[10] In other words, if God must do the work, why must a man preach?

To begin to answer this question requires recognition that, though his esteem for John Calvin is immense, Spurgeon refused to acknowledge Calvin or any other hero of the faith as the source for needed spiritual power. He believed that, 'All teaching which lifts up Wesley, or Calvin, or any man, living or dead, in the place of *the* authorized Teacher, and which says that their dicta are to be taken as though they were the infallible revelations of Christ, is not of the Spirit of God.'[11] To this end, Spurgeon sought to distinguish himself from some types of Calvinism resident and vocal in his community. For Spurgeon, predestination, rather than minimizing human responsibility, offered a framework for understanding its true nature. Spurgeon felt strongly on this point: 'I hope I shall never belong to that class of

Calvinists,' he said, 'who do the devil's work by excusing sinners in their sins.'[12]

The paradox finds its roots in Calvin's own teaching. For example, Book Four of Calvin's *Institutes* is entitled 'The External Means or Aids By Which God Invites Us into the Society of Christ and Holds Us Therein.' That God uses the means of preaching is 'doubly useful' because it both 'proves our obedience by a very good test' and it 'provides for our weakness' in drawing us to Himself. Then, referring to 'those who think the authority of the Word is dragged down by the baseness of men called to teach,' Calvin noted that though God's power 'is not bound to outward means,' He has 'nonetheless bound us to this ordinary manner of teaching.'[13] Notice that Spurgeon urged the same opinion. We are bound to use God-given means even though God's power is not bound or always given to these means.

Spurgeon's 'inconsistency' can at least find an explanation when the critic addresses Spurgeon's practice in the light of his Calvinistic theology. Spurgeon assumes that the same God who ordains all things also ordains the means by which He will bring all things to pass. The same God who elects His people also predestines responsible means for reaching His people. These concepts are conjoined by the secret influence of the Holy Spirit of God who sovereignly uses instruments to accomplish His purposes. So, even though 'The Spirit of God works...according to his own will,'[14] the Spirit of God does not violate the will of man in His working. Spurgeon explained:

The Spirit of God never acts by the human heart as you and I might act by a box of which we have lost the key. He does not wrench it and break it open. According to the laws of nature he acts with men as men. He draws with cords, but they are cords of love, – with bands, but they are bands of a man. It is by enlightening the judgment that he influences the will. He leads us to see things in a different light by the instruction which he gives to us, and by that clearer light he influences the understanding and the heart; the things [we once] loved we see to be evil, and we hate them; and the things we once hated we see to be good, and we choose them.[15]

The *Puritan Catechism* locates the foundations for this sovereign-instrument-conviction within the Calvinistic doctrine of 'effectual calling':

> 30. Q. What is effectual calling?
>   A. Effectual calling is the work of God's Spirit (2 Timothy 1:9) whereby, convincing us of our sin and misery (Acts 2:37), enlightening our minds in the knowledge of Christ (Acts 26:18), and renewing our wills (Ezekiel 36:26), he does persuade and enable us to embrace Jesus Christ freely offered to us in the gospel (John 6:44, 45).

Spurgeon believed that the Spirit of God is sovereignly and actively convincing and persuading people to embrace Jesus Christ by means of His being freely offered to them in the gospel through the instrumental reading of, but especially through the instrumental preaching of, that same gospel by designated human agents. God works by means. But His power is not demanded by those means.

Waiting and Watching for God to Give the Text
This paradox is clearly demonstrated when one views how Spurgeon prepared his sermons. He believed that each week he must submit to 'what topics the Holy Spirit would have' him 'bring before the congregation.'[16] To discern the leading of the Spirit, Spurgeon turned to the vigorous work of appointed means. Throughout the week and during his multiple labors in ministry, he would stay 'on the look out for material' that he could use for Sunday's messages. Then, on Saturday evenings by six o'clock, after guests had left and family worship had ended, Spurgeon would retire to his study. The time to choose his sermon texts for the morning and the evening was at hand. Once finding them, he would prepare for the Sunday morning sermon – the Sunday evening sermon being left for Sunday afternoon preparation. Susannah would hear her husband, and Charles and Thomas would hear their Dad, through the study door, pleading with God for himself and the people of his congregation. Spurgeon would search the Scriptures and those books which dealt with the Scriptures he had in mind. The greatest difficulty he admitted was in

choosing what texts the Spirit of God would have him preach. 'As soon as any passage of Scripture really grips my heart and soul,' he said. 'I concentrate my whole attention upon it.' By this focused attention, Spurgeon meant that he would look at the original language, closely examine the context of the passage and then write down all of the thoughts that would come to him for the passage. Then he would turn to commentaries and search them out. Sometimes, he did this with multiple Scripture passages, putting several aside and laboring to find which one was most suitable for the next morning.

As he labored in the appointed means of prayer and the Bible to determine his sermon, Spurgeon would also turn to the co-labor of his wife Susannah. She was his fellow worker in searching through commentaries. Spurgeon described this aspect of her help. 'I am glad to call my dear wife to my assistance. She reads to me until I get a clear idea of the whole subject; and, gradually, I am guided to the best form of outline, which I copy out, on a half-sheet of notepaper, for use in the pulpit.'[17] It is interesting to hear Susannah describe these same moments. She recalls:

> Will you come and help me to-night, wifey? He would say on those memorable Saturday evenings.... I always found, when I went into the study, an easy chair drawn up to the table, by his side, and a big heap of books piled upon the other, and opened at the place where he desired me to read...and I was, in this pleasant fashion, introduced to many of the Puritan and other divines whom, otherwise, I might not have known.[18]

Another help that Spurgeon found from his wife was her advice regarding which text to choose. She says of these occasional times, 'he would leave the study for a few moments, to seek me and say, with a troubled tone of voice, "Wifey, what shall I do? God has not given me my text yet? I would comfort him as well as I could," she continues, 'and, after a little talk, he would return to his work, and wait and watch for the Word to be given.'[19] For Mrs. Spurgeon, these moments were a cause of a 'peculiar thankfulness' that she had to God. Sometimes her husband was pleased to say to his fellow-worker, after God had blessed the morning sermon, 'Wifey, you gave me that text.'

What is apparent is that to 'wait and watch for God to give' was a thing which required a directed activity. This is why Spurgeon worked hard in the appointed means of praying, searching the Scripture, vigorously using his nearer and remote tools, and turning for help to his fellow-worker. In addition, he was practically mindful of providence. Spurgeon would turn to the inside cover of his Bible after he had worked through the initial stages of a text that had grabbed his heart. If he had preached the text before or one very nearly like it, he would assume that he was not to preach it. The reality that his sermons were published weekly kept him mindful not to repeat texts or themes too closely together for the sake of his readers.

The result is that while Spurgeon believed that God would give him the text for each week's sermons, his view of waiting on God meant a directed activity in the means that God has given to demonstrate His power. Within this mixture of an agonized searching and a practical method, Spurgeon's view of the 'free Spirit' is illustrated. Such a paradoxical illustration is also given in Spurgeon's work-habits. Spurgeon's view of waiting on God and depending upon the power of the Holy Spirit was forged within the sixty plus organizations that were under his founding and/or oversight, the five hundred letters he sought to answer each week, the six to eight books that he read each week, the weekly publications of his sermons, the editing and arranging of his books and regular periodicals, the fact that he often preached up to ten times a week, and his daily pastoral labors for his congregation. For Spurgeon, because God's Spirit is active and can be depended on, the preacher is lulled out of passivity and given courage to work as if real power is possible in the ministry of the gospel. Therefore, 'we ought to prepare the sermon as if all depended upon us.' But we are to hope for power from God alone. 'We are to trust the Spirit of God knowing that all depends upon Him.'[20]

Conclusion

Spurgeon offered two sides of the same coin to preachers. He urged preachers, amid the powerlessness of their times, to give their utmost efforts to God-ordained labors. He believed that 'The Holy Spirit will not come to rescue us from the consequences of willful neglect of the Word of God and study.' Spurgeon's practice of sovereign instrumentality allowed no rival to the glory of God in His work and yet required the preacher to give himself to God in faithful submission. In short, the apparent tension created by his paradoxical preaching approximates the same paradoxical tension he actively upheld in his theology. 'Instruments shall be used,' he declared, 'but their intrinsic weakness shall be clearly manifested; there shall be no division of the glory, no diminishing the honor due to the Great Worker. The man shall be emptied of himself and then filled with the Holy Ghost.'[21] 'Kindled fire' comes from surrendering to the free spirit's will amid the duty and delight of His appointed means.

Questions for Learning and Discussion

1. What strikes you most from this chapter?

2. How does Spurgeon's paradox of the 'free Spirit' challenge you?

3. How does Spurgeon's method of sermon preparation compare or contrast with your own?

4. What suggestions does his paradox make for your preaching and labors?

5. What will you take with you from this chapter?

11

SEEKING A FRESH BAPTISM:

Pursuing the Spirit's Fellowship

What is the use of a sermon if there is no unction in it? What is unction but the Holy Ghost?[1]

As the nineteenth century drew to a close, it was apparent that Charles Spurgeon was not alone in his concern that preachers give a renewed attention to the necessity of dependence on the Spirit. In 1881, D. L. Moody observed: 'There has been much inquiring of late on the subject of the Holy Spirit. In this and other lands thousands of persons have been giving attention to the study of this grand theme.'[2] G. Campbell Morgan agreed. 'During the last quarter of this 19th century,' he said, 'men in all parts of the Christian church have spoken and written about the ministry and work of the Holy Spirit.'[3]

As we have noted, for Spurgeon the antidote for church infection was the igniting of the 'old truth' with a 'fresh baptism of the Holy Spirit.' This kindled fire of the Spirit and Word of God, he believed, would form the means by which preachers could 'hold fast' the 'sound words' of the Scripture and preach with more than mental power to their generation. Because Spurgeon regularly prayed for the Spirit's power and sought to preach in fellowship with that Spirit, clarification is needed regarding how Spurgeon's view of the Spirit and preaching compared or differed from other movements of renewed interest in the Holy Spirit in the nineteenth century. Such clarifications may also help

Spurgeon's theological grandchildren who, in light of their cultural contexts, may find his longing for a fresh baptism of the Spirit strange.

The Power of the Holy Ghost in the Midst of His People
Spurgeon believed that the minister not only must study his text for his sermon, but must also 'ask for a baptism of the Holy Ghost' for his sermon.[4] By the term, 'Baptism of the Holy Ghost,' Spurgeon had at least three things in mind. First, 'baptism' of the Spirit was synonymous with conversion to Christ and not synonymous with water baptism.

> Remember, my dear friends, that into the Holy Ghost you and I, when we professed our faith in Jesus, were baptized. We were immersed 'into the name of the Father, and of the Son, and of the Holy Ghost;' and this day, without the Holy Spirit, you and I are fraudulent professors, baptized deceivers, and arrant hypocrites. If we were not, indeed, baptized into the Holy Ghost, how dare we be baptized into the outward symbol?[5]

More to the point for preachers, when Spurgeon urged preachers to seek a fresh baptism, he was not asking them to seek a fresh conversion. At Pentecost in Acts 2, Jesus baptized His people in the Holy Spirit. 'From that moment,' Spurgeon said, 'the Church of God was baptized into the Holy Spirit.'[6] Jesus had given her 'the fiery element of his Spirit' so that she now 'dwells in the everlasting burnings of the divine power.'[7] A preacher, therefore, does not 'need to pray to have the Spirit poured out. For,' Spurgeon said, 'that has been done.' What the preacher does need however, is 'a baptism of the Holy Spirit.' 'Baptism' is different from 'outpouring' in that the Spirit is already with us. What is needed is that the preacher must walk in light of that presence and relationship. He must 'go down personally into that glorious flood which has been poured forth.' To go down into that which has been poured forth is 'to be immersed into the Holy Ghost, and into fire, covered with his holy influence.'[8] Therefore, to 'go down' into this influence is for Spurgeon to 'walk in the power bestowed upon' the church 'at Pentecost.'[9]

To walk in the Spirit's power means to resist grieving and quenching the Spirit, and to give oneself to the Spirit's appointed ways. From this standpoint, when preachers turn to their own devices they forfeit the greater measure of fellowship with the divine person and lose power for life and ministry effectiveness. A fresh baptism describes a repentance toward the Spirit's person and His appointed means. It is an immediate and local application of what has been available since Pentecost.

But there is another side to this coin. At other times, Spurgeon refers to a fresh baptism of God's Spirit as if the Spirit had actually withdrawn His manifest power from even His appointed means. Following the Westminster Assembly's Confession of Faith, Spurgeon agreed that 'sometimes the Lord purposely leaves his children, withdraws the divine inflowings of his grace, and permits them to begin to sink, in order that they may understand that faith is not their own work, but is at first the gift of God, and must always be maintained and kept alive in the heart by the fresh influence of the Holy Spirit.'[10]

From this view, a grieving and quenching can persist such that the Spirit simply allows His people to go on in their own way. He withdraws, not ultimately, but locally, from their ministerial efforts. The result is that the effect seen by the preacher is merely mental in origin. The need here is for preachers and people not only to repent toward the appointed means and thereby to disrupt the measures of grieving and quenching that have taken place, but also to receive a fresh returning of the Spirit's local manifestation or attendance to those appointed means. When such an absence is noticed, an inquiry with God is needed. In this sense, to pray for a fresh baptism is not only to ask for a local application of what began at Pentecost, but also to ask for a return of the manifest presence of the Spirit. It is to ask for an intensified demonstration of the Spirit's presence and power in a way that was not manifested before in the preacher's life. Spurgeon says:

The mainspring of everything good and gracious is the Holy Spirit. Where he comes, everything prospers; but when he has gone, nothing but failure and disaster will come. I believe that, at this present moment, God's people ought to cry to him day and night that there may be a fresh baptism into the Holy Ghost. There are many things that are desirable for the Church of Christ, but one thing is absolutely needful; and this is the one thing, the power of the Holy Ghost in the midst of his people.

From the first vantage point, to pray for God to arrive on the scene and unite His voice for the soul with the preacher's voice for the ear, is simply to ask God to do what Pentecost has made possible. From the second vantage point, to pray for the dual voice in preaching may require recognition that God has withdrawn a sense of His presence and power. 'There are times,' he said, 'when a want of success or a withering of our cherished hopes will help to make us feel most keenly how barren and unfruitful we are until the Lord endows us with his Spirit.'[11]

This kind of fresh baptism also arises when the nature of the difficulty facing the church requires a measure of manifest power that earlier generations may have known, but that would be new to the churches in the current generation. By asking for a fresh baptism, the preacher acknowledges this absence of needed grace and power. The preacher returns again to an active awareness that all of his hopes in preaching rest with God Himself and that nothing but God's intensified presence will sustain the church in her present trial. In essence, preachers need an analogy of Pentecost, not because God has ultimately gone, but because He is gone in a manifest way or because the nature of the times warrants greater measures of God's grace in working.

The Higher Life
Spurgeon's threefold way of referring to the baptism of the Spirit (conversion, walking in the pentecostal power, being interrupted by a fresh infiltration of a pentecostal analogy) can seem confusing at times. But what is certain is that when Spurgeon spoke of a fresh baptism or intensification of the Spirit's power, he did not refer to a one-time event, but an occurrence that could be repeated. Furthermore, Spurgeon's understanding of this baptism, while its fruit would include growth in holiness, was in the main a renewal of effectiveness

for preaching and hearing the Word. Rather than a blessing for sanctification, it was a blessing of empowerment for ministry. Therefore, there were many baptisms needed by the church in order for God's people to have God's power for the needs of the hour. Thus, Spurgeon's view was separate from those Higher Life views of Spirit-baptism and sanctification that were contemporary to Spurgeon and still remain in our day. This view asserted that Spirit-baptism was a matter of a crisis moment of complete surrender in which a person was made habitually perfect to live a victorious and sanctified life in Christ. Such an experience from the Spirit enables the believer to experience a habitual victory over all known sins. Such an experience is referred to by some as 'the second blessing.' Spurgeon's sentiments expose his longing for many blessings and his caution for those who pride themselves in their second experience. Speaking of the second blessing, Spurgeon says:

> I wish that they would get beyond that also, and reach the third blessing.... To go on from a second to a third, and a fourth, and a fifth, and a sixth, and a seventh, and an eighth, and a ninth, and a tenth blessing, is the thing for a child of God to do; but to get into a state of pride, and cry that he has got a second blessing, is a poor way of growing.[12]

Spurgeon was also pastorally concerned with the effect of self-deceiving or inward deadening that such a teaching could have on a person.

> Whatever doctrinal views you may hold as to the higher life, I will not dispute with you, but practically I beseech you to shun the spirit which lulls the heart into soft slumbers by the music of spiritual flattery. Whoever you are, I make bold to say that you are not all you should be, nor all you can be.[13]

Therefore Spurgeon cautioned his hearers. 'Depend upon it, the moment we conclude that we have overcome, and can say what Paul could not say – that he had attained and was already perfect – we are in an evil case.'[14]

Spurgeon's view of Spirit-baptisms included empowerment for service and required multiple applications. Holiness for Spurgeon was a matter of daily growth by the power
of the Spirit through faith in Christ. It was to be pursued
diligently and great measures of it could be obtained in
this life by the grace of Christ. However, he charitably but
strongly cautioned the Higher Life movement's emphasis on
a one-time experience of the Spirit for the perfect life.

That being said, however, it is important to note that
Spurgeon was mostly charitable in his cautions and correc-
tions. Actually, he seems to speak more strongly in rejection
of those who criticized the Higher Life movement.

> Somebody asked me the other day whether I thought
> Christians could be quite perfect, and, I have no doubt,
> expected a long harangue from me; but I cut him short,
> for my secret thought was, 'Well, you are a fine fellow
> to be asking such a question, for there is no danger of
> your coming anywhere near that condition....' I am sick
> of seeing a set of beggarly professors, whose poverty of
> grace is manifest to everybody but themselves, shaking
> their heads at those good brethren who preach up a high
> standard of grace. They need be under no alarm about
> growing too devout, too prayerful, or too holy. They may
> go a long way before they will be mistaken for perfect.[15]

Thus, Spurgeon's perspective on Spirit-baptism was both
disparate and confluent with those in his culture. Some
agreed with Spurgeon's first vantage point that there was no
need to ask for an outpouring of the Spirit as that Spirit was
already poured out at Pentecost. James Henry McConkey,
for example, stated: 'We already have the baptism of the
Holy Spirit. We are not waiting on God to do something,
God is waiting on us to do something.'[16]

In contrast, others believed that continued fillings and/or
baptisms of the Spirit were required and intended for the
believer. Therefore, continued fresh givings from the Spirit
were to become the regular experience of the preacher and
the people. G. Campbell Morgan, for example, used the term
'filling' to describe what Spurgeon meant by his third use of
the term 'baptism.'[17] Morgan simply said that the believer

has one baptism but needs many fillings. Spurgeon seems to follow this line of thinking. Preachers need to disrupt grieving the Spirit and to walk in the provision already given by their Spirit-baptism. But they also may need a more immediate and local return or intensification of God's power which requires fresh applications or baptisms of the Spirit's power.

What is clear from both sides of Spurgeon's perspective is this: Spurgeon insisted throughout the whole of his ministry that preachers and people continuously need a fresh attendance of power from the Holy Spirit. He called it a baptism, an influence, and 'the unction.' Morgan's terminology may possess greater clarity than Spurgeon's. But it is reasonable to conclude from Spurgeon's practice that he more often resembled the second side of his Pentecost coin in his ministry. That is the side which looks to continued intensifications of power rather than the side which simply looks back to the power already given. Though he said that believers did not require requests for further outpourings of the Spirit, in practice this is actually what he seemed to model and teach. This point can be made more clearly by showing how Spurgeon viewed Pentecost and by the criticisms that he had to answer.

Tongues of Fire

Whenever Spurgeon mentioned the term 'tongues,' he generally referred to one's use of ordinary speech, akin to the New Testament book of James which says, 'the tongue is a fire, a world of unrighteousness' (3:6). In this regard, Spurgeon meant the term 'tongues' to refer to human language when used at its best or worst. Often he warns of licentious tongues, forked tongues, cruel tongues, and our need of learning to hold our tongues. Perhaps this kind of usage is best demonstrated in Spurgeon's 'John Ploughman' talks. 'Beware of those who come from the town of Deceit,' he said. 'Mr. Facing-both-ways, Mr. Fair-speech, and Mr. Two-tongues are neighbors who are best at a distance.'[18] The preacher must learn to practice and teach how godliness informs his speech (tongues).

Centrally, however, preachers are meant by Spurgeon to turn regularly and earnestly to the pentecostal tongues of the New Testament, not for ecstatic-language seeking, nor for a gift to receive and practice, but for a picture of the nature and necessity of the Spirit's anointing for preaching and preachers. Such a turn may surprise some. But for Spurgeon, 'tongues of fire' pictures the power and outcomes of a preaching that is attended by the Holy Spirit. For example, in his sermon, 'Death and Life in Christ,' Spurgeon called preachers to resist seeking novelties for power in the Christian life and return instead to Pentecost. Such a statement sounds foreign to twenty-first-century ears who associate pentecostal tongues with a gift, a novelty or an error. Spurgeon surprises his theological grandchildren by considering pentecostal tongues as the proof text for getting back to preaching the old paths. As we have already noted, the lenses by which he sees Pentecost require no 'reaction' to perceived pentecostal abuses by some and no adherence to the required assumptions of others. Quoting John Newton, Spurgeon reminded preachers that their task must never stray from 'the work of Christ for us and his work in us by the Holy Spirit.' Our business, he said, 'is the old labor of apostolic tongues, to declare that Jesus, who is the same yesterday to-day and for ever.'[19] Spurgeon saw the 'old labor of apostolic tongues' as a picture of preaching, because in the Acts passage, when those disciples are filled with the Spirit, they immediately preach and declare the wonders of God to the community. Spurgeon saw the preaching of God to the community in power as the direct outworking of the attending Spirit. In this exhortation, preachers learn from Spurgeon that (1) Pentecost pictures an 'old labor' which belongs to preachers today, (2) that labor finds its parallel in the 'Apostolic tongues' which is (3) a given power of the Holy Spirit to declare Christ.

Spurgeon viewed the gift of tongues while Peter preached to Cornelius' house in Acts 10 the same way. He points out that Peter's sermon 'was never finished, but closed abruptly.' Then Spurgeon longs that 'our sermons were incomplete for the same cause that Peter's was.' By this Spurgeon did not mean that he wished that our sermons would be interrupted by congregational members suddenly breaking forth into ecstatic utterances of other languages. What Spurgeon appreciated was the picture of the Holy Spirit's power. As Peter preached, there was a divine interruption. 'The Holy Ghost fell on all them which heard the word...and the sermon was stopped.' Spurgeon then calls out, 'Oh that the Spirit of God would in the same manner interrupt us!'[20]

Such biblical pictures help to explain why Spurgeon would regularly and publicly ask for the pentecostal fire to come again in his day. He was not referring to our contemporary discussions concerning speaking in other languages. He was referring to the need for the fresh unction of God's Spirit to empower preachers and give power to their proclamation. As Peter preached the Spirit fell. This was Spurgeon's longing for his own generation. 'Give us men who know experimentally those things that they labor to teach,' he beckons, 'and let their tongues be set on fire of the Holy Ghost, and ye shall then see London as full of the glory of the Lord as was Jerusalem of old.'[21]

The Inward Monitions of the Spirit

Spurgeon's room for immediate, fresh, local and new[22] applications of the Spirit's power included what he called the Spirit's 'monitions' outside of the pulpit and in the life of the believer. 'When believers come into difficult circumstances, they bow the knee,' says Spurgeon, 'and cry for guidance.' Often, in this circumstance, 'in some way not always to be explained, the Spirit of God guides our steps through life, if we are willing to obey his monitions.'[23] Spurgeon defines these 'monitions' as emotional impressions: 'There are feelings and emotions, tendernesses and tremblings, joys and delights, which we cannot quite link with any special portion of Scripture laid home to the heart,' he said. Rather, they 'seem to steal upon us unawares by the direct operation of the Spirit of God upon the heart.'[24] Spurgeon did not mean that these local and personal applications of the Spirit took place without a life-context of the Bible. He meant that they may take place with no recognized connection or immediate reading of the Bible. 'Keep to the Word of God,' he said. 'Moreover...be attentive to that mind of Christ, which is often expressed by the Holy Spirit in divine monitions in our minds.' Spurgeon meant to keep the working of the Spirit with the Bible while recognizing that the Spirit functions even when the person does not have the Bible in his hands. In this way, 'the law of the book may be with us and the law of the Spirit within us.'[25]

But what are these inward monitions? They can come in the form of inward inclinations that can indicate a second, temporally binding command built upon, guarded by, and informed by the prior and always binding commands given in the Bible. An inward impulse to pray, for example, is recognized by Spurgeon as no new revelation, but rather as a present and immediate application by the Spirit of the command to pray which is already revealed by that same Spirit in the Bible. Spurgeon explains:

> You feel on a sudden, possibly in the midst of business, the pressing thought that you must retire to pray. It may be, you do not at first take particular notice of the inclination, but it comes again, and again, and again – 'Retire and pray!'... Now, it strikes me that whenever our Lord gives you the special inclination to pray, that you should double your diligence. You ought always to pray and not to faint; yet when He gives you the special longing after prayer, and you feel a peculiar aptness and enjoyment in it, you have, over and above the command which is constantly binding, another command which should compel you to cheerful obedience.[26]

Why Not Follow George Fox?

Spurgeon's emphasis upon the immediate and local movements of the Spirit by fresh baptisms in preaching and inward monitions in living was critically challenged by some. One primary challenge that Spurgeon received was that he was in actual practice, a Quaker. The Quakers believed in an immediate leading of the Spirit in life and the immediate inspiration of the preacher for the sermon. Some critics heard Spurgeon's descriptions of the Spirit's power in preaching and living, and identified him as such. Referring to his own views, Spurgeon acknowledged that 'Some people call this fanaticism,' and they say, 'You are a Quaker, why not follow George Fox?' Spurgeon's answer might surprise some today as it surely did then. He countered his challenger, 'Well we would not mind that much, we would follow any one who followed the Holy Ghost.'[27]

Spurgeon did not mind association with this particular idea that the Spirit can prompt a person. After identifying 'monitions' as impulses, Spurgeon suggested that 'every man should look and see whether God is making him do a certain thing; and when once he feels the impulse, let him by no means ever check it.... I am somewhat of a believer in the doctrine of the Quakers, as to the impulses of the Spirit,' Spurgeon continued, 'and I fear lest I should check one of them.'

Spurgeon concluded therefore that: 'If a thought crosses my mind, "Go to such a person's house," I always like to do it, because I do not know but what it may be from the Spirit.'[28] Similarly, Spurgeon elsewhere explains, though with 'great caution,' that 'the Spirit of God does, I believe, directly, even apart from the word, speak in the hearts of the saints.' Monitions therefore are movements from God in the midst of life to do something in accordance with the Word even though the person is not currently reading the Bible. By this means the Spirit may urge the believer to pray or visit a stranger, both of which are clearly commanded truths applied to a specific moment in one's life.

These monitions could also come in the form of a restraint – an inward sense that something is not right with a particular circumstance. Spurgeon goes on to explain:

There will come to you sometimes, you know not why, certain inward checks.... Do not violate that inward restraint. 'Quench not the Spirit.' It is not to every man that the Holy Ghost speaks in such a way; but he has his favored ones, 'Why,' says one, 'you run into Quakerism.' I cannot help that. If this is Quakerism I am so far a Quaker: names – do not concern me one way or another.[29]

To the sure consternation of his friends and colleagues who wished he might clarify himself, Spurgeon did not mind if some considered him an adherent of Quakerism. If any of his friends voiced their desire for him to clarify, their concern may not have been unfounded. Spurgeon regularly and consistently taught his students that 'The Spirit speaks to people by means of the Word of God.'[30] In fact,

Spurgeon could be quite adamant about this point. I offer one example in full.

> I have heard many fanatical persons say the Holy Spirit revealed this and that to them. Now that is very generally revealed nonsense. The Holy Ghost does not reveal anything fresh now. He brings old things to our remembrance...the canon of revelation is closed, there is no more to be added. God does not give a fresh revelation, but he rivets the old one. When it has been forgotten, and laid in the dusty chamber of our memory, he fetches it out and cleans the picture, but does not paint a new one. There are no new doctrines, but the old ones are often revived. It is not, I say, by any new revelation that the Spirit comforts. He does so by telling us old things over again; he brings a fresh lamp to manifest the treasures hidden in Scripture; he unlocks the strong chests in which the truth had long lain, and he points to secret chambers filled with untold riches; but he coins no more, for enough is done.[31]

These convictions become blatantly clear when speaking of preaching. In contrast to the Quakers, for example, Spurgeon limited inward monitions when referring to the actual preaching event. As he describes the role of 'inspiration' from the Spirit when preaching, he offered a negative anecdote about an approach to immediate inspiration practiced among an unnamed local gathering:

> I need scarcely warn any brother here against falling into the delusion that we may have the Spirit so as to become inspired. Yet the members of a certain litigious modern sect need to be warned against this folly. They hold that their meetings are under the 'presidency of the Holy Spirit': concerning which notion I can only say that I have been unable to discover in Holy Scripture either the term or the idea....[32]

Referring to these same gatherings, Spurgeon then makes a distinction between the immediate *inspiration* of the Spirit upon the preacher and the immediate *influence* of the Spirit upon the preacher. Speaking to those who may have attended such gatherings, Spurgeon says:

> I greatly question whether you have been more edified by the predilections produced under celestial presidency, than you have been by those ordinary preachers of the Word, who only consider themselves to be under the influence of the Holy Spirit, as one spirit is under the influence of another spirit, or one mind under the influence of another mind.[33]

Spurgeon clearly believed and taught that the Spirit of God speaks through the instrumentality of the Bible. Yet, he believed that the Spirit could give a direct impulse, apart from the Bible, in the moments of life. Spurgeon did not believe that these impulses qualified as direct inspiration nor that they had authority over the Bible. It seems, rather, that Spurgeon believed that God's Spirit would directly apply a prior command in His word to those who were willing to listen, for a particular circumstance in life. The Spirit who commanded prayer urges a person to pray at an odd moment during a day. The Spirit who commanded that the poor are cared for inwardly compels a person to go at an unplanned moment to help the poor. Such impulses, while direct and apart from the locality of the Bible, coincide with the clear teaching of the Bible. Moreover, far from a binding authority upon the people of God in the manner of inspiration, the application is personal and, as Spurgeon seemed to see it, it was binding to his conscience and worthy of obeying.

Perhaps his willingness not to distance himself from Quakerism was simply due to an unwillingness to take time and energy to get into a round of arguments with these particular critics. After all, pastorally, Spurgeon did have enough to do already and plenty of other critics from among whom to choose his battles. Another reason might lie in Spurgeon's belief that fresh intensifications of the Spirit's power among God's people were found at the core of his Puritan theological heritage, and he simply was not concerned about proving his point.

But it is also possible that Spurgeon's disinclination toward distancing himself from the Quakers on this point was more personal. Quakers were in his family ancestry, and at least one of them that Spurgeon knew about was a faithful man of God and a source of inspiration for Spurgeon. Referring to how he handled the difficult sufferings of body that he oftentimes felt, Spurgeon once remarked:

> Personally, when my bones have been tortured with rheumatism, I have remembered Job Spurgeon, doubtless of my own stock, who in Chelmsford Jail was allowed a chair, because he could not lie down by reason of rheumatic pain. That Quaker's broad-brim overshadows my brow. Perhaps I inherit his rheumatism; but that I do not regret if I have his stubborn faith, which will not let me yield a syllable of the truth of God.[34]

Like his response to the Higher Life movement, Spurgeon charitably identified with those aspects of Quaker theology which emphasized the need for active and regular dependence upon the Spirit of God. In so doing, he was not always as clear on his details as students may have liked. But there is no mistaking what students of Spurgeon would have learned from him about preaching. They were not only to study diligently, but they were to do so with an active awareness that they needed the immediate power of God's Spirit for their effectiveness in their life and ministry. This awareness was to lead them to seek daily fresh empowerments from the Spirit for their preaching and their generation.

Conclusion
In sum, Spurgeon felt that 'The lack of distinctly recognizing the power of the Holy Ghost' lay 'at the root of many useless ministries.'[35] Spurgeon was by no means alone in this conviction. By the end of the nineteenth century, multiple movements of interest in the Holy Spirit had arisen in England and America. Clarifying his views of Spirit-baptism exposes his interactions with his critics and with other views such as the Quakers and the Higher Life movements of his time. Clarity remains wanting in the details, but not in the main. Spurgeon believed that a preacher was meant to live in an active and ongoing daily fellowship with the Spirit of God. Preaching was meant to be lived out by seeking continually the kindled fire of the fresh power of the Spirit of God.

Questions for Learning and Discussion

1. How do you understand Spurgeon's view on the baptism of the Spirit?

2. What are inward monitions? How do you interact with Spurgeon's views?

3. How did Spurgeon's views on Spirit-baptism differ from Quaker and Higher Life perspectives?

4. What was the role of pentecostal tongues for Spurgeon's convictions about preaching?

5. What does it mean when God's Spirit withdraws from a preacher or a people?

6. Connect Spurgeon's view of Spirit-baptism with his earlier discussed views of the virtual preaching of Christ in the preaching-event, his distinctions between mental and spiritual power, and his view on the appointed ways of the Spirit. How do these ideas correspond to one another?

7. What will you take with you from this chapter?

PART FOUR:
The Preacher's Limitations

Key Points to Look for in Chapters Twelve and Thirteen

- A preacher's weakness is felt when temperament, criticism, sickness and circumstances converge.

- Criticism can be constructive. It can also be very cruel. A preacher needs help to learn how to handle criticism.

- Preachers need to learn the sources and manifestations of depression. Depression is something that most preachers will face. God is near to the depressed.

- A preacher partners with his wife in order to handle criticism, sickness and depression. They lean on each other and support each other in the common cause of the gospel.

- The ministry of the Spirit attends not only the preacher, but the members of the congregation whom He has gifted in Christ. Preaching takes place in the context of a Spirit-gifted community.

- Preachers and people play an interdependent role in ministering the gospel to a community.

- Preachers need a team. Preachers need to learn how to lean on and support that team.

- Spirit attended ministry does not necessarily remove depression, criticism and sickness. Rather, it teaches and enables men and women to walk by empowered faith through these trials.

Overview for Part Four

Unique to Spurgeon's pastoral theology for his students are discussions concerning the nature of criticism, depression and hardship, which often attend the preacher's life and the lives of those he serves. Preachers depend upon others to help them. The ministry of the Spirit in preaching is not an individual but a communal event in which preacher and people play interdependent roles. When the Spirit comes with power, He strengthens community. 'Kindled fire' does not promote isolated and doing-it-alone ministry. Nor does it take people from the earth to heaven. Rather, God's power is manifest within the earthbound limitations of a fallen world until Christ comes again, so that the strength of a community can be clearly seen as having been given by God. This is one way that a preacher and people testify with power to the watching world.

12

THE FAINTING FITS:

Handling Criticism and Depression

Fits of depression come over the most of us. Usually cheerful as we may be, we must at intervals be cast down. The strong are not always vigorous, the wise not always ready, the brave not always courageous, and the joyous not always happy.[1]

Sometimes Sunday evenings are emotionally complex for preachers. The combination of adrenaline, fatigue and a full heart can make it an evening affording a deep sense of satisfaction and nearness to God. It can at other times offer an evening in which it is difficult to sleep, rendering the pastor vulnerable to late night temptations, and filling his conscience with guilt and grief.

Such emotional mixtures were not any different for Charles Spurgeon. On Sunday evenings, after all was done for the week and for the day, he and his wife, Susannah, would sit together by the fire. Charles would prop his feet up and sit back in the easy chair. 'Shall I read to you to-night, dear?' Susannah would ask. If his conscience was free and the only fatigue fighting him was physical, Charles would ask his 'wifey' if she would read 'a page or two of good George Herbert.' 'Yes,' he'd say, 'that will be very refreshing, wifey; I shall like that.' Susannah would then read for an hour or more interspersed with their conversation regarding 'the sweet mysteries hidden within the gracious words.' The result of their companionship on these particular evenings would leave them with 'the peace of heaven' flowing into their souls. When this occurred, Charles would lose his 'sense of fatigue' and rejoice in the Lord with Susannah after all of his ministerial labors. Sleep would come easy that night as the new week began.

Other Sunday evenings were not so pleasant. Sometimes for Spurgeon the fatigue fighting him was more than physical. He could be 'sorely depressed in spirit' following the ministry of the day. 'Oh, darling!' he'd say to Susannah, 'I fear I have not been as faithful in my preaching to-day as I should have been; I have not been as much in earnest after poor souls as God would have me be. O Lord, pardon Thy servant!' Then he'd ask Susannah to read, but not poetry or *The Country Parson* – not on these occasions. 'Go, dear,' he'd say. Go 'to the study, and fetch down Baxter's *Reformed Pastor*, and read some of it to me; perhaps that will quicken my sluggish heart.' Mrs. Spurgeon would 'read page after page' of Baxter's 'solemn pleadings.' As she read, he would break into moments of 'heart-sobs.' She too would begin to cry and they would weep together. According to Mrs. Spurgeon, Charles would weep 'from the smitings of a very tender conscience towards God.' She would cry 'simply and only' because she loved her husband and wanted 'to share his grief.' She believed there was no legitimate cause for the way he sometimes upbraided himself, but she sought to comfort her husband by her 'quiet sympathy.'[2]

Any apprentice of Spurgeon's would soon learn that preaching in the midst of a fallen world will dismantle one's romanticism. Preaching is sometimes romantic, but never is it ideal. This is because the preacher must preach amid the sometimes harsh realities of the fall. One of the riches of Spurgeon's talks to his students and alumni is that he gave time to discussing how a preacher can learn to handle criticism, trials and physical and emotional sicknesses. He referred to some of these pains as 'the fainting fits.' He reminds us that a preacher needs the Spirit of God not only for the power by which God makes sermons effective but also because the preacher himself faces trials of many kinds. A preacher must not only learn to boast in his weakness as a Christian; he must learn to preach amid his weakness as a pastor.

The Sharp Knife

The trials begin with the challenge to a man's inner being to preach the gospel. Someone might ask: 'What is there difficult about preaching God's gospel?' First of all, there is the courage required. Preachers do what few people are required to do in their lives. Preachers stand up week upon week in a public forum and declare where they stand. Preaching 'is difficult,' Spurgeon admits, because 'you are afraid of displeasing the rich in your congregation.' Or 'you think' that if you 'say such-and-such a thing, so-and-so will be offended.' Or 'perhaps you will happen to win the applause of the multitude, and you must not say anything that will displease them.'[3]

Another trial is handling criticism inwardly while preaching in the presence of your critics and among those who have heard your critics' remarks. Spurgeon called criticism 'the sharp knife.' Even though the preacher may 'put on his armor' and tell himself that it doesn't matter, 'he cannot help feeling it sometimes.'[4]

Criticism can come in the form of a small annoyance like a fly that keeps buzzing around your head. 'You have been pleading as for life and death and they have been calculating how many seconds the sermon occupied.'[5]

But sometimes, criticism can simply be cruel in its attack on the character of the preacher. Throughout Spurgeon's ministry, many such attacks came his way. For example, one critic wrote: 'Mr. Spurgeon preaches *himself.* He is nothing unless he is an actor.... He is a nine days' wonder, – a comet that has suddenly shot across the religious atmosphere. He has gone up like a rocket, and ere long will come down like a stick.'[6] Another questioned whether Spurgeon was a Christian at all and implied worse. 'Whose servant is he?' asked the critic. 'As to the Divine reality of his conversion I have my doubts.' Then, after using the picture of the serpent who deceived Eve, and who presented himself as an angel of light, the critic among his numerous other attacks asserted that Spurgeon's ministry was not a true ministry of the Holy Spirit.[7] Another wrote:

I fear there is very little difference between the Church and the world. In both, the tide seems strongly set in favour of ignorance, presumption, and charlatanism. In the case of Mr. Spurgeon, they have both agreed to worship the same idol. Nowhere more abound the vulgar, be they great or little, than at the Surrey Music Hall on Sunday morning.[8]

Perhaps the cruellest of Spurgeon's criticisms is best illustrated by the great tragedy that took place early in his ministry. Upwards of twelve thousand people were sitting and standing, with many others standing outside unable to gain admittance to the Music Hall for worship. As Charles was praying during the service, someone cried out, 'Fire!' 'The galleries are giving way!' 'The place is falling!' There erupted a panic. Spurgeon cried out in vain to stop it. Several were killed and many were injured as the crowds trampled on one another to the exits. Charles actually did not know what the disturbances were. Because of the size of the building, he was unaware at the moment that people were dying. He tried to preach but to no avail. He eventually called for a hymn, dismissed the crowds and then nearly fainted, being carried out by friends amid the loud cries and weeping. It was not until later that he heard that there were 'seven corpses lying on the grass.'

In response, the daily papers gave a forum for Spurgeon's critics. This man is 'nothing more than a ranting charlatan,' said one. 'We would keep apart the theatre and the church,' he continued. 'Above all, would we place in the hand of every right-thinking man, a whip to scourge from society the authors of such vile blasphemies, as, on Sunday night, above the cries of the dead and the dying, and louder than the wails of misery from the maimed and suffering, resounded from the mouth of Spurgeon in the Music Hall of Surrey Gardens.'[9] Temperament, circumstance and criticism had converged in a seeming conspiracy from which those closest to Charles believed he never fully recovered. He himself said of that time in his young life, 'Perhaps never a soul went so near the burning furnace of insanity and yet came away unharmed.'

How does a preacher handle the buzzing flies, the cruel slanders and the unexplainable traumas that he encounters during the life of his ministry?

Practically, as he got older, Spurgeon used a private secretary, J.W. Harrald. In the peak of his ministry, he was receiving around 500 letters each week, not all of which were friendly. Harrald would read and filter these letters and prevented Spurgeon from reading the most abusive among them. They were simply too much to bear for Spurgeon amid the demands of his ministry and the regular challenges to his character.

At home, another practical step was taken. Mrs. Spurgeon had Matthew 5:11-12 'printed in large Old English type and enclosed in a pretty Oxford frame.' It hung in their bedroom so that Charles could read over it every morning.

> Blessed are ye, when men shall revile you and persecute you and shall say all manner of evil against you falsely for my sake. Rejoice and be exceedingly glad: for great is your reward in Heaven: for so persecuted they the prophets which were before you.

In a sample of Spurgeon's letters, a glimpse is offered as to how he personally tried to apply during the day what he read from his bedroom each morning. To his father, he once wrote, 'Do not be grieved at the slanderous libel in this week's *Express*...the devil is roused, the Church is awakening, and I am now counted worthy to suffer for Christ's sake.' Such declarations did not mean that Spurgeon arrived at them easily. He acknowledges to his father the pain that the public slander at that time had caused him. 'Last night I could not sleep till morning light, but now my Master has cheered me, and I hail reproach and welcome shame.'[10]

This same method of pouring out his pained heart to his Master in the night and there finding eventual strength is revealed in another letter he wrote to Susannah. He spoke first of the strength Susannah was to him. 'My love,' he said, 'Were you here, how you would comfort me.' Her partnership, companionship and love formed part of the personal way that he found strength amid the critics. Then in his letter, he reveals to Susannah how he will fundamentally cope with two particular slanders in the London papers. 'I shall go upstairs alone and pour out my griefs into my Saviour's ear. Jesus Lover of my soul, I to thy bosom fly!'[11]

Taking his deep wounds in full-hearted conversation to his Savior was Spurgeon's way. In the agony of grief, he said, 'Down on my knees I have often fallen, with the hot sweat rising from my brow under some fresh slander poured upon me.'[12] On his knees, amid the practical steps and personal help of his wife, Spurgeon found strength from personal communion with his Lord.

This point seems important for a student of Spurgeon's preaching; for criticism exposes a preacher to a further temptation which makes preaching difficult. It is the temptation to 'come out and defend' oneself. The reason why Spurgeon urged his father and others not to respond publicly to his attackers was that Spurgeon felt that whoever tries to defend himself 'is a great fool.' Instead, 'he who lets his detractors alone and like the eagle cares not for the chattering of the sparrows...he is the man and he shall be honored.' But 'oh!' he bellowed. 'Who is sufficient to steer clear from these rocks of danger?'[13] The preacher personally needs the ministry of the Spirit in these times. He must look to Christ for defense.

Inward Bleeding

In addition to the need for courage and the criticism often experienced by a preacher, the work of preaching is difficult because it entails seasons with no seeming 'success' and can inflict wounds described by Spurgeon as 'inward bleeding.' Overcoming such ailments requires more than oratorical skill, and preparation for such wounds tempts the preacher to desertion. He remarks: 'To go on tilling a thankless soil, to continue to cast bread upon the waters, and to find no return, has caused many a true heart to faint with inward bleeding.... Faint hearts of that kind there may be among my fellow-soldiers, ready to lay down the weapons of their warfare because they win no victory at this present.'[14]

Poignantly, even successful battles in preaching can dull the heart-condition of the maturing preacher. Spurgeon searchingly lamented this fact. 'We know,' he said, 'that there is more thought and more accuracy in our sermons, and that we use better elocution than we did in our young days; but where are the tears of our early ministry? Where is the heart-break...the passion...the self-annihilation that we often felt when we poured out our very life with every syllable we spoke?' Then, referring to God's withdrawing of power from Samson in the Old Testament, Spurgeon penetratingly asked maturing pastors: 'Brethren, what if the Lord should depart from us? Alas for us, and for our work! Nothing can be done if the Holy Spirit be withdrawn; indeed, nothing truly good will be attempted.'[15]

Sorrowful Spiritual Diseases
A preacher's temperament can also add to the inward conflict of preaching. 'Some are full of rejoicing,' Spurgeon observed, while 'others are often depressed.' 'A few keep the happy medium' but 'many soar aloft, and then dive into the deeps again.'[16] These moods of individual temperament can affect a person in surprising ways through an ordinary day. Spurgeon observes: 'There are a thousand different sorrows that cross over men's minds.' Spurgeon then explained what he meant. 'A working-man, for instance, may during the day feel depressed, and he does not know why. Some recollections of his early childhood may come across him, but he cannot tell why....'[17]

Spurgeon himself knew this kind of 'causeless' crying in a day. He testified that his 'spirits were sunken so low that' he 'could weep by the hour like a child, and yet not know what he wept for.'[18] Spurgeon wanted his students to know about the difficulty of trying to handle 'cause-less depression.' It 'cannot be reasoned with,' he said.[19] He felt that it was important for his students and hearers to know that sometimes believers can 'fall into sorrowful spiritual diseases' which have no connection to sin. Such depression, nervousness, fear and timidity, the kinds which make persons feel that they will despair, can take place in a person, he explained, 'without any particular sin as the cause.'[20]

Spurgeon understood depression because he himself suffered with ongoing and serious bouts of it. What is important for our study is to note that he did not hide this fact. Unique to older literature for preaching and pastors is Spurgeon's chapter for his ministerial students entitled, 'The Minister's Fainting Fits.' Spurgeon's view of testimony and redemptive transparency enabled him to speak plainly to students about the nature of depression in the pastoral ministry. 'Knowing by most painful experience what deep depression of spirit means, being visited there-with at seasons by no means few or far between,' Spurgeon said, 'I thought it might be consolatory to some of my brethren if I gave my thoughts thereon.'

Then Spurgeon offered his penetrating purposes for doing so. He first wanted to disrupt an idealistic view of preaching and preachers and help prepare men for its reality. He said that he desired that 'younger men might not fancy that some strange thing had happened to them when they became for a season possessed by melancholy.' He also wanted to disrupt idealistic views that struggling brethren might have about himself. He said to his class that he wanted 'sadder men [to] know that one upon whom the sun has shone so joyously did not always walk in the light.'[21] He listed and explained for them at least ten reasons why preachers can become depressed.

- Because preachers are human and broken

- Because preachers encounter various kinds of physical illness

- Because of the nature of a preacher's work with people

- Because a preacher's job is often a lonely one

- Because a preacher often does not exercise sufficiently

- Because a preacher does not know how to handle success

- Because God sometimes uses humbling to prepare preachers

- Because preachers do not get enough rest

- Because preachers are sometimes betrayed by friends

- Because preachers must sometimes handle multiple troubles

- Sometimes preachers are depressed with no apparent cause.

But Spurgeon extended his transparent desire to help the depressed beyond his students to those who came to hear him preach. A brief glance at Spurgeon's sermons elicits titles such as, 'Consolation for the Despairing,' 'A Call to the Depressed,' 'For the Troubled,' 'Songs for Desolate Hearts,' 'Encouragement for the Depressed,' and 'No Tears in Heaven.' He makes his hope for such preaching explicit. 'I shall be well rewarded this morning if I shall minister comfort to one heavy spirit.'[22]

Spurgeon generally identified three basic kinds of grief which form the experience of Christian people; (1) that grief which is incidental to all men; (2) that grief which arises from a sense of our sin; (3) that holy grief which cries for what Jesus cried for.[23] Each of these three sources for grief has a ready counselor because God cares for the sad heart and has made provision for it. Referring to Matthew 11:28, which says, 'Come unto me all you who are heavy laden,' Spurgeon said that God had provided promises of rest in Christ 'even to those who are most dark.'[24]

For those who doubted this, Spurgeon explained to them that God's character is different from the character of people. The tendency of people is to 'despise the broken heart.' But God's priority is to look after the broken hearted and to heal them. 'It is the nature of men to seek the cheerful and the happy and to avoid the broken-hearted. God does not do so.... He goes where they are, and he reveals himself to them as the Comforter and the Healer.'[25]

Spurgeon would also assure his hearers that God's care for the sad heart was thoroughly demonstrated in the Bible. The Scripture mourns with us and rejoices with us. He testified that Lamentations and Jeremiah and Job had mourned with him; whereas portions of the Psalms or the Songs of Solomon had rejoiced with him. Even the Apostle Paul 'was also often depressed by that which came daily upon him, the care of all the churches,' said Spurgeon. 'Yet, while he looked in the face of the evils which surrounded him, he was able to see beyond them, and to believe that the consequences of all his trials would be real and lasting good.'[26] For these reasons, the Bible was made intentionally by God to suit the realities of the broken. 'It tells us all what is in our heart, and talks to us as a living thing that has been in the deeps, and has been on the heights, that has known the overwhelming of affliction, and has rejoiced in the triumphs of delight.'[27]

Furthermore, the priority of care from God's character is not only demonstrated in the written Word but also in the person and work of Jesus. Jesus 'is One who can feel our grief because he has felt the same,' Spurgeon would say.[28] Jesus 'feels at his heart the sorrows of his people.' Therefore we must 'not think he is ever hard or unfeeling towards his poor, his afflicted, his depressed disciples. Nay, brethren, the heart of Jesus is full of tenderness.'[29]

For these reasons, Spurgeon even assured the 'mentally depressed' who were not Christians that their depression would not disqualify them from God's saving grace toward them. 'We say to despairing souls, we are personal witnesses that Christ has saved such as you are.... Be of good courage, there is hope for you.'[30]

God Redeems These Depressions
Spurgeon believed that God ruled over the depressions and trials of preachers and congregations. Because of this, they need not fear taking their trials to God nor need they fear that He will bring their good out of the ugly which challenges them in this life.

Perhaps the way Spurgeon spoke to others opens windows into his own inner dealings with his own sufferings. The Christian must surrender to the good fact that his trial is held in God's hand. This does not mean that God is the author of evil. No, Spurgeon believed fully in an actual devil and in actual evil of choice. But even these evils must bow before God. Therefore, Spurgeon would call upon the depressed or those in trial to remember that 'God is full of love, and therefore nothing that God sends can harm his child.' Profoundly, Spurgeon urged his hearers to come to the conviction that everything that God does in the life of His people is 'as a love-token.' Even if the trial seems like 'a stroke of his rod, or a cut of his knife,' everything 'from that dear hand must mean love.' Spurgeon rooted this conviction in the promises of God in the Bible. 'I have graven thee on the palms of my hands,' the Bible says. Therefore, when a person accepts 'every affliction as a love-token,' their fear can be overcome.[31]

Because of God's sole intention of love for His people, Spurgeon would also say that God will bring the sweetness of His joy alongside of and into the affliction. In a mysterious way, a follower of Jesus will grow into experiencing a 'connection between sorrow and joy,' such that sorrow always has 'a joy wrapped in it.' Not because the source of the grief is necessarily good; it might, in fact, be very evil. But, because evil cannot do anything to conquer the love of God in one's life, 'within the black envelop of affliction there is a love-token from God.' At times, this love-token is the discovered treasure of a sweet closeness to Christ amid 'the vessel of sorrow.'[32]

Or it is the presence of a kindling of fire that is somehow burning in the midst of the dark hail, thunder, and terrible rains of the soul. 'The creature can do little' due to its 'barrenness and desolation.' 'The more we try the more we sink', Spurgeon said. Often 'it seems' in this condition 'as if all human energy were but the energy to sin.' Where then is the love-token? How can such a miserable place picture a kindled fire? It is because our barrenness is 'the platform of his Divine power.' The flesh may profit nothing, but 'it is the Spirit' that quickens us. When this takes place, our desolation becomes, by His grace, the ugly 'setting for the sapphire of his everlasting love.'[33] In other words, 'God redeems these depressions.'[34]

He redeems them for preachers by using such infirmities to strengthen others. 'You will not be worth a pin as a preacher,' Spurgeon cautions, if you have never had difficulties yourselves. 'You cannot lift others out of despondency and depression,' he continues, 'unless you yourself have sometimes needed to be lifted out of such experiences.' For this reason, God allows infirmities for his preachers so that they can grow in the compassion needed to minister to His people.[35]

That God uses infirmities to strengthen preachers does not mean that preachers are meant to pursue or tackle infirmities alone. Students of Spurgeon learned that they are meant to lean on their 'fellow-workers' for encouragement amid their trials. Spurgeon's own transparency models this. Conversely, 'fellow-workers' are instructed by Spurgeon to grow in their ministry of encouragement to their pastors. 'To serve in any part of the spiritual army is dangerous, but to be a captain is to be doubly exposed,' Spurgeon explains. 'The most of the shots are aimed at the officers.' Therefore, Spurgeon urges those around the minister to pray for him and encourage him. They should pray for him regarding criticism, Satan's accusations, handling his own weakness, and the emotional demand of bearing with the troubles of those under his care. The preacher 'may be sighing and crying in his closet, while you, perhaps, are thanking God that your souls have been fed under him. Encourage your minister, I pray you.' See that he is resting upon God and receiving his divine power, and you will all know, each Sabbath day, the benefit of it.'[36]

Then Comes the Hissing Serpent
The preacher must learn to recognize when he most needs his fellow-workers. Often these times will arise when difficult circumstances, the sheer amount of work, continued criticisms, and personal temperament converge in a seeming conspiracy of assault. One such time in Spurgeon's life was the tragedy already mentioned at the Music Hall. But there were others. Spurgeon's sicknesses were not only emotional. He and his wife both struggled severely and continuously with physical sickness. Susannah was bedridden or nearly so for much of their married life. Charles suffered from a debilitating gout for the last twenty years of his ministry and it was coupled with rheumatism and inflammations of the kidneys. These physical infirmities often limited his ability to be in the pulpit and forced him at times to co-ordinate all the varying ministries under his charge from Mentone, France, where he and Susannah would go for physical recuperation. Amid these physical and emotional trials, Spurgeon's workload was immense. The orphanage, pastoring the four thousand members of the church, sermons, marriages, burials, weekly printed sermons, prayer meetings, editing *The Sword and Trowel*, the 500 weekly letters written to him, the Pastors' College, overseeing alumni and churches planted from their ministry, and the counsel sought daily from him by other ministers and ministries, joined the physical and emotional labor of him and his wife, such that by 1869, amid his wife's increasing

decline in health, Spurgeon was impaired by overwork. 'By the age of thirty, he had been used to do much more than is usually expected from a life-time of ministry.'[37] Amid these realities, Spurgeon describes how the convergence of trials could severely test his faith.

> When I was exceedingly ill in the South of France, and deeply depressed in spirit – so deeply depressed and so sick and ill that I scarce knew how to live, – one of those malicious persons who commonly haunt all public men, and especially ministers, sent me anonymously a letter, openly directed to 'That unprofitable servant C. H. Spurgeon.' This letter contained tracts directed to the enemies of the Lord Jesus, with passages marked and underlined, with notes applying them to myself. How many Rabshekahs have in their day written to me! Ordinarily I read them with the patience which comes of use, and they go to light the fire. I do not look for exemption from this annoyance, nor do I usually feel it hard to bear, but in the hour when my spirits were depressed, and I was in terrible pain, this reviling letter cut me to the quick. I turned upon my bed and asked – Am I, then, an unprofitable servant? I grieved exceedingly, and could not lift up my head, or find rest... I wonder that any human being should find pleasure in trying to inflict pain upon those who are sick and depressed; yet are there persons who delight to do so.[38]

Spurgeon attributes such convergences ultimately to the warfare that is not against flesh and blood, but is spiritual. 'Satan is a great coward,' Spurgeon observes. 'He will generally meddle with God's people when they are down.' Then Spurgeon explains what he means from his own experience. 'I find that when I am in good physical health, I am not often tempted of Satan to despondency or doubt; but whenever I get depressed in spirit, or the liver is out of order, or the head aches, then comes the hissing serpent.'[39]

Clinging to Christ's Dear Skirts
Fundamental to Spurgeon's approach to handling the hissing serpent amid his own depression and trials was remembering that those trials did not change the fact that

a Christian is a child whom God dearly and everlastingly loves. Satan's strategy is to whisper when you are down. He wants to say to you that 'God has forsaken you, you are no child of God, you are unfaithful to your Master, yea have no part in the blood of sprinkling.' For Spurgeon, it is the doctrine of justification personally applied and experienced that Satan seeks to undo in the Lord's preachers. Spurgeon exhorted Christians that they must expect that when they lose sight of their sense of justification, when they are conscious of sin and feel unfit to minister before God, 'just then,' the enemy 'will come to accuse' them.[40]

Two examples offer insight for preaching students regarding how we fight the challenges of the moment and the harassments of Satan. Two foes who seek to rob us of our due sense of the fatherly love and forgiving grace of God for us in Christ.

> I have been very sick and full of pain, and depressed in spirit, and I have judged myself to be of all men most unworthy, and I judged truly. I stand to that judgment still. I felt myself only worthy to be shaken like dust from off the feet of my Lord, and cast into the bottomless pit for ever. Then it was that my Substitute was my hope, and in my lonely chamber at Mentone I clung to his dear skirts; I looked into his wounds; I trusted myself with him again, and I know that I am a saved man. I tell you there is no salvation in any other, but only in Jesus.[41]

This 'clinging to Christ's dear skirts' refers to the believer turning afresh to the old truths about himself in God. 'I have found it a blessed thing in my own experience, to plead before God that I am His child,' Spurgeon said.[42] One of the most compelling glimpses of Spurgeon clinging in this way, trusting the truth that his pains did not undo the love of God for him, is an experience that Spurgeon had in Mentone during 1871, which became a story he sometimes told to encourage others.

> When some months ago, I was racked with pain to an extreme degree, so that I could no longer bear it without crying out. I asked all to go from the room and leave me

alone; and then I had nothing I could say to God but this, 'Thou are my Father, and I am Thy child; and Thou, as a Father, art tender and full of mercy. I could not bear to see my child suffer as Thou makest me suffer; and if I saw him tormented as I am now, I would do what I could to help him and put my arms under him to sustain him. Wilt Thou hide Thy face from me, my Father? Wilt Thou still lay on me Thy heavy hand, and not give me a smile from Thy countenance?'[43]

Spurgeon testified how his Heavenly Father comforted him and eased his pain. He said then to his hearers, 'I think this is why that prayer, "Our Father which art in heaven," is given to us, because, when we are lowest, we can still say, "Our Father." And 'when it is very dark, and we are very weak, our childlike appeal can go up, "Father, help me! Father, rescue me!"'[44]

The Motto of the Gospel Preacher

In the context of the fainting fits, Spurgeon established a motto for the gospel preacher. It is a motto which assumes more than mental power as the resource for the preacher. The motto derives from the Apostle Paul who asked, 'Who is sufficient for these things?' Such a motto leads the preacher away from himself and on to a God-ward hope. 'God has not taken his heart from us, nor his care from us, nor his interest from us,' Spurgeon declares. God 'is bound up heart and soul with his people, and their holy warfare.'[45]

Consequently, the preacher must learn to live humbly with what God has not made him to be while pursuing boldly what God has given him to do. To avoid ministry for fear of exposing weakness or not measuring up to another's gifts is to misunderstand the nature of divine calling. A man's temperament, providential story, measures of depressions and infirmities, all form the context of his God-given gifts and are meant to be stewarded for joining others in glorifying God until Christ comes. Therefore, Spurgeon assures the faithful that they are God's children and have His love. With this confidence he says to preachers, 'Friend, be true to your own destiny! Apollos has the gift of eloquence; why must he copy blunt Cephas?'[46] In other words, 'Be yourself, dear brother! Do not be a mere copyist, a borrower, a spoiler of other men's notes. Say what God has said to you, and say it in your own way; and when it is so said, plead personally for the Lord's blessing upon it.'[47]

The student of preaching must come to terms with the fact that kindled fire arises amid the weakness of a man called by God. God demonstrates His strength in our weakness. This principle must inform our views of what a kindled fire will look like.

Conclusion

Spurgeon certainly encountered kindled fire throughout his ministry and experienced profound waves of the Spirit's power. But none of this took away the trials of a fallen world – its sickness, emotional struggles, criticism, and difficult circumstances. Kindled fire takes place in the midst of, and not in spite of, our need for a new Kingdom to come. The Spirit will demonstrate His power so that our preaching will exhibit more than that which is merely mental and common to rhetorical study. But it will be the lame, the depressed, the broken, the accused, who will exhibit this flame. 'Rainbows are delightful sights, and a vision of Jesus is rapturous and transporting,' Spurgeon counseled, 'but we cannot expect to see him, I say, unless it is when the storm is over or when another storm is coming on.'[48]

Sometimes when seeking what Spurgeon sought for relevant and powerful preaching, students might tend to approach it naively. But kindled fire manifests the strength of God alongside the preacher's weakness so that the power can be seen as having its origin in God. 'Without the Spirit of God we can do nothing; we are as ships without wind, or chariots without steeds; like branches without sap, we are withered; like coals without fire we are useless.' May we desire both to feel and confess this fact whenever we attempt to preach.[49]

Questions for Learning and Discussion

1. How do you handle criticism?

2. What do you think about how Spurgeon spoke about his trials?

3. What provisions has God made for our depressions? What depressions have you known? How has God ministered to you?

4. What is the role of fellow-workers in facing criticism and depression?

5. Do you agree with Spurgeon about the role of experiencing the benefit of our justification amid our trials? Do you know this 'sense' of it?

6. How does Spurgeon's inclusion of 'the Fainting Fits' in his instruction of students shape the way he wanted us to learn about the manifestation of the Spirit's power?

7. What will you take with you from this chapter?

13

OUR FELLOW WORKERS:

Sharing the Ministry

With 'the Holy Spirit' as 'the actual agent,' says Spurgeon, with 'the Word preached, and the prayers of the people as the instruments...'we have thus explained the cause of a true revival of religion.[1]

Bishop Lightfoot, the famed Anglican, upon giving an address to a meeting of junior clergy in 1884, lamented the spiritual decline evident in his times. One answer to this decline, according to Lightfoot, was that his Anglican brethren must recognize again the power of a mobilized laity. 'An untold mine of missionary power is here,' he said. Such a power, he felt, would enable the Anglican Church to 'cope with the spiritual destitution' of the age.[2]

Spurgeon would have agreed with such a sentiment. Human 'agents' who are to use their remote and near tools are categorized, not just as 'public teachers,' but also as 'private believers.'[3] Both public teachers and private believers are 'fellow workers' who have spiritual work to do.

A student of the Pastors' College would witness the practice of this theology in the daily life of the Metropolitan Tabernacle. Such a theology assumes that power in the pulpit is interconnected and interdependent on an analogous power from God's Spirit in the congregation. Yes, it is true and fundamental that God, who is the primary preacher, intends to arrive upon the scene and demonstrate His power upon that preacher in the preaching. But equally true is that God pairs His voice with the preacher's *in community.*

The fact that God 'works by instrumentalities' means that He may move, not just one, but 'a number of persons to act together' for the sake of 'a soul.' 'In this way,' both 'people and ministers may unite in bringing sinners to the Savior.'[4] For this reason, as hinted at earlier, one cannot delve very long into Spurgeon's literature before discovering the phrase, 'my fellow-workers.' Borrowing the phrase from Paul (Colossians 4:11), Spurgeon was convinced that preachers and members are meant to work side by side in seeking the spiritual power necessary from God to revive and transform their communities.

The Ordinary Call of Private Believers

If you had applied to the Pastors' College and your application had been denied by President Spurgeon, the letter which informed you of your status with the College would have given instruction as to the value of your current vocation. To 'Dear Mr. Tooke,' for example, Spurgeon wrote: 'In your present calling you can serve the Lord and maintain yourself.... I would counsel you to go on as you are, and do all you can for our Lord. I must decline your application.'[5]

Spurgeon's beliefs concerning the value of the laity are rooted in John Calvin and the Puritan stream. Calvin stated, for example, that God calls every person to a place with a purpose for living. These 'various kinds of living' are given by God to each of His children as a kind of 'sentry post' in the world.[6] The beneficent consequence of such a calling is that a person can know that 'no task will be so sordid or base, provided you obey your calling in it, that it will not shine and be reckoned very precious in God's sight.'[7]

Spurgeon seems to have taken this concept of calling and connected it to the concept of instrumentality. When one places the 'appointed ways' of the Spirit within the locale of individual callings, a community ministry emerges. The preacher's work as an instrument in the Spirit's hands, though central to rediscovering lasting pulpit-power in a generation, does not usurp the necessary and God-glorifying work of daily labor by so-called 'private believers.' The value of 'private believers' in their daily work formed the rationale for student housing at the Pastors' College. Students would live during the two to three years of their course-work with a families who were members of the Tabernacle. Responding to a nervous father regarding this strange arrangement for his son, Spurgeon makes his conviction on this point clear. He believed that pastoral training often invited an unwitting evil to become a part of a young man's life and ministry; mainly, the emergence of a 'levity' which arises from separating a man from 'common social life.' Deeming this separation a 'serious injury' to the ministry, Spurgeon explained to the inquiring father that 'when a young man resides in a Christian family, not only is he under the most vigilant oversight, but he never ceases to be one of the people.'[8] That ministers must 'never cease to be one of the people' remained a hallmark of Spurgeon's approach to pastoral training. Even when a building was finally erected for the college in 1874, residential facilities were intentionally left out of the plans.

Toward this end, Spurgeon instructed his hearers that their calling in the world was 'God's work' for them. He said to them: 'The truest religious life is that in which a man follows the ordinary calling of life in the spirit of a Christian.'[9] Spurgeon pointed to the Christmas shepherds, or the Apostle Peter fishing, in order to illustrate his idea of 'ordinary' calling. The evident strength of Christianity in an age is demonstrated in the vibrancy of Christian testimony amid ordinary callings. 'Our Christianity,' said Spurgeon, 'shows itself more...to the world, in the pursuits of daily life, than it does in the engagements of the house of God.' What a profound statement. A Christian's life outside of church has as much power for the gospel in the world as that which takes place within the church walls. Consequently, Spurgeon not only urged men and women to attend church, but he also identified mothers, fathers, and people of business as doing meaningful work for the Lord. He even lamented that 'some people seem to think that hard work in attending to ordinary business is not spiritual-minded in a Christian.'[10] In Spurgeon's thinking, then, every Christian 'sanctifies his ordinary calling to the cause of Christ, and makes himself the Lord's servant in everything.' No matter what his post in life, the Christian says, 'Here, Lord, I give myself to thee.'[11]

For this reason, Spurgeon was concerned to correct what he thought was an errant notion. 'It has *come* to be a dreadfully common belief in the Christian Church that the only man who has a "call",' he said, 'is the man who devotes all his time to the "ministry".' 'Christian service is ministry,' Spurgeon countered, 'and every Christian has a call to some kind of ministry or another.'[12] As seen in chapter 2, Spurgeon maintained the centrality of the sacred office of preacher. He would never let his students forget this. A student of President Spurgeon would also learn that as a pastor, one must dignify, encourage and even depend upon the working of God amid the ordinary callings of one's church members.

Clergy and Laity

There is no more central place for demonstrating the inter-dependence of fellow-workers than in the pastor's relation-ship with his elders and deacons. Spurgeon's relationship with his fellow officers of elder and deacon was real in its devotion and real in its human nature. The devotion his fellow-workers had for Spurgeon is evidenced by the nick-name they gave to him, 'The Governor.' They referred to him as such and often the repeated refrain among them was that 'there must only be one captain of the ship.'[13] That the relationship was real in its human nature is evidenced by an anecdote Spurgeon told of his days at the Tabernacle. On one occasion, as a deacon came down to the commun-ion table during a Sunday morning service, the Governor inquired how many new members were to be received that morning. To this the deacon replied, 'only seven.' He then said to Spurgeon, 'This won't pay, Governor; running all this big place for seven new members in a month!' Spur-geon muses that such comments, though they were hurtful, were taken in the context of mutual respect. He implies in his autobiography that if the minister and the deacon were each vying for who had more authority, then such a comment could divide them. In contrast, Spurgeon believed he and his officers were on equal footing in terms of value and calling. Their relational devotion toward one another seemed to allow them to weather conflicts together. Hints of these conflicts are ample in his autobiography. But they are placed into the context of anecdotes such as this one. Spurgeon recounts how after a long bout with illness, which kept him out of the pulpit for weeks, the Governor said to one of the deacons, 'I am afraid you will get quite tired of your poor crippled minister.' But one of the men spoke quickly in response. 'Why, my dear sir, we would sooner have you for one month in the year than anyone else in the world for the whole twelve months!'[14]

Spurgeon's relational pursuit of his officers seems to have evidenced itself in his approach to the people of his congregation. Perhaps this feeling of camaraderie and value was regularly reinforced by how Spurgeon spoke of his officers and members from the pulpit. While Spurgeon strenuously upheld his conviction of a sacred office, he did not mean that those who are called to the sacred office have more value or favor with God. As it relates to one's value to God and one's capacity for ministry, he surprisingly said: 'We know nothing of any distinction between "clergy" and "laity".' 'All God's people are God's clergy or if there be any laity, any common people, all God's people are the laity.'[15]

Spurgeon's concerns on this point were global, theological, practical and natural. Globally, he felt that nothing was more disastrous to the cause of Christianity than leaving the work of the gospel on only a few shoulders. The cause of Christ is hindered when the people of Christ are little aware of their role in spreading the good news. Theologically, he believed that the unction of the Spirit was meant not just for the sacred office of preacher but also for the callings of every believer. 'We shall never see the world turned upside down as it was in apostolic times until we get back to the apostolic practice, that all the saints are filled with the Holy Ghost, and speak for Christ as the Spirit gives them utterance.'[16] The Spirit's presence should be sought in every sphere of calling. Spurgeon expected the attendant power of God to fall, not only in the moment of preaching, but also in varying degrees in the ordinary moments of life. He could say: 'I fear that the presence of God is not often felt as it ought to be at a dinner-table, when a number of people are met together and are enjoying themselves.'[17] His concern was also a practical one. The needs of any given community are too great for the sacred officers to handle

alone. 'What can one overseer do? What could twenty pastors do?' Spurgeon asked, 'It is impossible if you leave this
work entirely to us that it will ever be properly discharged.
Oh no! Let each member have his own office in the body.'[18]
Furthermore, the nature of some callings meant that the
weight of their tasks required recognition beyond that of
the preacher. Spurgeon often made this point with Sunday
school teachers.

> But when you teach in Sabbath-schools, you are, if it
> be possible, in a more responsible situation even than
> a minister occupies. He preaches to grown-up people,
> to men of judgment, who, if they do not like what he
> preaches, can go somewhere else; but you teach children
> who have no option of going elsewhere. If you teach the
> child wrongly, he believes you; if you teach him heresies,
> he will receive them; what you teach him now, he will
> never forget.[19]

Your Various Spheres of Service

For these global, theological, practical and natural reasons
Spurgeon believed that when he came into the pulpit his
'dear friends' who heard him would likewise go into their
'various spheres of service with the comforting thought'
that neither the preacher nor the people were 'laboring in
vain' or spending their 'strength' for nothing.[20] He commonly
described his congregants as 'fellow workers' or 'fellow
members.' He would remind these 'fellow workers,' that the
Lord can use feeble instruments. Therefore any believer in
Christ can say to God, 'Why not me?' Spurgeon believed
that God may use persons who are not commonly called
to great public engagements for great purposes. He often
pointed in his sermons to ordinary people in the Bible who
were used greatly by God. Turning to the Old Testament
book of Judges, for example, Spurgeon pointed out that
the woman who slew Sisera was 'no orator but a woman
who milked the cows and made butter.' Then Spurgeon
asked his hearers: 'May not the Lord use any one of us to
accomplish his purpose?' Then making a contrast between
that cow-tender's purpose and Sisera's own intention, he
gave instruction:

Somebody may come to the house today, even as Sisera came to Jael's tent. Be it ours, not to slay him, but to save him. Let us receive him with great kindness, and then bring forth the blessed truth of salvation by the Lord Jesus, our great Substitute, and press home the command, 'Believe and live.'[21]

For Spurgeon, therefore, the preacher's hearers possess an ordinary calling by God which leads them into the instrumental agency of the Spirit of God. Prior to the preaching event, therefore, many of the preacher's hearers are laboring instrumentally in the hands of the Spirit, as 'fellow workers' in the common cause of the gospel. Therefore, the purpose of the preacher gains a community orientation. The preacher must not think that his task is merely to inform and educate. Rather, the pulpit is meant to be 'a fountain from which streams of beneficence flow forth' into the surrounding community. Spurgeon applied this point to his own preaching:

This Tabernacle is not a mere theological lecture platform. It is a fountain from which streams of beneficence are ever flowing forth. Our friend would never be satisfied with crowds listening to his eloquent voice, if those crowds were not prompted to go away to do all the good they can, imitating his example, and blessing the neighborhood round about.[22]

Consequently, the congregation is meant to learn a community orientation from the preacher. They too know that their church is not their own but meant for the gospel in community. Not only is Spurgeon not afraid to speak openly of the Holy Spirit from the pulpit, but he publicly declares value and casts a vision for the daily life of God's people. For example, he calls them not to try to be preachers. Theirs is not 'to seek precedence in public assemblies.' Rather he says to them, you are called:

To exert influence in private society...by a good conversation, with a speech seasoned with salt, at home among friends, kinsfolk, or companions, to the dozen or to one,

make known what love has done, what grace has done,
what Christ has done. Make it known; make it known.
Among your servants, among your children, among your
tradespeople – wherever you go make it known; make it
known.[23]

In other words, all believers in their sphere of calling has a
testimony of life and words to bring to their God-given place
in the world. Such testimonies fill the community with those
who speak and live with people for God and who speak and
live with God for people.

Ministries of Individual Earnestness to the Outside World
First, the sacred office is not meant to be alone in its proclamation of the gospel in a community. The congregation
is meant to speak and live with people for God. This means
that every Christian, alongside the preacher, is called to
communicate the gospel in his or her ordinary, public
or private spheres of human agency. Though Spurgeon
limits the formal and public proclamation of the Bible to
called men, he honors and urges the gospel-declarations
of women and non-publicly called men in other spheres of
instrumentality. Both 'brethren and sisters' are his 'fellow-
workers,' and he considers such 'workers and...sufferers'
as 'the cream of the church.'[25] He therefore calls upon all
Christian men and women to take an awakened posture of
communication in their spheres of calling. Church officers
and church members are meant to labor alongside him for
the gospel.

> My fellow workers – deacons and elders, honored Church
> officers – will you draw back in this day of hopefulness,
> and refrain to sow the seed, when the field is ploughed
> and ready for the grain? Church members – ye young
> men that can speak in public, ye women that can in your
> households talk of Christ – will any of you be dull and
> lethargic *now*?[26]

The preacher is not the only one seeking the Spirit of God
through the week. Actually, the preacher stands up to
preach in the context of a Spirit-active community. What

the preacher intends to do centrally for his sacred office, the hearer intends supplementally by his spheres of calling in the world. The Spirit is active in every member of His people toward the larger goal of God's glory in the community. 'The Holy Spirit waters us by the admonitions of parents, by the kind suggestions of friends, by the teaching of his ministers, by the example of all his saints...he takes care to do it by our fellow-workers, putting an honor upon his own servants by using them in instrumentality.'[27]

Important, therefore, is the recognition that the gospel preacher proclaims his message by the power of the Holy Spirit, in a context in which that same Spirit is presently active in the private spheres of proclamation that have been given by God to non-preachers amid their ordinary callings. Spurgeon applies the doctrine of unction, usually ascribed to the calling of the preacher, to extend in some sense to every member of the church for their callings.

> The divine Spirit blows also from other quarters. Sometimes he uses one man, sometimes another...it comes through different instrumentalities in the same Church. Sometimes the wind blows from this pulpit: God blesses me to your conversion. Another time it is from my good sister, Mrs. Bartlett's class; on a third occasion it is the Sunday-school; again, it may be another class, or the preaching of the young men, or from the individual exertion of private believers. God causes that wind to blow just which way he wills.[28]

Therefore, the preacher not only must look for endowments of power for his ministry but he must look for them also for the callings of his fellow workers in the world. 'Let the Spirit of God be in the church,' Spurgeon exhorted. 'Then there is power given to all her ministries; whether they be ministries of public testimony in the preaching of the word, or ministries of holy love amongst the brethren, or ministries of individual earnestness to the outside world.'[29] The result is that Spurgeon urged every Christian, both the public preachers and private communicators, to their instrumental agency within their various spheres of proclamation:

Any Christian has a right to disseminate the gospel who has the ability to do so; and more, he not only has the right, but it is his duty...the propagation of the gospel is left, not to a few, but to all the disciples of the Lord Jesus Christ: according to the measure of grace entrusted to him by the Holy Spirit....[30]

That which distinguishes 'public teachers' from 'private believers' does not reside, therefore, in the fact that one communicates the gospel message and the other does not. Rather, both are called to gospel communication within their appropriate places. Spurgeon never equates the testimony of private spheres with the necessary preaching of the sacred office. The nature of one's sphere of calling determines the nature of one's speaking ministry. But the kind of calling one has received, far from negating gospel communication outside of the pulpit, actually anticipates and requires appropriate spheres of life in which the Spirit of God regularly demonstrates instrumental gospel influence. The preacher gives himself to public proclamation, therefore, while audience-members are giving themselves to non-pulpit and private testimony of the gospel. Power in preaching resides in communal interactivity of God's people. Spurgeon asks:

What is the preacher to do, what is the church to do, if the workers are half asleep? Sunday-school teachers going through their duty with great regularity and no spirituality; people going about with their tracts when they might almost as well go about with Sunday newspapers, for they have no love to the souls of the people! What is the result if we have deacons and church-officers going about without any life or spiritual power?[31]

This communal activity of the Spirit explains why Spurgeon commends the 'laboring man, a suffering woman, a servant-girl, a chimney-sweeper, or a crossing sweeper' as 'servants of God' and 'soul winners.' Soul winning, Spurgeon declared, 'belongs not to the learned doctor of divinity, or to the eloquent preacher alone, but to you all who are in Christ Jesus.'[32] Consequently, while the preacher labors in the appointed means of communicating Christ from the Bible, so the 'fellow worker' in his or her daily calling serves by speaking a gospel testimony in the world.

At Home Pleading Earnestly
Therefore, the preacher doesn't speak of Christ by himself. Neither then does the preacher pray to God by himself. Spurgeon assumes that the work of God has a community orientation. When asked by some American visitors to the Tabernacle what was the secret of his success, Spurgeon replied: 'My people pray for me.'[33] Spurgeon's reply was no mere sentimentality. He meant it. 'We poor mortals, whom God has called to be preachers,' he declared, 'are desperately dependent upon our congregations. I do not say that we rest on you first, our chief dependence must be upon God; but a praying; loving, earnest, wakeful people will keep the minister awake.'[34] Therefore, Spurgeon looked actively to the prayers of the congregation as an 'aid' to his preaching: 'I shall feel it a joyous work,' he said, 'to be the lamplighter to-night for my Master, if I know that I have you at home pleading earnestly on my behalf. Give me this aid this morning.'[35]

The basis for such a view returns one to the themes of insufficiency, the Spirit's power, instrumentality, and the presence of sin and spiritual warfare.

> The minister is sent to be God's messenger for the quickening of the dead. What can he do in it? He can do nothing whatever unless the Spirit of God be with him through the prayer of his brethren...and if we be put to this work but have not your prayers, and in consequence have not the supply of the Spirit, we are of all men the most miserable.[36]

A preacher fulfilling his sacred office depends upon the people in their private offices. A community of prayer must form as God's appointed means of demonstrated power.

> No army fights well when its camp is unguarded.... While some of us are teaching in the school or preaching in the street, we have great comfort in knowing that a certain

number of our friends are praying for us. To me it is a boundless solace that I live in the prayers of thousands.... Therefore, as for those who cannot come into the front places of warfare, deny them not seats of honor, since, after all, they may be doing the greater good.[37]

The lack of this 'congregational warfare' leaves many ministers weak. 'How many ministers are weak for warfare with sin,' Spurgeon lamented, 'because they are not supported by a godly people, and their hands are not held up by praying brethren!'[38]

Just as a community of proclamation fills the neighborhoods with gospel speech to people, so a community of supplication will fill the neighborhoods surrounding the pulpit with gospel speech to God. In this way, Godward speaking begins to surround the pulpit hour. Every act of labor in every place is meant to sound forth conversation with God. Spurgeon described what surrounded his labor in England:

> The true Christian will pray in business; he will pray in labor; he will pray in his ordinary calling: like sparks out of the smithy chimney short prayers fly up all day long from truly devout souls. Not thus is it with the mere pretender. The hypocrite prays at prayer-meetings, and his voice is heard in the assembly, sometimes at tedious length; but will he pray with ejaculatory prayer? Will he speak with God at the counter? Will he draw near to God in the field? Will he plead with his Lord in the busy street with noiseless pleadings? When he finds that a difficultly has occurred in his daily life, will he without saying a word breathe his heart into the ear of God?[39]

Because of this, the preacher never steps up to preach alone. He steps up to preach in the context of a gospel-speaking and gospel-praying people. This context of daily prayer culminates in instrumental aid as preacher and people approach the pulpit-event: 'If we acted aright, we should never come even to the hearing of a sermon without prayer; were our hearts in a proper spiritual condition, we should never leave our houses to go to the house of prayer, without first supplicating God to help the minister and to help us.'[40]

Moreover, Spurgeon assumes that prayer will take place during the worship service. Spurgeon describes the kinds of praying that he means. Such praying fellow-workers ask God to aid the preacher: 'Lord, help him to speak the truth out-right, and put thy power into it to send it home to the hearts and consciences of the hearers.' Spurgeon then encourages his hearers 'to pick out some one in the congregation, and pray, "Lord, bless the word to him."'[41]

Spurgeon was convinced that prayer formed the heart of the Spirit's appointed ways. Divine power for the gospel in a generation required this communal praying. The depth of his conviction was demonstrated during a time when he was absent from the pulpit due to various and severe illness. Upon hearing that attendance was less when he was not the one preaching that morning, Spurgeon wrote a moving exhortation to his fellow-workers. His statements highlight the direct correlation that prayer in spheres of calling has to preaching power:

> Have you begun to be of Spurgeon? This will never do. God can bless one man as well as another. I do not know that he always does do so, but he can; and perhaps if you expected him to do so he would do so. If you came up to this house with the same prayerfulness for others as you apportion me, you would get the same blessing. I am weakest of the weak apart from God, therefore pray for me; but others are weak too, therefore pray for them also. Do let us pray mightily for a blessing. Pray always. Pray in your bed-chambers, at your family altars, at your work, and in your leisure, and also in this place. Come in larger numbers to pray for a blessing.[42]

Mysterious Agencies Cooperating with the Ministries of Grace

Within this communal activity are spheres of proclamation: 'It is the Holy Spirit, then, who is everywhere in the midst of his Church, who comes forth and puts himself into direct contact with a human spirit.'[43] This communal activity of interdependence between preacher and people, between the sacred and private offices of ordinary believers, forms the context in which providence works. Harkening back to our exploration of mysterious agencies in chapter one, Spurgeon looks to this unseen working of God to form a basis for hope larger than the labor of the pulpit itself.

'We do not reckon that the forces engaged upon our side are confined to the pulpit,' he said. 'We know that, all the week long, God is, by care, and affliction, and trouble, and sometimes by joy and consolation, making the people ready to receive what He has charged us to teach them.'[44] God uses the testimony and prayers of His people in a community to prepare individuals within that community to embrace the gospel proclaimed by the preacher. Spurgeon assumes that his words are not the first movements of God in a person's life. After referring to the prayers of a mother, the words of a friend or the afflictions of living, Spurgeon can say to his hearers: 'Perhaps the chance words of this night are no chance words to some of you now present, but the very words of God sent straight to your soul.' He then speaks to God in their presence. 'God grant that it may be so, and he shall have the praise. O eternal Spirit, thus let it be.'[45]

Conclusion
The spiritual power of gospel preaching is a community concern. Each believer according to his or her sphere of calling testifies as a fellow worker of Christ and prays through Christ to God in the world. The result is a community of interdependent proclamation and prayer in local neighborhoods which God providentially will use to bring power to the preaching of His Word. God intends to arrive upon the scene of a community and work in lives of individuals. President Spurgeon sought to inculcate this view of ministry into his students by their living arrangements and by the example of ministry they saw lived out. Kindled fire ultimately is a corporate event. The fruition of a longing for kindled fire will demonstrate a re-ignition of spiritual power in the pulpit and beyond it. That a preacher must carry out his ministry within an interdependent Spirit-gifted community reminds preachers of every generation that more than one man's skills of oratory are necessary for true gospel power.

These assumptions lie at the root of Spurgeon's view of preaching. All that we've explored throughout this book assumes a communal context. When the Spirit attends with power, He promotes community and minimizes an isolated individualism. Preachers and people, in their various callings and with their various weaknesses, each have a role to play for the glory of God manifested in a generation. Thus, Spurgeon leaned on the community as they leaned on him, each crying out for God to kindle a fire for their world.

Before the turn of the twentieth century, Charles Spurgeon had gone home to be with His Lord. But his earnest exhortation for a kindled fire among an interdependent community of preachers and peoples remains with us:

> I ask you, then, dear brethren and sisters who are alive to God, to pray that Jesus would speak while the preacher speaks. Be lifting up your hearts and silently crying: 'Oh! Let the dead now hear thy voice, Bid, Lord, thy banished ones rejoice; Their beauty this, their glorious dress, Jesus, the Lord, our righteousness.'[46]

Questions for Learning and Discussion

1. What strikes you most from this chapter?

2. What is it that distinguishes the callings of preachers and lay people?

3. Why do you need community if you are going to seek spiritual power for your preaching? What changes does this suggest to your approach to preaching power?

4. How can you remind your congregation of their callings and how theirs relates to yours?

5. How does the preacher's need of community inform a preacher's view of relevance and power for a generation?

6. What will you take with you from this chapter?

7. What will you take you with from this book?

Appendix

A Summary of Spurgeon's View of Preaching

	Mental Power	Spiritual Power
Identifying Traits	Natural Talent and Skill	Gifts and Grace from God
Theory of Preaching	• Speaker, Message, Audience • Five Canons of rhetoric • Instruct, Please, Move	• Speaker, Message, Audience, and God • Six Canons of Rhetoric • Pray, Instruct, Please, Testify, and Move
Theorists for Preaching	Aristotle, Demosthenes, Cicero, Bacon, Blair, etc	The Holy Spirit via Biblical Prophets, Apostles, and Jesus
Manuals for Preaching	*Rhetoric, De Oratore,* etc	The Bible
Purpose of Preaching	Natural and temporal persuasion for a purpose	Soul and eternal persuasion in Christ
Problems for Preaching	Media proliferation, Loss of authority, Skepticism/Unbelief, Attention spans, Time pressures, Plagiarism, Seminary training, Logic, Sermon length, and Story needs	These plus a trans-generational spiritual war in the souls of both preacher and people.
Solutions for Preaching	Find available means for Persuasion, Less or no sermons, Shorter sermon length, Plagiarism, Stories, Seminary training, Art, Music, Architecture, Less Bible/Darwin, Less Authoritative, Victorian Decorum	The appointed instrumental means of the Spirit, The appointed Scripture manner of the Spirit, Plain Talk, Direct, Familiar, Vulgar, Soul Conditions, Sacred Emotion, Holy Fancy, Opening Mercy's Door
Sermon Preparation	The preacher's invention	The communal instrumentality of the Spirit, Spheres of calling, Spheres of proclamation, Spheres of prayer
Sermon Delivery	The preacher's skills and the human voice	The Scripture manner and the Dual voice
Sermon Evaluation	Immediate response/effects common to non-gospel oratory	Christ-ward, Soul-movement, not necessarily immediate
Implications	Changing assumptions	Nothing new under the sun

References

Introduction

[1] See 'How to Meet the Evils of the Age', 'The Evils of the Present Time and our Object, Necessities, and Encouragements', 'The Preacher's Power and the Conditions of Obtaining It', and 'The Minister in These Times', in *An All Around Ministry* (1900 reprint, Edinburgh: Banner of Truth, 1986).

[2] Spurgeon, *An All Around Ministry*, 296.

[3] Charles Spurgeon, *The Downgrade Controversy* (Ages Digital Library, 1998), 77.

[4] See Anthony Wilson Thorold, 'The Evangelical Clergy of 1868', *The Contemporary Review* 8 (1868): 583, B. G. Johns, 'The Traffic in Sermons', *The Nineteenth Century* 31 (1892): 198. See also, A. P. Peabody, 'Sermons and Sermonizers', *Fraser's Magazine for Town and Country* 55 (1857): 88, J. Baldwin Brown, 'Is the Pulpit Losing its Power?', *The Living Age* 133 (1877): 304, 310, John M. Titzel, 'The Pulpit: Its Province and its Power', *The Reformed Quarterly Review* 31 (1884): 134, Louisa A. Merivale, 'Modern Preaching', *Fraser's Magazine for Town and Country* 79 (1869): 257.

[5] Vincent E. Bacote, *The Spirit in Public Theology: Appropriating the Legacy of Abraham Kuyper* (Grand Rapids, Michigan: Baker Academic, 2005), 56.

[6] Charles Spurgeon, 'Eyes Right', *Metropolitan Tabernacle Pulpit*, Vol. 34 (Ages Digital Library, 1998), 885.

[7] For a full exploration of these discussions in the literature of the times, see Zachary Eswine, 'The Role of the Holy Spirit in the Preaching Theory and Practice of Charles Haddon Spurgeon', Ph.D. Dissertation (Virginia Beach, Virginia: Regent University, 2003), 58-88.

[8] Charles Spurgeon, *The Letters of Charles Haddon Spurgeon* (Ages Digital Library, 1998), 213.

[9] Robinson, 'Sermons and Preaching', 413-14.

[10] Evans, 'Discourse upon Sermons', 59, 62.

[11] Robinson, 'Sermons and Preaching', 411.

[12]William Davies, 'The English Pulpit', *Littell's Living Age* 120 (1874): 67.

[13]Merivale, 'Modern Preaching', 268.

[14]Author Unknown, 'The Pulpit', *Tait's Edinburgh Magazine* (1859): 413.

[15]Ibid., 416.

[16]Fanny Fern, 'Notes Upon Preachers and Preaching', in *Folly as It Flies* (New York: G.W. Carleton and Co., 1869), 90.

[17]Ibid.

[18]Henry Allon, 'What is Evangelical Preaching?', *The Congregational Review* 2 (1888): 1067.

[19]Alfred Garvie, *The Christian Preacher* (New York: Charles Scribner's Sons, 1921), 4.

[20]See Spurgeon's 'Attention!' in *Lectures to My Students.*

[21]Charles Spurgeon, 'Harvest Men Wanted', in *The Metropolitan Tabernacle Pulpit*, Vol. 19 (Ages Digital Library, 1998), 567.

[22]Charles Spurgeon, 'The Miracles of our Lord's Death', in *The Metropolitan Tabernacle Pulpit*, Vol. 34 (Ages Digital Library, 1998), 895.

[23]Charles Spurgeon, *Autobiography*, Vol. 2, The *Full Harvest* (reprinted, Edinburgh: Banner of Truth, 1995), 48.

[24]Charles Spurgeon, 'Pentecost', in *The Metropolitan Tabernacle Pulpit*, Vol. 9 (Ages Digital Library, 1998), 364.

[25]Charles Spurgeon, 'The Abiding of the Spirit in the Glory of the Church', in *The Metropolitan Tabernacle Pulpit*, Vol. 32 (Ages Digital Library, 1998), 613.

[26]Charles Spurgeon, 'Signs of the Times', in *The Metropolitan Tabernacle Pulpit*, Vol. 19 (Ages Digital Library, 1998), 688.

[27]G. C. Needham, *The Life and Labors of Charles H. Spurgeon, the Faithful Preacher, the Devoted Pastor, the Noble Philanthropist, the Beloved College President, and the Voluminous Writer, Author, Etc.* (Boston: D. L. Guernsey, 1881), 185.

[28]Spurgeon, *The Full Harvest*, 96.

[29]'The length of course was fixed at two years. This was lengthened to three years in 1880.' M. Niclholls, 'Charles Haddon Spurgeon, Educationalist: Part 2 – the Principles and Practice of Pastors' College', *The Baptist Quarterly* Vol. 22/2 (April 1987): 79.

[30]L. E. Elliott-Binns, *Religion in the Victorian Era* (London: Lutterworth Press, 1953), 457.

[31]Charles Spurgeon, *The Early Years,* Autobiography, Vol. 1 (reprint; Edinburgh, Banner of Truth, 1994), 384.

[32]Ibid., 388.

[33]Arnold Dallimore, *Spurgeon: A New Biography* (Edinburgh: Banner of Truth Turst, 1999), 78.

[34]Needham, *The Life and Labors*, 178.

1. Mysterious Agencies: *Preparing our Heart*

[1]Charles Spurgeon, 'Two Visions', in *The Metropolitan Tabernacle Pulpit*, Vol. 10 (Ages Digital Library, 1998), 786.

[2]Spurgeon, *The Early Years*, 19.

[3]Ibid., 185.

[4]Spurgeon, *The Full Harvest*, 120.

[5]Spurgeon, *The Early Years*, 182.

[6]Ibid., 188.

[7]Ibid., 206.

[8]Spurgeon says: 'I am persuaded that the use of a good Catechism in all our families will be a great safeguard against the increasing errors of the times, and therefore I have compiled this little manual from the Westminster Assembly's and Baptist Catechisms, for the use of my own church and congregation. Those who use it in their families or classes must labor to explain the sense; but the words should be carefully learned by heart, for they will be understood better as years pass.'

[9]Charles Spurgeon, *A Puritan Catechism* (Ages Digital Library, 1998), 9.

[10]Spurgeon, *The Early Years*, 183.

[11]Spurgeon, *The Early Years*, 159.

[12]Ibid., 184.

[13]Spurgeon, *The Early Years*, 22.

[14]Charles Spurgeon, *Letters of Charles Spurgeon: Selected with Notes by Iain H. Murray* (Edinburgh: Banner of Truth, 1992), 26.

[15]Spurgeon, *The Early Years,* 26-27.

[16]Ibid., 55-56.

[17]Ibid., 40.

[18]Ibid., 110.

[19]Spurgeon, *Letters Selected with Notes*, 24-25.

[20]Spurgeon, *The Early Years*, 15.

[21]Ibid., 21.

[22]Ibid.

[23]Ibid.

[24]Ibid., 7.

[25]Ibid., 6.

[26]Ibid., 73.

[27]Ibid., 18.

[28]Ibid., 130.

[29]Ibid., 89.

[30]Ibid., 21.

[31]Ibid., 12.

[32]See Spurgeon's letter to Richard Knill, *Letters Selected with Notes*, 38.

[33]Spurgeon, *The Early Years*, 27.

[34]Ibid., 210.

[35]Ibid., 37.

[36]Charles Spurgeon, 'The Two Talents', in *The Park Street Pulpit*, Vol. 4 (Ages Digital Library, 1998), 140.

[37]Charles Spurgeon, 'Spiritual Transformations', in *The Metropolitan Tabernacle Pulpit*, Vol. 53 (Ages Digital Library, 1998), 365.

[38]Spurgeon, *An All Around Ministry*, 13.

[39]Charles Spurgeon, 'Two Visions', in *The Metropolitan Tabernacle Pulpit*, Vol. 10 (Ages Digital Library, 1998), 786.

[40]Charles Spurgeon, 'Understandest Thou?' in *The Metropolitan Tabernacle Pulpit*, Vol. 30 (Ages Digital Library, 1998), 526.

[41]Charles Spurgeon, 'Good News for the Lost', in *The Metropolitan Tabernacle Pulpit*, Vol. 19 (Ages Digital Library, 1998), 177.

Chapter 2. The Call of Heaven: *Clarifying our Work*

[1]Charles Spurgeon, 'The Unsearchable Riches of Christ', in *The Metropolitan Tabernacle Pulpit*, Vol. 13 (Ages Digital Library, 1998), 250.

[2]Charles Spurgeon, 'Have you Forgotten Him?', in *The Metropolitan Tabernacle Pulpit*, Vol. 12 (Ages Digital Library, 1998), 184.

[3]Charles Spurgeon, 'The Sound in the Mulberry Trees', in *The Park Street Pulpit*, Vol. 3 (Ages Digital Library, 1998), 531.

[4]Spurgeon, *The Early Years*, 388.

[5]Charles Spurgeon, *Lectures to My Students*, *Ministry Resources Library* (Grand Rapids, Michigan: Zondervan, 1954), 23.

[6]Spurgeon, *Lectures*, 22.

[7]Spurgeon, 'Mulberry Trees', 530.

[8]Spurgeon, *Lectures*, 22.

[9]Charles Spurgeon, 'Fallen Angels a Lesson to Fallen Man', in *The Metropolitan Tabernacle Pulpit*, Vol. 31(Ages Digital Library, 1998), 67.

[10]Spurgeon, *An All Around Ministry*, 67.

[11]Charles Spurgeon, *Spurgeon's Commentary on Matthew* (Ages Digital Library, 1998), 361.

[12]Spurgeon, *The Early Years*, 388.

[13]Spurgeon, *Lectures*, 31.

[14]Spurgeon, 'Mulberry Trees', 531.

[15]Spurgeon, *Lectures*, 24.

[16]Charles Spurgeon, 'The Holy Spirit in the Covenant', in *The Metropolitan Tabernacle*, Vol. 53 (Ages Digital Library, 1998), 426.

[17]Spurgeon, *A Puritan Catechism*, 30.

[18]Charles Spurgeon, 'Christ Crucified', in *The Park Street Pulpit*, Vol. 1 (Ages Digital Library, 1998), 108.

[19]Charles Spurgeon, 'Early and Late, or Horae Gratiae', in *The Metropolitan Tabernacle Pulpit*, Vol. 11 (Ages Digital Library, 1998), 861.

[20]Charles Spurgeon, *The Great Change – Conversion* (Ages Digital Library, 1998), 8-9.

[21]Charles Spurgeon, 'Regeneration', in *The Park Street Pulpit*, Vol. 3 (Ages Digital Library, 1998), 311.

[22]Charles Spurgeon, 'June 18-AM', in *Morning and Evening* (Ages Digital Library, 1998), 341.

[23]Spurgeon, *Lectures*, 26.

[24]Spurgeon, *An All Around Ministry*, Stewards, 182.

[25]Spurgeon, *Letters Selected with Notes*, 26.

[26]Spurgeon, *The Early Years*, 19.

[27]Spurgeon, *Lectures*, 27.

[28]Ibid.

[29]Charles Spurgeon, 'The Cry of the Heathen', in *The Park Street Pulpit*, Vol. 4 (Ages Digital Library, 1998), 342.

[30]'Mulberry Trees', 532.

[31]'Mulberry Trees', 531.

[32]Spurgeon, *Lectures*, 31.

[33]Spurgeon is probably following Calvin's two-fold designation of an 'outward' and communal call from the body of believers joined with a 'secret' and internal call personal to the would-be-preacher; both of which are necessary for a 'ministry approved by God.' See *Institutes* Vol. 2, 1063.

[34]Spurgeon, *Lectures*, 26.

[35]Spurgeon, 'Mulberry Trees', 532.

[36]Spurgeon, *The Early Years*, 156.

[37]Ibid., 158.

[38]Charles Spurgeon, 'Preach the Gospel', in *The Park Street Pulpit*, Vol. 1 (Ages Digital Library, 1998), 473.

Chapter 3. The Old Truth: *Settling Our Convictions*

[1]Charles Spurgeon, 'Preface', in *The Metropolitan Tabernacle Pulpit*, Vol. 7 (Ages Digital Library, 1998), 3.

[2]Spurgeon, *The Early Years*, 387.

[3]Ibid.

[4]Spurgeon, *An All Around Ministry*, 318.

[5]For a brief summary of this controversy see Ernest W. Bacon, *Spurgeon, Heir of the Puritans* (Arlington Heights, Illinois: Christian Liberty Press, 1996), 127-44.

[6]Lewis Brastrow, *Representative Modern Preachers* (New York: The Macmillan Company, 1904), vii, 383, 401.

[7]Bacon, *Heir of the Puritans*, 110.

[8]Spurgeon, *The Early Years*, 390.

[9]For further exploration of Spurgeon's Calvinism, see Iain Murray, *The Forgotten Spurgeon* (Edinburgh: Banner of Truth, 1994).

[10]Charles Spurgeon, 'A Chat About Commentaries', in *Lectures to My Students*, Vol. 3 (Ages Digital Library, 1998), 10.

[11]Theodore Nelson, 'Charles Haddon Spurgeon's Theory and Practice of Preaching', *Quarterly Journal of Speech*, 32 (1946): 175.

[12]Charles Spurgeon, 'Doctrines of Grace', in *The Metropolitan Tabernacle Pulpit*, Vol. 7 (Ages Digital Library, 1998), 547.

[13]Charles Spurgeon, 'Meeting the Unfinished Tabernacle', in *Autobiography*, Vol. 3 (Ages Digital Library, 1998), 393-94.

[14]Spurgeon, 'Pentecost', 372.

[15]Charles Spurgeon, 'Christ, the Body of Divinity', in *The Metropolitan Tabernacle Pulpit*, Vol. 7 (Ages Digital Library, 1998), 308.

[16]'Righteous Hatred', *PSP*, Vol. 4, 616.

[17]Charles Spurgeon, 'The Silver Trumpet', in *The Metropolitan Tabernacle Pulpit*, Vol. 7 (Ages Digital Library, 1998), 271.

[18]Charles Spurgeon, 'Heavenly Worship', in *The Park Street Pulpit*, Vol. 3 (Ages Digital Library, 1998), 48.

[19]Spurgeon, *Letters Selected with Notes*, 56-57.

[20]Charles Spurgeon, 'Faith', in *The Park Street Pulpit*, Vol. 3 (Ages Digital Library, 1998), 5-6.

[21]Charles Spurgeon, 'Preaching for the Poor', in *The Park Street Pulpit*, Vol. 3 (Ages Digital Library, 1998), 98.

[22]Spurgeon, 'Mulberry Trees', 536.

[23]Spurgeon, *A Puritan Catechism*, 3.

[24]Charles Spurgeon, 'The Comforter', in *The Park Street Pulpit*, Vol. 1 (Ages Digital Library, 1998), 73.

[25]Charles Spurgeon, 'Revival Work', *The Sword and the Trowel* (March 1898): 350.

[26]Ibid., 349-50.

[27]Charles Spurgeon, 'The Statute of David for the Sharing of the Spoil', in *The Metropolitan Tabernacle Pulpit*, Vol. 37 (Ages Digital Library, 1998), 405.

[28]Spurgeon, 'Revival Work', 351.

[29]Ibid.

[30]Charles Spurgeon, 'The Great Revival', in *The Park Street Pulpit*, Vol. 4 (Ages Digital Library, 1998), 283.

[31]Spurgeon, 'Revival Work', 350.

[32]Spurgeon, *The Early Years*, 348.

[33]Spurgeon, *An All Around Ministry*, 177.

[34]E.W. Hayden, *Spurgeon on Revival: A Biblical and Theological Approach* (Grand Rapids, Michigan: Zondervan, 1962), 10.

[35]Charles Spurgeon, 'The Minister's Plea', in *The Metropolitan Tabernacle Pulpit*, Vol. 1 (Ages Digital Library), 753.

Chapter 4. A Scripture Manner: *Examining our Sermon Delivery*

[1]Tait, 'Preachers and Preaching', 692-693.

[2]Eric Hayden, *Highlights in the Life of Charles Haddon Spurgeon* (Ages Digital Library, 1998), 124.

[3]Spurgeon, 'First Visit to Scotland', in *Autobiography* Vol. 2(Ages Digital Library, 1998), 120.

[4]Charles Spurgeon, 'All of One', in *The Metropolitan Tabernacle Pulpit*, Vol. 41 (Ages Digital Library, 1998), 396.

[5]Charles Spurgeon, 'Spurgeon as a Literary Man', in *Autobiography*, Vol. 4 (Ages Digital Library, 1998), 292.

[6]Brastow, *Representative Modern Preachers*, 410.

[7]Spurgeon, *Lectures*, 363.

[8]Peabody, 'Sermons and Sermonizers', 94.

[9]Spurgeon, 'Literary Man', 292.

[10]Charles Spurgeon, 'Come My Beloved', in *The Metropolitan Tabernacle Pulpit*, Vol. 40 (Ages Digital Library, 1998), 298.

[11]Charles Spurgeon, 'A Sore Grievance', in *The Metropolitan Tabernacle Pulpit*, Vol. 60 (Ages Digital Library, 1998), 596.

[12]Quoted in Davies, *Worship and Theology in England*, 337.

[13]Brastow, *Representative Modern Preachers*, 400.

[14]John R. Knott, Jr., *The Sword of the Spirit: Puritan Responses to the Bible* (Chicago and London: The University of Chicago Press, 1980), 5.

[15]Spurgeon, 'Pentecost', 376.

[16]Charles Spurgeon, 'Heman's Sorrowful Psalm', in *The Metropolitan Tabernacle Pulpit*, Vol. 41 (Ages Digital Library, 1998), 623.

[17]Charles Spurgeon, 'Penitence, Pardon, and Peace', in *The Metropolitan Tabernacle Pulpit*, Vol. 59 (Ages Digital Library, 1998), 374.

[18]Charles Spurgeon, 'A Sacred Solo', in *The Metropolitan Tabernacle* Pulpit, Vol. 24 (Ages Digital Library, 1998), 489.

[19]Charles Spurgeon, 'The Gracious Lips of Jesus', in *The Metropolitan Tabernacle* Pulpit, Vol. 54 (Ages Digital Library, 1998), 134.

[20]Charles Spurgeon, 'The Miracles of our Lord's Death', in *The Metropolitan Tabernacle* Pulpit, Vol. 34 (Ages Digital Library, 1998), 895.

[21]Charles Spurgeon, 'A Sermon of Personal Testimony', in *The Metropolitan Tabernacle* Pulpit, Vol. 44 (Ages Digital Library, 1998), 373.

[22]Spurgeon, *The Early Years*, 348.

[23]Charles Spurgeon, 'The Crisis of this World', in *The Metropolitan Tabernacle* Pulpit, Vol. 39 (Ages Digital Library, 1998), 805.

[24]Charles Spurgeon, 'The Cloud of Doves', in *The Metropolitan Tabernacle* Pulpit, Vol. 48 (Ages Digital Library, 1998), 65.

[25]Patricia Stallings Kruppa, 'Charles Haddon Spurgeon: A Preacher's Progress', Unpublished Dissertation (Columbia University, 1971), 166.

[26]Spurgeon, *An All Around Ministry*, 112.

[27]Charles Spurgeon, 'Invitation to a Conference', in *The Metropolitan Tabernacle Pulpit*, Vol. 49 (Ages Digital Library, 1998), 69.

[28]Notice John Calvin, 'If we heard God speaking to us in His majesty, it would be useless for us, for we would understand nothing. Therefore, since we are carnal, He has to stutter or otherwise he would not be understood by us.' Sermon on John 1:1-5, quoted in Ronald Wallace, *Calvin's Doctrine of the Word & Sacrament* (Grand Rapids, Michigan: Eerdmans, 1957), 3.

[29]Charles Spurgeon, 'The Approachableness of Jesus', in *The Metropolitan Tabernacle Pulpit*, Vol. 14 (Ages Digital Library, 1998), 315.

[30]Charles Spurgeon, 'Christ Receiving Sinners', in *The Metropolitan Tabernacle Pulpit*, Vol. 50 (Ages Digital Library, 1998), 397.

[31]Charles Spurgeon, 'The Secret Food and the Public Name', in *The Metropolitan Tabernacle Pulpit*, Vol. 18 (Ages Digital Library, 1998), 779.

[32]Charles Spurgeon, 'The Fainting Soul Revived', in *The Metropolitan Tabernacle Pulpit*, Vol. 62 (Ages Digital Library, 1998), 197.

[33]Charles Spurgeon, 'Longing to Find God', in *The Metropolitan Tabernacle Pulpit*, Vol. 38 (Ages Digital Library, 1998), 546.

[34]Charles Spurgeon, 'Out of Darkness into Light', in *The Metropolitan Tabernacle Pulpit*, Vol. 41 (Ages Digital Library, 1998), 53.

[35]Charles Spurgeon, 'There is Forgiveness', in *The Metropolitan Tabernacle Pulpit*, Vol. 41 (Ages Digital Library, 1998), 459.

[36]Charles Spurgeon, *Able to the Uttermost* (Ages Digital Library, 1998), 195.

[37]Charles Spurgeon, 'Sovereignty and Salvation', in *The Park Street Pulpit*, Vol. 2 (Ages Digital Library, 1998), 100.

[38]Charles Spurgeon, 'Effectual Calling', in *The Park Street Pulpit*, Vol. 2 (Ages Digital Library, 1998), 257.

[39]Charles Spurgeon, 'The Shadow of a Great Rock', in *The Metropolitan Tabernacle Pulpit*, Vol. 53 (Ages Digital Library, 1998), 173.

[40]Merivale, *Modern Preaching,* 263.

[41]Charles Spurgeon, 'Feeding on the Word', in *The Metropolitan Tabernacle Pulpit*, Vol. 38 (Ages Digital Library, 1998), 650.

[42]Charles Spurgeon, 'Choice Teaching for the Chosen', in *The Metropolitan Tabernacle Pulpit*, Vol. 45 (Ages Digital Library, 1998), 60.

[43]Charles Spurgeon, 'Man's Extremity God's Opportunity', in *The Metropolitan Tabernacle Pulpit*, Vol. 47 (Ages Digital Library, 1998), 152.

[44]Charles Spurgeon, 'The Prosperous Man's Reminder', in *The Metropolitan Tabernacle Pulpit*, Vol. 24 (Ages Digital Library, 1998), 761.

[45]Charles Spurgeon, 'A Sermon for Gleaners', in *The Metropolitan Tabernacle Pulpit*, Vol. 8 (Ages Digital Library, 1998), 559.

[46]Charles Spurgeon, 'Tender Words of Terrible Apprehension', in *The Park Street Pulpit*, Vol. 6 (Ages Digital Library, 1998), 835.

[47]Charles Spurgeon, 'The Prosperous Man's Reminder', in *The Metropolitan Tabernacle Pulpit*, Vol. 24 (Ages Digital Library, 1998), 761.

[48]Charles Spurgeon, 'The Saddest Cry from the Cross', in *The Metropolitan Tabernacle Pulpit*, Vol. 48 (Ages Digital Library, 1998), 656.

[49]Charles Spurgeon, 'Peace Perfect Peace', in *The Metropolitan Tabernacle Pulpit*, Vol. 55 (Ages Digital Library, 1998), 782.

[50]Spurgeon, 'Tender Words of Terrible Apprehension', 836.

[51]Charles Spurgeon, 'An All Important Question', in *The Metropolitan Tabernacle Pulpit*, Vol. 52 (Ages Digital Library, 1998), 628.

[52]Charles Spurgeon, 'Unwillingness to Come to Christ', in *The Metropolitan Tabernacle Pulpit*, Vol. 22 (Ages Digital Library, 1998), 806.

[53]Charles Spurgeon, *Pictures from Pilgrim's Progress* (Ages Digital Library, 1998), 25.

[54]Charles Spurgeon, 'Impotence and Omnipotence', in *The Metropolitan Tabernacle Pulpit*, Vol. 38 (Ages Digital Library, 1998), 500.

[55]Kruppa, 'A Preacher's Progress', 166.

[56]Charles Spurgeon, *Faith's Checkbook* (Ages Digital Library, 1998), 3.

[57]Charles Spurgeon, *Gleanings from Among the Sheaves* (Ages Digital Library, 1998), 2.

[58]Peabody, 'Sermons and Sermonizers', 85.

[59]Charles Spurgeon, 'God Beseeching Sinners', in *The Metropolitan Tabernacle Pulpit*, Vol. 19 (Ages Digital Library, 1998), 527.

[60]Peabody, 'Sermons and Sermonizers', 85.

[61]Ibid.

[62]Charles Spurgeon, 'Invitation to a Conference', in *The Metropolitan Tabernacle Pulpit*, Vol. 49 (Ages Digital Library, 1998), 75.

[63]Charles Spurgeon, 'Faith Working by Love', in *The Metropolitan Tabernacle Pulpit*, Vol. 26 (Ages Digital Library, 1998), 596.

[64]Spurgeon, 'The Talking Book', 754.

[65]Tait, 'Preachers and Preaching', 692.

[66]Spurgeon, *The Early Years*, 316.

[67]Ian Maclaren, *The Cure of Souls: Lyman Beecher Lectures on Preaching at Yale University, 1896* (New York: Hodder & Stoughton, 1896), 54.

[68]Lewis Drummond, *Spurgeon: Prince of Preachers* (Grand Rapids, Michigan: Kregel, 1992), 302.

[69]Charles Spurgeon, *The Saint and His Savior* (Ages Digital Library, 1998), 82.

[70]Charles Spurgeon, 'How Can I Obtain Faith', in *The Metropolitan Tabernacle Pulpit*, Vol. 18 (Ages Digital Library, 1998), 57.

[71]Charles Spurgeon, 'Testimony and Experience', in *The Metropolitan Tabernacle Pulpit*, Vol. 18 (Ages Digital Library, 1998), 381-382.

[72]Spurgeon, *The Early Years*, 377.

[73]Charles Spurgeon, *According to Promise* (Ages Digital Library, 1998), 56.

[74]Charles Spurgeon, 'Fellowship with God', in *The Metropolitan Tabernacle Pulpit*, Vol. 7 (Ages Digital Library, 1998), 904.

[75]Charles Spurgeon, 'Exposition of the Doctrines of Grace', in *The Metropolitan Tabernacle Pulpit*, Vol. 7 (Ages Digital Library, 1998), 552.

[76]Charles Spurgeon, *Conversion the Great Change* (Ages Digital Library, 1998), 7.

[77]Charles Spurgeon, *The Sword and the Trowel*, Vol. 7 (Ages Digital Library, 1998), 154.

[78]Spurgeon, *The Early Years*, 378.

Chapter 5. The Holy Fancy: *Engaging our Imagination*

[1]Charles Spurgeon, 'Three Homilies from One Text', in *The Park Street Pulpit*, Vol. 6 (Ages Digital Library, 1998), 677.

[2]Daniel P. Kidder, *Treatise on Homiletics: Designed to Illustrate the True Theory and Practice of Preaching the Gospel* (New York: Carlton & Porter, 1866), 299.

[3]R. L. Dabney, *Sacred Rhetoric* (1870; reprint, *Evangelical Eloquence* Carlisle, Pennsylvania: The Banner of Truth Trust, 1999), 243.

[4]Spurgeon, *Lectures*, 412.

[5]Ibid.

[6]Ibid., 411.

[7]Ibid., 410.

[8]Ibid., 412.

[9]Charles Spurgeon, 'Preaching for the Poor', in *The Park Street Pulpit*, Vol. 3 (Ages Digital Library, 1998), 97.

[10]Spurgeon, *Lectures*, 362.

[11]Charles Spurgeon, 'The Remembrance of Christ', in *The Park Street Pulpit,* Vol. 1 (Ages Digital Library, 1998), 30-31.

[12]Spurgeon, *Lectures*, 143.

[13]Charles Spurgeon, 'Human Inability', in *The Park Street Pulpit*, Vol. 4 (Ages Digital Library, 1998), 236.

[14]Spurgeon, *Lectures*, 32.

[15]Charles Spurgeon, 'The Tabernacle – Without the Camp', in *The Metropolitan Tabernacle Pulpit*,Vol. 7, (Ages Digital Library, 1998), 169.

[16]Charles Spurgeon, 'Grieving the Holy Spirit', in *The Park Street Pulpit*, Vol. 5 (Ages Digital Library, 1998), 737.

[17]Charles Spurgeon, *The Sword and the Trowel*, Vol. 5 (Ages Digital Library, 1998), 639.

[18]Charles Spurgeon, 'The Drawings of Love', in *The Metropolitan Tabernacle Pulpit*, Vol. 63 (Ages Digital Library, 1998), 191.

[19]Spurgeon, *Lectures*, 363.

[20]Charles Spurgeon, *The Bible and the Newspaper* (Ages Digital Library, 1998), Preface.

[21]Spurgeon, *Lectures*, 16.

[22]Charles Spurgeon, 'Books of Fables, Emblems and Parables', in *Lectures to My Students*, Vol. 2 (Ages Digital Library, 1998), 109.

[23]Spurgeon, *Lectures*, 13.

[24]Ibid., 17.

[25]Spurgeon, 'Preaching for the Poor', 97.

[26]Spurgeon, *Lectures*, 63.

[27]Ibid., 32.

[28]Ibid., 63.

[29]Davies, *Worship and Theology*, 298.

[30]Nicholls, 'C. H. Spurgeon, Educationalist', 86.

[31]Charles Spurgeon, 'God in Nature and in Revelation', in *The Metropolitan Tabernacle Pulpit*, Vol. 58 (Ages Digital Library, 1998), 472.

[32]Spurgeon, *Lectures*, 408.

[33]Charles Spurgeon, *The Teaching of Nature in the Kingdom of God* (Ages Digital Library, 1998), 3.

[34]Spurgeon, *Lectures*, 65-66.

[35]Ibid., 67.

[36]Spurgeon, *The Bible and the Newspaper*, 2.

[37]Ibid., 2-3.

[38]Spurgeon, *Lectures*, 94.

[39]Charles Spurgeon, 'The Cast-Off Girdle', in *The Metropolitan Tabernacle Pulpit*, Vol. 29 (Ages Digital Library, 1998), 125.

[40]Spurgeon, *An All Around Ministry*, 274.

[41]Spurgeon, *Lectures*, 81.

[42]Spurgeon, *Lectures*, 56.

[43]Ibid., 13.

[44]Ibid., 54.

[45]Ibid., 13.

[46]Spurgeon, *Lectures*, 54.

[47]Ibid., 29.

[48]Charles Spurgeon, 'Not Now but Hereafter', in *The Metropolitan Tabernacle Pulpit*, Vol. 7 (Ages Digital Library, 1998), 908-09.

[49]Charles Spurgeon, 'The Blood', in *The Park Street Pulpit*, Vol. 5 (Ages Digital Library, 1998), 49.

Chapter 6. The Soul Running Over at the Mouth: *Anchoring our Emotions*

[1]Spurgeon, 'Testimony and Experience', 380.

[2]Charles Spurgeon, 'A Preacher from the Dead', in *The Park Street Pulpit*, Vol. 3 (Ages Digital Library, 1998), 484.

[3]Spurgeon, *The Early Years*, 348.

[4]Spurgeon, *The Full Harvest*, 109.

[5]Charles Spurgeon, 'The Joyous Return', in *The Metropolitan Tabernacle Pulpit*, Vol. 37 (Ages Digital Library, 1998), 158.

[6]Charles Spurgeon, 'Plenary Absolution', in *The Metropolitan Tabernacle Pulpit*, Vol. 19 (Ages Digital Library, 1998), 292.

[7]Charles Spurgeon, 'The Entreaty of the Holy Ghost', in *The Metropolitan Tabernacle Pulpit*, Vol. 20 (Ages Digital Library, 1998), 157.

[8]Charles Spurgeon, 'The Voice Behind Thee', in *The Metropolitan Tabernacle Pulpit*, Vol. 28 (Ages Digital Library, 1998), 530.

[9]'The Sermon of the Seasons', in *The Metropolitan Tabernacle Pulpit*, Vol. 32 (Ages Digital Library, 1998), 206.

[10]Charles Spurgeon, 'Small Rain for Tender Herbs', in *The Metropolitan Tabernacle Pulpit*, Vol. 33 (Ages Digital Library, 1994), 904.

[11]Charles Spurgeon, 'The Lowly King', in *The Metropolitan Tabernacle Pulpit*, Vol. 31 (Ages Digital Library, 1998), 676.

[12]Charles Spurgeon, 'Migratory Birds', in *The Metropolitan Tabernacle Pulpit*, Vol. 49(Ages Digital Library, 1998), 737.

[13]Charles Spurgeon, 'The Bellows Burned', in *The Metropolitan Tabernacle Pulpit*, Vol. 15 (Ages Digital Library, 1998), 616.

[14]Charles Spurgeon, 'The Resurrection of the Dead', in *The Park Street Pulpit*, Vol. 2 (Ages Digital Library, 1998), 179.

[15]Charles Spurgeon, 'Vanities and Verities', in *The Metropolitan Tabernacle Pulpit*, Vol. 23 (Ages Digital Library, 1998), 740.

[16]Charles Spurgeon, 'The Students Prayer', in *The Metropolitan Tabernacle Pulpit*, Vol. 23 (Ages Digital Library, 1998), 305.

[17]Charles Spurgeon, 'Jesus in Gethsemane', in *The Metropolitan Tabernacle Pulpit*, Vol. 48 (Ages Digital Library, 1998), 122.

[18]Charles Spurgeon, *Spurgeon's Prayers* (Ages Digital Library, 1998), 4.

[19]Spurgeon, *The Full Harvest*, 310.

[20]Charles Spurgeon, 'Characteristics of Faith', in *The Park Street Pulpit,* Vol. 6 (Ages Digital Library, 1998), 442.

[21]Charles Spurgeon, 'Where True Prayer is Found', in *The Metropolitan Tabernacle Pulpit*, Vol. 24 (Ages Digital Library, 1998), 329.

[22]Charles Spurgeon, 'The Ship on Fire – A Voice of Warning', in *The Metropolitan Tabernacle Pulpit*, Vol. 10 (Ages Digital Library, 1998), 49.

[23]Spurgeon, *Lectures*, 174.

[24]Spurgeon, *An All Around Ministry*, 176.

[25]'The Minister's Stock-Taking', in *The Metropolitan Tabernacle Pulpit*, Vol. 9 (Ages Digital Library, 1998), 439. Spurgeon says elsewhere, 'Do not play upon the mind by exciting feelings which are not spiritual...[W]hat is the good of opening up a mother's grief or a widow's sorrows? I do not believe that our merciful Lord has sent us to make men weep over their departed relatives by digging anew their graves and rehearsing past scenes of bereavement and woe...it is granted that you may profitably employ the death-bed of a departing sinner for proof of the rest of faith in the one case and the terror of conscience in the other, but it is out of the fact proved and out of the illustration itself that the good must arise. Natural grief is of no service in itself; indeed, we look upon it as a distraction from higher thoughts, and as a price too great to exact from tender hearts, unless we can repay them by engrafting lasting spiritual impressions upon the stock of natural affection.'

[26]Ibid.

[27]Spurgeon, 'Election', 67.

[28]Ibid.

[29]Charles Spurgeon, 'The Glorious Gospel of the Blessed God', in *The Metropolitan Tabernacle Pulpit*, Vol. 13 (Ages Digital Library, 1998), 451.

[30]Charles Spurgeon, 'My Own Personal Holdfast', in *The Metropolitan Tabernacle Pulpit*, Vol. 35 (Ages Digital Library, 1998), 107.

[31]Spurgeon, 'Bochim; or, The Weepers', 657.

[32]Ibid.

[33]Spurgeon, *An All Around Ministry*, 176.

[34]Charles Spurgeon, 'The Minister's Stock-Taking', in *The Metropolitan Tabernacle Pulpit*, Vol. 9 (Ages Digital Library, 1998), 439.

[35]Spurgeon, 'The Glorious Gospel of the Blessed God', 451.

[36]Charles Spurgeon, *The Treasury of David*, Vol. 1 (Grand Rapids, Michigan: Zondervan, 1957), 272-273.

[37]Charles Spurgeon, 'Sow to Yourselves', in *The Metropolitan Tabernacle Pulpit*, Vol. 21 (Ages Digital Library, 1998), 757.

[38]Charles Spurgeon, 'The Superlative Excellence', in *The Metropolitan Tabernacle Pulpit*, Vol. 10 (Ages Digital Library, 1998), 420.

[39]Charles Spurgeon, 'Temple Glories', in *The Metropolitan Tabernacle Pulpit*, Vol. 7 (Ages Digital Library, 1998), 408.

[40]Charles Spurgeon, 'Sincere Seekers Assured Finders', in *The Metropolitan Tabernacle Pulpit*, Vol. 61 (Ages Digital Library, 1998), 571.

Chapter 7. Opening Mercy's Door: *Motivating our Hearers*

[1]Spurgeon, 'Able to the Uttermost', 83.

[2]Spurgeon, *The Early Years*, 43.

[3]Spurgeon, 'Books of Fables', 125.

[4]Charles Spurgeon, 'The Bridgeless Gulf', in *The Metropolitan Tabernacle Pulpit*, Vol. 9 (Ages Digital Library, 1998), 472.

[5]Charles Spurgeon, 'Great Spoil' in *The Metropolitan Tabernacle Pulpit*, Vol. 28 (Ages Digital Library, 1998), 71.

[6]Charles Spurgeon, 'A Blow at Self Righteousness', in *The Metropolitan Tabernacle Pulpit*, Vol. 7 (Ages Digital Library, 1998), 42.

[7]Charles Spurgeon, *The Covenant of Grace* (Ages Digital Library, 1998), 6.

[8]Ibid.

[9]Spurgeon, *Puritan Catechism*, 13.

[10]Charles Spurgeon, 'The Stern Pedagogue', in *The Metropolitan Tabernacle Pulpit*, Vol. 20 (Ages Digital Library, 1998), 686.

[11]Charles Spurgeon, 'Acceptable Service', in *The Metropolitan Tabernacle Pulpit*, Vol. 28 (Ages Digital Library, 1998), 36.

[12]Charles Spurgeon, 'The Touch', in *The Metropolitan Tabernacle Pulpit*, Vol. 28 (Ages Digital Library, 1998), 57.

[13]Charles Spurgeon, *All of Grace* (Ages Digital Library, 1998), 12.

[14]Spurgeon, *Covenant of Grace*, 28.

[15]Spurgeon, 'Grace Abounding', in *The Metropolitan Tabernacle Pulpit*, Vol. 9 (Ages Digital Library, 1998), 218.

[16]Spurgeon, *A Puritan Catechism*, 15.

[17]Spurgeon, 'Acceptable Service', 46.

[18]Charles Spurgeon, 'The Gift Unspeakable', in *The Metropolitan Tabernacle Pulpit*, Vol. 26 (Ages Digital Library, 1998), 549.

[19]Charles Spurgeon, 'Marah Better than Elim', in *The Metropolitan Tabernacle Pulpit*, Vol. 39 (Ages Digital Library, 1998), 205.

[20]Spurgeon, 'Books of Fables', 125.

[21]Spurgeon, *A Puritan Catechism*, 20.

[22]Spurgeon, 'Marah Better than Elim', 205.

[23]Spurgeon, 'All for Jesus,' in *The Metropolitan Tabernacle Pulpit*, Vol. 20 (Ages Digital Library, 1998), 833.

[24]Spurgeon, *A Puritan Catechism*, 15.

[25]Spurgeon, 'The Reward of the Righteous', in *The Metropolitan Tabernacle Pulpit*, Vol. 12 (Ages Digital Library, 1998), 58.

[26]Charles Spurgeon, 'The Sacred Love Token', in *The Metropolitan Tabernacle Pulpit*, Vol. 21 (Ages Digital Library, 1998), 610.

[27]Charles Spurgeon, 'Do You Know Him', in *The Metropolitan Tabernacle Pulpit*, Vol. 10 (Ages Digital Library, 1998), 76.

[28]Spurgeon, 'The Double-Come', in *The Metropolitan Tabernacle Pulpit*, Vol. 27 (Ages Digital Library, 1998), 501.

[29]Charles Spurgeon, 'The Entreaty of the Holy Ghost', in *The Metropolitan Tabernacle Pulpit*, Vol. 20 (Ages Digital Library, 1998), 58.

[30]Charles Spurgeon, 'Satan's Banquet', in *The Park Street Pulpit*, Vol.5 (Ages Digital Library, 1998), 3.

[31]Spurgeon, 'The Bridgeless Gulf', 472.

[32]Charles Spurgeon, 'The New Heart', in *The Park Street Pulpit*, Vol. 4 (Ages Digital Library, 1998), 661.

[33]Charles Spurgeon, 'Spiritual Liberty', in *The Park Street Pulpit*, Vol. 1 (Ages Digital Library, 1998), 126.

[34]Spurgeon, *Morning and Evening*, 528.

[35]Charles Spurgeon, 'Prodigal Love for the Prodigal Son',

in *The Metropolitan Tabernacle Pulpit*, Vol. 37 (Ages Digital Library, 1998), 883.

[36]Charles Spurgeon, 'Why They Leave Us', in *The Metropolitan Tabernacle Pulpit*, Vol. 32 (Ages Digital Library, 1998), 227.

[37]Spurgeon, *Lectures*, 176.

[38]Charles Spurgeon, 'The Blind Man's Earnest Cries', in *The Metropolitan Tabernacle Pulpit*, Vol. 11 (Ages Digital Library, 1998), 583.

[39]Charles Spurgeon, 'Altogether Lovely', in *The Metropolitan Tabernacle Pulpit*, Vol. 17 (Ages Digital Library, 1998), 508.

[40]Charles Spurgeon, 'Kicking Against the Pricks', in *The Metropolitan Tabernacle Pulpit*, Vol. 12 (Ages Digital Library, 1998), 624.

Chapter 8. The Lord's Ways: *Trusting the Spirit's Appointed Means*

[1]'Harvest Men Wanted', *The Metropolitan Tabernacle Pulpit*, Vol. 19, 566.

[2]'Pricked in their Heart', 597.

[3]*Lectures to My Students*, Vol. 1, 20.

[4]Spurgeon, *Farm Sermons*, 108.

[5]Charles Spurgeon, 'The Light of the World', in *The Metropolitan Tabernacle Pulpit*, Vol. 19 (Ages Digital Library, 1998), 299.

[6]Spurgeon, *Lectures*, 7-8 .

[7]Ibid., 12.

[8]Spurgeon, *Lectures*, 199.

[9]Ibid., 200-01.

[10]Charles Spurgeon, 'The Leading of the Spirit: The Secret Tokens of the Sons of God', in *The Metropolitan Tabernacle*, Vol. 21 (Ages Digital Library, 1998), 159.

[11]Charles Spurgeon, 'The Word a Sword', in *The Metropolitan Tabernacle Pulpit*, Vol. 34 (Ages Digital Library, 1998), 149.

[12]Charles Spurgeon, 'The Spirit and the Wind', in *The Metropolitan Tabernacle Pulpit*, Vol. 35 (Ages Digital Library, 1998), 73.

[13]Calvin, *Institutes*, 3.2.33.

[14]Charles Spurgeon, 'Revelation and Conversion', in *The Metropolitan Tabernacle Pulpit*, Vol. 50 (Ages Digital Library, 1998), 97.

[15]Charles Spurgeon, 'North and South', in *The Metropolitan Tabernacle*, Vol. 17 (Ages Digital Library, 1998), 597.

[16]Charles Spurgeon, 'Our Manifesto', in *The Metropolitan Tabernacle Pulpit*, Vol. 37 (Ages Digital Library, 1998), 59.

[17]Charles Spurgeon, 'Order is Heaven's First Law', in *The Metropolitan Tabernacle Pulpit*, Vol. 52 (Ages Digital Library, 1998), 135.

[18]Charles Spurgeon, *The Sword and the Trowel*, Vol. 3 (1871) (Ages Digital Library, 1998), 107.

[19]Spurgeon, *Lectures*, 146-47.

[20]Charles Spurgeon, *Commenting on Commentaries* (Ages Digital Library, 1998), 27.

[21]Spurgeon, *Commenting and Commentaries*, 28.

[22]Charles Spurgeon, 'Spiritual Religion', in *The Metropolitan Tabernacle Pulpit*, Vol. 46 (Ages Digital Library, 1998), 336.

[23]Ibid.

[24]Spurgeon, *An All Around Ministry*, 26.

[25]John Broadus, *On the Preparation and Delivery of Sermons*, 4th ed. (San Francisco, California: HarperCollins, 1979), 58.

[26]Charles Spurgeon, 'Four Choice Sentences', in *The Metropolitan Tabernacle Pulpit*, Vol. 27 (Ages Digital Library, 1998), 827.

[27]Charles Spurgeon, 'First Literary Friends', in *Autobiography*, Vol. 2 (Ages Digital Library, 1998), 70.

[28]Spurgeon, *Commenting and Commentaries*, 4.

[29]Charles Spurgeon, 'The Power of the Risen Saviour', in *The Metropolitan Tabernacle Pulpit*, Vol. 20 (Ages Digital Library, 1998), 756.

[30]Charles Spurgeon, 'Our Heavenly Father's Pity', in *The Metropolitan Tabernacle Pulpit*, Vol. 45 (Ages Digital Library, 1998), 577.

[31]Charles Spurgeon, 'Scriptural Salvation', in *The Metropolitan Tabernacle Pulpit*, Vol. 36 (Ages Digital Library, 1998), 350.

[32]Charles Spurgeon, 'The Holy Spirit's Chief Office', in *The Metropolitan Tabernacle Pulpit,* Vol. 34 (Ages Digital Library, 1998), 661.

[33]Charles Spurgeon, 'The Hospital of Waiters Visited with the Gospel', in *The Metropolitan Tabernacle Pulpit*, Vol. 21(Ages Digital Library, 1998), 20.

[34]Spurgeon, 'The Holy Spirit's Chief Office', 661.

[35]Charles Spurgeon, 'The Mediator, Judge, and Savior', in *The Metropolitan Tabernacle Pulpit*, Vol. 26 (Ages Digital Library, 1998), 403.

[36]Charles Spurgeon, 'The Apple Tree in the Wood', in *The Metropolitan Tabernacle Pulpit*, Vol. 19 (Ages Digital Library, 1998), 467.

[37]Charles Spurgeon, *Christ's Incarnation the Foundation of Christianity* (Ages Digital Library, 1998), 96.

[38]Ibid., 97.

[39]Charles Spurgeon, 'Withholding Corn', in *The Metropolitan Tabernacle Pulpit*, Vol. 11 (Ages Digital Library, 1998), 531-32.

[40]Ibid.

[41]Charles Spurgeon, 'The Flight to Zoar', in *The Metropolitan Tabernacle Pulpit*, Vol. 45 (Ages Digital Library, 1998), 623.

[42]Charles Spurgeon, 'To You', in *The Metropolitan Tabernacle Pulpit*, Vol. 50 (Ages Digital Library, 1998), 566.

[43]Charles Spurgeon, 'Now', in *The Metropolitan Tabernacle Pulpit*, Vol. 10 (Ages Digital Library, 1998), 850.

[44]Charles Spurgeon, 'Jesus Affirmed to Be Alive', in *The Metropolitan Tabernacle Pulpit*, Vol. 34 (Ages Digital Library, 1998), 235.

[45]Spurgeon, 'The Holy Spirit's Chief Office', 664-65.

[46]Charles Spurgeon, 'Notable Lectures and Addresses', in *Autobiography*, Vol. 3 (Ages Digital Library, 1998), 47.

[47]Spurgeon, *Lectures*, 42.

[48]Charles Spurgeon, 'Intercessory Prayer', in *The Metropolitan Tabernacle Pulpit*, Vol. 18 (Ages Digital Library, 1998), 326.

[49]Spurgeon, 'A New Order', 373.

[50]*C. H. Spurgeon's Prayers*, 3.

[51]Charles Spurgeon, *The Sword and the Trowel*, Vol. 2 (Ages Digital Library, 1998), 158.

[52]Spurgeon, *Lectures*, 55.

[53]Spurgeon, *The Sword*, Vol. 2, 158.

[54]Charles Spurgeon, 'Jesus Knew What He Would Do', in *The Metropolitan Tabernacle Pulpit*, Vol. 27 (Ages Digital Library, 1998), 453.

[55]Charles Spurgeon, 'To Those who are Angry with Their Godly Friends', in *The Metropolitan Tabernacle Pulpit*, Vol. 32 (Ages Digital Library, 1998), 780.

[56]Spurgeon, *Lectures*, 55.

[57]Charles Spurgeon, 'Gospel Missions', in *The Park Street Pulpit*, Vol. 2 (Ages Digital Library, 1998), 302.

[58]Spurgeon, 'The Gospel of the Glory', 228.

[59]Spurgeon, 'The Sword of the Spirit', 226.

[60]Spurgeon, 'The Gospel of the Glory', 243.

[61]Spurgeon, 'Prayer – Its Discouragements and Encouragements', in *The Metropolitan Tabernacle Pulpit*, Vol. 49 (Ages Digital Library, 1998), 464.

[62]Charles Spurgeon, 'The Agreement of Salvation by Grace with Walking in Good Works', in *The Metropolitan Tabernacle Pulpit*, Vol. 37 (Ages Digital Library, 1998), 441.

[63]George Herbert, 'The Country Parson', in *The Complete English Works, Everyman's Library Series* (New York: Alfred A. Knopf, Inc, 1995), 205.

[64]Charles Spurgeon, 'Looking for One Thing and Finding Another', in *The Metropolitan Tabernacle Pulpit*, Vol. 54 (Ages Digital Library, 1998), 42.

[65]Spurgeon, *An All Around Ministry*, 208.

[66]Ibid.

[67]Ibid.

[68]Spurgeon's critics called this 'discouragement.' Spurgeon clarifies that such 'discouragement' is a vital road to saving faith. What his critics referred to as 'discouragement' referenced Spurgeon's insistence that saving faith was not achievable by the good efforts of a human soul. 'Oh, but, I want to set a man working!' says one. Do you? I want to set him not working; that is to say, I want him to have done with any idea that salvation is of himself...discouragement of this sort is the very thing I always aim at in my preaching. Oh, if I could but bring all my hearers, not only into a state of discouragement, but into a condition of despair about themselves, then I should know that they were on the road to a simple faith in the Lord Jesus Christ! Our extremity is God's opportunity. Oh, how I long to get you all to that extremity! It is absolute helplessness and death that lays the sinner where Christ can deal with him. When he is nothing, Christ shall be everything' ('Good Reasons for a Good Resolution', in *The Metropolitan Tabernacle Pulpit*, Vol. 43 [Ages Digital Library, 1998], 735). See also, Benjamin Franklin, the eighteenth-century father of America, who hinted at the affront that such a preached message offers an audience. Franklin observed the 'extraordinary influence of' the 'oratory' of George Whitefield, whom Spurgeon so much admired, and he marveled that under the power of Whitefield's oratory 'it seem'd as if all the world were growing religious; so that one could not walk thro' the town in an evening without hearing Psalms sung in different families of every street.' Yet, this power was demonstrated, Franklin added with surprise, 'notwithstanding' Whitefield's 'common abuse' of his hearers 'by assuring them they were naturally half beasts and devils' (*The Autobiography and Other Writings* [New York, N.Y.: Penguin Books, 1986], 116-17).

[69]Spurgeon, *Lectures*, 336-48.

Chapter 9. Lips Touched by the Live Coal: *Seeking the Spirit's Attendant Power*

[1]Charles Spurgeon, 'The Story of God's Mighty Acts', in *The Park Street Pulpit*, Vol. 5 (Ages Digital Library, 1998), 522.

[2]Spurgeon, *The Early Years*, v.

[3]Charles Spurgeon, 'Intimate Knowledge of the Holy Spirit', in *The Metropolitan Tabernacle Pulpit*, Vol. 35 (Ages Digital Library, 1998), 178.

[4]Spurgeon, 'Intimate Knowledge', 171.

[5]Charles Spurgeon, *The Greatest Fight in the World* (Ages Digital Library, 1998), 37.

[6]Charles Spurgeon, 'The Private Tutor', in *The Metropolitan Tabernacle Pulpit*, Vol. 31 (Ages Digital Library, 1998), 383.

[7]Spurgeon, 'Intimate Knowledge', 179.

[8]Charles Spurgeon, 'The Talking Book', in *The Metropolitan Tabernacle Pulpit*, Vol. 17 (Ages Digital Library, 1998), 750.

[9]Charles Spurgeon, 'How to Read the Bible', in *The Metropolitan Tabernacle Pulpit*, Vol. 58 (Ages Digital Library, 1998), 534.

[10]Spurgeon, 'Intimate Knowledge', 188.

[11]Charles Spurgeon, 'The Gospel of the Glory of Christ', in *The Metropolitan Tabernacle Pulpit*, Vol. 35 (Ages Digital Library, 1998), 228.

[12]Charles Spurgeon, 'A Family Sermon', in *The Metropolitan Tabernacle Pulpit*, Vol. 23 (Ages Digital Library, 1998), 79.

[13]Spurgeon, 'The Gospel of the Glory of Christ', 228.

[14]Charles Spurgeon, 'The Withered Hand', in *The Metropolitan Tabernacle Pulpit*, Vol. 25 (Ages Digital Library, 1998), 544.

[15]Charles Spurgeon, 'Election: Its Defenses and Evidences', in *The Metropolitan Tabernacle Pulpit*, Vol. 51 (Ages Digital Library, 1998), 68-69.

[16]Ibid., 73-74.

[17]Ibid., 74.

[18]Charles Spurgeon, 'The Blessed Guest Detained', in *The Metropolitan Tabernacle Pulpit*, Vol. 28 (Ages Digital Library, 1998), 274.

[19]Charles Spurgeon, 'Divine Forgiveness Admired and Imitated', in *The Metropolitan Tabernacle Pulpit*, Vol. 31 (Ages Digital Library, 1998), 361.

[20]Calvin, *The Ministry of the Word*, 173.

[21]Spurgeon's theology of instrumentality will find exploration in Chapter 9.

[22]Charles Spurgeon, 'The Centurion: Of an Exhortation to the Virtuous', in *The Metropolitan Tabernacle* Pulpit, Vol. 10 (Ages Digital Library, 1998), 816.

[23]Spurgeon, *Lectures*, 187.

[24]Charles Spurgeon, 'Election: Its Defenses and Evidences', 69.

[25]Charles Spurgeon, 'Magdalene at the Sepulchre: An Instructive Scene', in *The Metropolitan Tabernacle Pulpit*, Vol. 35 (Ages Digital Library, 1998), 856.

[26]Charles Spurgeon, 'Right Replies to Right Requests', in *The Metropolitan Tabernacle Pulpit*, Vol. 16 (Ages Digital Library, 1998), 780.

[27]Spurgeon, 'Intimate Knowledge, 179.

[28]Charles Spurgeon, 'The Sword of the Spirit', in *The Metropolitan Tabernacle Pulpit*, Vol. 37 (Ages Digital Library, 1998), 296.

[29]Spurgeon, *An All Around Ministry,* 315.

[30]Charles Spurgeon, 'Gospel Missions', in *The Metropolitan Tabernacle Pulpit*, Vol. 2 (Ages Digital Library, 1998), 302.

[31]Charles Spurgeon, 'Strength and Recovery', in *The Metropolitan Tabernacle Pulpit*, Vol. 30 (Ages Digital Library, 1998), 726.

[32]Charles Spurgeon, 'Our Omnipotent Leader', in *The Metropolitan Tabernacle Pulpit*, Vol. 42 (Ages Digital Library, 1998), 319.

[33]Charles Ray, *A Marvellous Ministry: The Story of C. H. Spurgeon's Sermons 1855-1905* (Ages Digital Library, 1998), 22.

[34]Spurgeon, *The Early Years*, 355.

[35]Charles Spurgeon, 'The Master', in *The Metropolitan Tabernacle Pulpit*, Vol. 20 (Ages Digital Library, 1998), 718.

[36]Charles Spurgeon, 'The Outpouring of the Holy Spirit', in *The Park Street Pulpit*, Vol. 4 (Ages Digital Library, 1998), 513.

[37]Spurgeon, *Eccentric Preachers,* 37.

[38]Spurgeon, 'Pentecost', 376.

[39]Charles Spurgeon, 'Stephen's Martyrdom', in *The Metropolitan Tabernacle Pulpit*, Vol. 13 (Ages Digital Library, 1998),179.

[40]Spurgeon, *An All Around Ministry,* 322.

[41]Charles Spurgeon, 'Self Sufficiency Slain', in *The Park Street Pulpit*, Vol. 6 (Ages Digital Library, 1998), 863.

[42]Spurgeon, *A Puritan Catechism*, 10.

[43]Charles Spurgeon, 'The Spirit's Work in the New Creation', in *The Metropolitan Tabernacle Pulpit*, Vol. 55 (Ages Digital

Library, 1998), 146. Note John Calvin's similar remark: 'We clearly see how destitute and devoid of all good things man is, and how he lacks all aids to salvation. Therefore, if he seeks resources to succor him in his need, he must go outside himself and get them elsewhere...for in Christ [God] offers all happiness in place of our misery' (*Institutes*, Vol. *2*, 850).

[44]Charles Spurgeon, 'The Church's Probation', in *The Metropolitan Tabernacle Pulpit*, Vol. 51 (Ages Digital Library, 1998), 796

[45]Charles Spurgeon, 'The Reason Why Many Cannot Find Peace', in *The Metropolitan Tabernacle Pulpit*, Vol. 24 (Ages Digital Library, 1998), 266.

[46]Spurgeon, *Lectures*, 165.

[47]Charles Spurgeon, 'Not Sufficient and Yet Sufficient', in *The Metropolitan Tabernacle Pulpit*, Vol. 36 (Ages Digital Library, 1998), 582.

[48]Charles Spurgeon, 'A Homily for Humble Folks', in *The Metropolitan Tabernacle*, Vol. 36 (Ages Digital Library, 1998), 283.

[49]Spurgeon, *An All Around Ministry*, 216.

[50]Revelation 3:17-18

[51]I Corinthians 2:4-5.

[52]'While the Lamp Holds on to Burn,' in *Able to the Uttermost* (Ages Digital Library, 1998), 212.

[53]'Faith Purifying the Heart,' in *The Metropolitan Tabernacle Pulpit*, Vol. 23 (Ages Digital Library, 1998), 279.

[54]Spurgeon, *Lectures*, 336.

[55]Ibid., 337.

[56]Charles Spurgeon, 'A Message from God', in *The Metropolitan Tabernacle Pulpit*, Vol. 61 (Ages Digital Library, 1998), 182. Elsewhere, Spurgeon urges that 'We must, having our heart glowing, and our souls on fire with love to [our hears], seek to bring the truth to be upon them, to impress it upon their hearts and consciences, as in the sight of God and in the stead of Christ' ('The True Aim of Preaching,' 208).

[57]Charles Spurgeon, 'The Holy Ghost – the Great Teacher', in *The Park Street Pulpit*, Vol. 1 (Ages Digital Library, 1998), 666.

[58]Ibid.

[59]Charles Spurgeon, 'Christ with the Keys of Death and Hell', in *The Metropolitan Tabernacle Pulpit*, Vol. 15 (Ages Digital Library, 1998), 679.

[60]Charles Spurgeon, 'The Spur', in *The Metropolitan Tabernacle Pulpit*, Vol. 19 (Ages Digital Library, 1998), 450.

[61]Charles Spurgeon, 'The Holy Spirit Compared to the Wind', in *The Metropolitan Tabernacle Pulpit*, Vol. 11 (Ages Digital Library, 1998), 336.

[62]Spurgeon, 'The Blessed Guest Detained', 272.

[63]Charles Spurgeon, 'Degrees of Power Attending the Gospel', in *The Metropolitan Tabernacle Pulpit*, Vol. 11 (Ages Digital Library, 1998), 622.

Chapter 10. The Free Spirit: *Bowing before the Spirit's Mysteries*

[1]Spurgeon, 'The Holy Spirit Compared to the Wind', 346.

[2]Spurgeon, 'The Light of the World', 299.

[3]Spurgeon, 'The Minister's Plea', 741.

[4]Charles Spurgeon, 'Pricked in their Heart', in *The Metropolitan Tabernacle Pulpit*, Vol. 35 (Ages Digital Library, 1998), 597.

[5]Charles Spurgeon, 'Iconoclast', in *The Metropolitan Tabernacle Pulpit*, Vol. 16 (Ages Digital Library, 1998), 788.

[6]Spurgeon, 'The Holy Spirit Compared to the Wind', 345-346.

[7]Drummond, *Prince of Preachers*, 32.

[8]Spurgeon, *Lectures*, 199.

[9]Nelson, 'Theory and Practice', 176.

[10]Charles Spurgeon, 'The Ethiopian', in *The Metropolitan Tabernacle Pulpit*, Vol. 43 (Ages Digital Library, 1998), 623.

[11]Charles Spurgeon, 'The Spirit's Office Towards Disciples', in *The Metropolitan Tabernacle Pulpit*, Vol. 53 (Ages Digital Library, 1998), 640.

[12]Charles Spurgeon, 'Making Light of Christ', *The Park Street Pulpit*, Vol. 2 (Ages Digital Library, 1998), 572.

[13]Calvin, *Institutes*, 1011.

[14]Spurgeon, 'The Spirit and the Wind', 72.

[15]Spurgeon, 'The Hospital of Waiters', 20.

[16]Spurgeon, *The Full Harvest*, 311.

[17]Ibid., 313.

[18]Ibid.

[19]Ibid., 311.

[20]Spurgeon, 'The Greatest Fight in the World', 14.

[21]Spurgeon, *Lectures*, 163.

Chapter 11. Seeking a Fresh Baptism: *Pursuing the Spirit's Fellowship*

[1]Charles Spurgeon, 'Salt for Sacrifice', in *The Metropolitan Tabernacle Pulpit*, Vol. 33 (Ages Digital Library, 1998), 57.

[2]D. L. Moody, 'Secret Power or the Secret of Success in Christian Life and Work', in *Late Nineteenth Century Revivalist Teachings on the Holy Spirit*, ed. Donald W. Dayton (New York & London: Garland Publishing, Inc., 1985), 9.

[3]Leona Frances Choy, *Powerlines: What Great Evangelicals Believed About the Holy Spirit 1850-1930* (Camp Hill, Pennsylvania: Christian Publications, 1990), 174.

[4]Charles Spurgeon, 'Witnessing Better than Knowing the Future', in *The Metropolitan Tabernacle Pulpit*, Vol. 39 (Ages Digital Library, 1998), 671.

[5]Charles Spurgeon, 'A Most Needful Prayer Concerning the Holy Spirit', in *The Metropolitan Tabernacle Pulpit*, Vol.16 (Ages Digital Library, 1998), 698.

[6]Charles Spurgeon, 'A Fatal Deficiency', in *The Metropolitan Tabernacle Pulpit*, Vol. 19 (Ages Digital Library, 1998), 653.

[7]Charles Spurgeon, 'One Greater than the Temple', in *The Metropolitan Tabernacle Pulpit*, Vol. 22 (Ages Digital Library, 1998), 69.

[8]Charles Spurgeon, 'Our Lord's Triumphant Ascension', in *The Metropolitan Tabernacle Pulpit*, Vol. 36 (Ages Digital Library, 1998), 317.

[9]Charles Spurgeon, 'A Fatal Deficiency', in *The Metropolitan Tabernacle Pulpit*, Vol. 19 (Ages Digital Library, 1998), 653.

[10]Charles Spurgeon, 'Mr. Fearing Comforted', in *The Park Street Pulpit*, Vol. 5 (Ages Digital Library, 1998), 292. See also, 'Chapter Five: Providence', in *The Westminster Confession of Faith* (Glasgow, Scotland: Free Presbyterian Publications, 1997), 36.

[11]Charles Spurgeon, 'Unstaggering Faith', in *The Metropolitan Tabernacle Pulpit*, Vol. 13 (Ages Digital Library, 1998),78.

[12]Charles Spurgeon, 'An Inscription for the Mausoleum of the Saints', in *The Metropolitan Tabernacle Pulpit*, Vol. 31 (Ages Digital Library, 1998), 142.

[13]Charles Spurgeon, 'Holy Water', in *The Metropolitan Tabernacle Pulpit*, Vol. 20 (Ages Digital Library), 782.

[14]Charles Spurgeon, 'Rubbish', in *The Metropolitan Tabernacle*, Vol. 20 (Ages Digital Library, 1998), 101-02.

[15]Charles Spurgeon, 'The Christian's Motto', in *The Metropolitan Tabernacle Pulpit*, Vol. 20 (Ages Digital Library, 1998), 238-39.

[16]Leona Francis Choy, *Powerlines: What Great Evangelicals Believe about the Holy Spirit, 1850-1930* (Camp Hill, Pennsylvania: Christian Publications, 1990), 135.

[17]Choy, *Powerlines*, 176.

[18]Charles Spurgeon, *John Ploughman's Talk* (Ages Digital Library, 1998), 72.

[19]Charles Spurgeon, 'Death and Life in Christ', in *The Metropolitan Tabernacle Pulpit*, Vol. 9 (Ages Digital Library, 1998), 245.

[20]Charles Spurgeon, 'The Mediator, Judge and Savior', in *The Metropolitan Tabernacle Pulpit*, Vol. 26 (Ages Digital Library, 1998), 402.

[21]Charles Spurgeon, 'The Chief of Sinners', in *The Metropolitan Tabernacle Pulpit*, Vol. 9 (Ages Digital Library, 1998), 660.

[22]The word 'new' here does not designate something 'essentially new' or new in kind, as the rest of the chapter will confirm. Rather, 'new' refers the Spirit's consistent practice that is new in experience for the individual person or generation.

[23]Spurgeon, 'Intimate Knowledge', 179.

[24]Charles Spurgeon, 'Speak Lord', in *The Metropolitan Tabernacle Pulpit*, Vol. 43 (Ages Digital Library, 1998), 451.

[25]Charles Spurgeon, 'Joshua's Vision', in *The Metropolitan Tabernacle*, Vol. 14 (Ages Digital Library, 1998), 120.

[26]*C. H. Spurgeon's Prayers*, 105.

[27]Charles Spurgeon, 'The Personality of the Holy Spirit', in *The Park Street Pulpit*, Vol. 1 (Ages Digital Library, 1998), 67.

[28]Charles Spurgeon, 'The Church of Christ', in *The Park Street Pulpit*, Vol. 1 (Ages Digital Library, 1998), 385.

[29]Spurgeon, 'The Leading of the Spirit', 160.

[30]Spurgeon, 'The Spirit and the Wind', 73.

[31]Spurgeon, 'The Comforter', 79.

[32]Spurgeon, *Lectures*, 187.

[33]Ibid.

[34]Charles Spurgeon, 'Holding Fast the Faith', in *The Metropolitan Tabernacle Pulpit*, Vol. 34 (Ages Digital Library, 1998), 109.

[35]Spurgeon, *Lectures*, 195.

Chapter 12. The Fainting Fits: *Handling Criticism and Depression*

[1]Spurgeon, *Lectures*, 154.

[2]Spurgeon, *The Early Years*, 416-17.

[3]Charles Spurgeon, 'The Two Effects of the Gospel', in *The Park Street Pulpit*, Vol. 1 (Ages Digital Library, 1998), 369.

[4]Ibid.

[5]Spurgeon, *Lectures*, 310.

[6]Spurgeon, *The Early Years*, 321.

[7]Spurgeon, *The Early Years*, 305.

[8]Spurgeon, *The Early Years*, 465.

[9]Ibid., 438.

[10]Ibid., 312.

[11]Charles Spurgeon, 'Love, Courtship and Marriage, Continued', in *Autobiography*, Vol. 2 (Ages Digital Library, 1998), 23.

[12]Quoted in John Piper, 'Charles Spurgeon: Preaching Through Adversity', Bethlehem Conference for Pastors, January 31, 1995.

[13]Spurgeon, 'The Two-Effects', 369.

[14]Charles Spurgeon, 'A Plain Talk Upon an Encouraging Topic,' in *The Metropolitan Tabernacle*, Vol. 54 (Ages Digital Library, 1998), 445.

[15]Spurgeon, *An All Around Ministry*, 148.

[16]Charles Spurgeon, 'Lessons from Nature', in *The Metropolitan Tabernacle Pulpit*, Vol. 17 (Ages Digital Library, 1998), 569.

[17]Charles Spurgeon, 'God's Mercy Going Before', in *The Metropolitan Tabernacle Pulpit*, Vol. 60 (Ages Digital Library, 1998), 406.

[18]Piper, 'Preaching through Adversity', 8.

[19]Spurgeon, *Lectures*, 49.

[20]Charles Spurgeon, 'Our Youth Renewed', in *The Metropolitan Tabernacle Pulpit*, Vol. 60 (Ages Digital Library, 1998), 462.

[21]Spurgeon, *Lectures*, 154.

[22]Charles Spurgeon, 'No Tears in Heaven', in *The Metropolitan Tabernacle Pulpit*, Vol. 11 (Ages Digital Library, 1998), 541.

[23]Ibid., 542-45.

[24]Charles Spurgeon, 'Light for those who sit in Darkness', in *The Metropolitan Tabernacle Pulpit*, Vol. 17 (Ages Digital Library, 1998), 642.

[25]Charles Spurgeon, 'Christ's Hospital', in *The Metropolitan Tabernacle Pulpit*, Vol. 38 (Ages Digital Library, 1998), 353.

[26]Spurgeon, 'The Minister's Plea', 740.

[27]Charles Spurgeon, 'Job's Regret and our Own', in *The Metropolitan Tabernacle Pulpit*, Vol. 17 (Ages Digital Library, 1998), 753.

[28]Charles Spurgeon, 'Our Compassionate High Priest', in *The Metropolitan Tabernacle Pulpit*, Vol. 38 (Ages Digital Library, 1998), 219.

[29]Charles Spurgeon, 'A Present Helper', in *The Metropolitan Tabernacle Pulpit*, Vol. 61 (Ages Digital Library, 1998), 80.

[30]Spurgeon, 'Light for those who sit in Darkness', 642.

[31]Charles Spurgeon, 'Sarah and her Daughters', in *The Park Street Pulpit*, Vol. 5 (Ages Digital Library, 1998), 882.

[32]Charles Spurgeon, 'Gladness for Sadness', in *The Metropolitan Tabernacle Pulpit*, Vol. 29 (Ages Digital Library, 1998), 54.

[33]Charles Spurgeon, 'Songs for the Desolate Heart', in *The Metropolitan Tabernacle Pulpit*, Vol. 11 (Ages Digital Library, 1998), 642.

[34]Spurgeon, 'Our Compassionate High Priest', 223.

[35]Ibid.

[36]Charles Spurgeon, 'Encourage Your Minister', in *The Metropolitan Tabernacle Pulpit*, Vol. 65 (Ages Digital Library, 1998), 765.

[37]Spurgeon, *The Full Harvest*, 193.

[38]Charles Spurgeon, 'Unprofitable Servants', in *The Metropolitan Tabernacle Pulpit*, Vol. 26 (Ages Digital Library, 1998), 415.

[39]Charles Spurgeon, 'Zechariah's Vision of Joshua the High Priest', in *The Metropolitan Tabernacle Pulpit*, Vol. 11 (Ages Digital Library, 1998), 66-67.

[40]Ibid.

[41]Charles Spurgeon, 'Men Bewitched', in *The Metropolitan Tabernacle Pulpit*, Vol. 26 (Ages Digital Library, 1998), 498.

[42]Spurgeon, *The Full Harvest*, 197.

[43]Ibid.

[44]Ibid.

[45]Charles Spurgeon, 'The Ascension and the Second Advent Practically Considered', in *The Metropolitan Tabernacle Pulpit*, Vol. 31 (Ages Digital Library, 1998), 29.

[46]Spurgeon, *An All Around Ministry*, 233.

[47]Ibid., 74.

[48]Charles Spurgeon, 'The Rainbow', in *The Metropolitan Tabernacle Pulpit*, Vol. 9 (Ages Digital Library, 1998), 463.

[49]Eric Hayden, *Highlights in the Life of Charles Haddon Spurgeon* (Ages Digital Library, 1998), 158.

Chapter 13. Our Fellow Workers: *Sharing the Ministry*

[1]Charles Spurgeon, 'The Great Revival', in *The New Park Street Pulpit*, Vol. 4 (Ages Digital Library, 1998), 279.

[2]Elliot-Binns, *Religion in the Victorian Era*, 451.

[3]Charles Spurgeon, 'Knowledge Commended', in *The Metropolitan Tabernacle Pulpit*, Vol. 11 (Ages Digital Library, 1998), 34.

[4]Charles Spurgeon, 'Bringing Sinners to the Savior', in *The Metropolitan Tabernacle Pulpit*, Vol. 47 (Ages Digital Library, 1998), 374.

[5]Spurgeon, *Letters Selected with Notes*, 128.

[6]Calvin, *Institutes*, Vol. 1, 724.

[7]Ibid., 725.

[8]Spurgeon, *Letters Selected with Notes*, 115.

[9]Charles Spurgeon, 'Strengthening Medicine for God's Servants', in *The Metropolitan Tabernacle Pulpit*, Vol. 21 (Ages Digital Library, 1998), 65-66.

[10]Charles Spurgeon, 'Peter's Three Calls', in *The Metropolitan Tabernacle Pulpit*, Vol. 12 (Ages Digital Library, 1998), 507-508.

[11]Charles Spurgeon, 'The Power of Aaron's Rod', in *The Metropolitan Tabernacle Pulpit*, Vol. 9 (Ages Digital Library, 1998), 524.

[12]Spurgeon, *The Sword and the Trowel*, Vol. 3, 370.

[13]Spurgeon, *The Full Harvest*, 71.

[14]Ibid.

[15]Charles Spurgeon, 'The Two Gatherings', in *The Metropolitan Tabernacle Pulpit*, Vol. 56 (Ages Digital Library, 1998), 588.

[16]Ibid.

[17]Charles Spurgeon, 'The Yoke Removed and the Lord Revealed', in *The Metropolitan Tabernacle Pulpit*, Vol. 25 (Ages Digital Library, 1998), 190.

[18]Charles Spurgeon, 'The Golden Lamp and its Goodly Lessons', in *The Metropolitan Tabernacle Pulpit*, Vol. 26 (Ages Digital Library, 1998), 839.

[19]Charles Spurgeon, *Come Ye Children* (Ages Digital Library, 1998), 56.

[20]Charles Spurgeon, 'The Two Gatherings', in *The Metropolitan Tabernacle Pulpit*, Vol. 56 (Ages Digital Library, 1998), 588-589.

[21]Charles Spurgeon, 'June 21st', in *Faith's Checkbook* (Ages Digital Library, 1998), 178.

[22]Charles Spurgeon, 'Report of the Proceedings at the Metropolitan Tabernacle', in *The Metropolitan Tabernacle: Its History and Work* (Ages Digital Library, 1998), 98.

[23]Charles Spurgeon, 'Speak for Yourself: A Challenge', in *The Metropolitan Tabernacle Pulpit*, Vol. 24 (Ages Digital Library, 1998), 31.

[24]Charles Spurgeon, 'A Feast for Faith', in *The Metropolitan Tabernacle Pulpit*, Vol. 12 (Ages Digital Library, 1998), 650.

[25]Charles Spurgeon, 'What Meanest Thou O Sleeper?', in *The Metropolitan Tabernacle Pulpit*, Vol. 8 (Ages Digital Library, 1998), 633.

[26]Charles Spurgeon, 'The Waterer Watered', in *The Metropolitan Tabernacle Pulpit*, Vol. 11 (Ages Digital Library, 1998), 285.

[27]Spurgeon, 'The Holy Spirit Compared to the Wind', 348.

[28]Charles Spurgeon, 'The Real Presence the Great Want of the Church', in *The Metropolitan Tabernacle*, Vol. 18 (Ages Digital Library, 1998), 107.

[29]Spurgeon, *Lectures*, 22.

[30]Charles Spurgeon, 'The Two I Wills in Isaiah 41', in *The Metropolitan Tabernacle Pulpit*, Vol. 38 (Ages Digital Library, 1998), 518.

[31]Charles Spurgeon, *The Soul Winner* (Ages Digital Library, 1998), 5.

[32]Eric Hayden, *Highlights*, 62.

[33]Spurgeon, 'Two I Wills in Isaiah 41', 518.

[34]Charles Spurgeon, 'Incense and Light', in *The Metropolitan Tabernacle Pulpit*, Vol. 29 (Ages Digital Library, 1998), 202.

[35]Spurgeon, 'The Minister's Plea', 743.

[36]Spurgeon, 'The Statute of David', 407.

[37]Spurgeon, *An All Around Ministry*, 191.

[38]Charles Spurgeon, 'The Touchstone of Godly Sincerity', in *The Metropolitan Tabernacle Pulpit*, Vol. 17 (Ages Digital Library, 1998), 266.

[39]Charles Spurgeon, 'Preparation Necessary for the Communion', in *The Metropolitan Tabernacle Pulpit*, Vol. 45 (Ages Digital Library, 1998), 709.

[40]Spurgeon, 'The Minister's Plea', 749.

[41]Charles Spurgeon, 'Farm Laborers', in *The Metropolitan Tabernacle Pulpit*, Vol. 27 (Ages Digital Library, 1998), 420.

[42]Charles Spurgeon, 'Spiritual Transformations', in *The Metropolitan Tabernacle Pulpit*, Vol. 53 (Ages Digital Library, 1998), 365.

[43]Spurgeon, *An All Around Ministry*, 13.

[44]Charles Spurgeon, 'A Gospel Sermon to Outsiders', in *The Metropolitan Tabernacle Pulpit*, Vol. 23 (Ages Digital Library, 1998), 888.

[45]Charles Spurgeon, 'The Soul's Awakening', in *The Metropolitan Tabernacle Pulpit*, Vol. 60 (Ages Digital Library, 1998), 39-40.

Subject Index

SCRIPTURE INDEX

The Saint and his Saviour

The work of the Spirit in the life of the Christian

C.H Spurgeon

This is the story of two friends on the journey of life.

One is the mentor to the other - a guide, a counsellor, but also a taskmaster and a judge. The other is a member of his family, loved despite their flaws.

In *The Saint and His Saviour,* Spurgeon takes us through the whole process of the work of the Spirit in a believer's life, from his first experience of the Lord, through the, often tumultuous, process of conversion, to the deepening knowledge of the presence of the Saviour with his people.

Captivating and challenging, Spurgeon examines how sin affects our relationship to Christ, and how we can cultivate a friendship with our Saviour.

Renowned for his love for people and his passion for the salvation of the lost, Spurgeon lays down a challenge to the unbeliever at every point. Extremely practical, **The Saint and his Saviour** also offers a hugely encouraging reminder to Christians that during the twists and turns of our spiritual walk the Lord is with us every step of the way.

ISBN 1-87167-601-0

Lectures to my Students

C.H Spurgeon

Preachers often quote Spurgeon today because he had an ability to explain Christian truth to ordinary people with pointed, memorable statements. The people who heard and read his words were effectively taught theology and enjoyed it. He was a dogged defender of the Bible as God's truth.

Another side to Spurgeon's character showed his sensitive and loving nature. It was this that spurred him to preach the gospel, so that as many people as possible could hear the good news about why Jesus Christ came to build a church for eternity. This passion showed through in his warm pastoring of his congregation and the setting up of a college for future ministers of the gospel - it still exists in London, England, today.

Spurgeon realised that he could influence the church beyond his own lifetime if he could encourage future pastors to trust the Bible, love people and preach the truth fearlessly. So he collected his lectures to his college students and published this book. It has been a classic of pastoral theology ever since and is still used to train ministers to this day.

If you need help in developing a love for your congregation, or need to spruce up the tools and abilities God has given you, then *Lectures to my Students* is a brilliant starting point.

ISBN 1-85792-417-7

Christian Focus Publications
publishes books for all ages

Our mission statement –
STAYING FAITHFUL
In dependence upon God we seek to help make His infallible Word, the Bible, relevant. Our aim is to ensure that the Lord Jesus Christ is presented as the only hope to obtain forgiveness of sin, live a useful life and look forward to heaven with Him.

REACHING OUT
Christ's last command requires us to reach out to our world with His gospel. We seek to help fulfill that by publishing books that point people towards Jesus and help them develop a Christ-like maturity. We aim to equip all levels of readers for life, work, ministry and mission.

Books in our adult range are published in three imprints.

Christian Focus contains popular works including biographies, commentaries, basic doctrine and Christian living. Our children's books are also published in this imprint.

Mentor focuses on books written at a level suitable for Bible College and seminary students, pastors, and other serious readers. The imprint includes commentaries, doctrinal studies, examination of current issues and church history.

Christian Heritage contains classic writings from the past.

Christian Focus Publications, Ltd
Geanies House, Fearn,
Ross-shire, IV20 1TW, Scotland, United Kingdom
info@christianfocus.com

For details of our titles visit us on our website
www.christianfocus.com